# The New World of Islam

Lothrop Stoddard

# PREFACE

The entire world of Islam is to-day in profound ferment. From Morocco to China and from Turkestan to the Congo, the 250,000,000 followers of the Prophet Mohammed are stirring to new ideas, new impulses, new aspirations. A gigantic transformation is taking place whose results must affect all mankind.

This transformation was greatly stimulated by the late war. But it began long before. More than a hundred years ago the seeds were sown, and ever since then it has been evolving; at first slowly and obscurely; later more rapidly and perceptibly; until to-day, under the stimulus of Armageddon, it has burst into sudden and startling bloom.

The story of that strange and dramatic evolution I have endeavoured to tell in the following pages. Considering in turn its various aspects—religious, cultural, political, economic, social—I have tried to portray their genesis and development, to analyse their character, and to appraise their potency. While making due allowance for local differentiations, the intimate correlation and underlying unity of the various movements have ever been kept in view.

Although the book deals primarily with the Moslem world, it necessarily includes the non-Moslem Hindu elements of India. The field covered is thus virtually the entire Near and Middle East. The Far East has not been directly considered, but parallel developments there have been noted and should always be kept in mind.

Lothrop Stoddard

# TABLE OF CONTENTS

THE NEW WORLD OF ISLAM

"Das Alte stürzt, es ändert sich die Zeit,
Und neues Leben blüht aus den Ruinen."
Schiller, Wilhelm Tell.

INTRODUCTION

THE DECLINE AND FALL OF THE OLD ISLAMIC WORLD

The rise of Islam is perhaps the most amazing event in human history. Springing from a land and a people alike previously negligible, Islam spread within a century over half the earth, shattering great empires, overthrowing long-established religions, remoulding the souls of races, and building up a whole new world—the world of Islam.

The closer we examine this development the more extraordinary does it appear. The other great religions won their way slowly, by painful struggle, and finally triumphed with the aid of powerful monarchs converted to the new faith. Christianity had its Constantine, Buddhism its Asoka, and Zoroastrianism its Cyrus, each lending to his chosen cult the mighty force of secular authority. Not so Islam. Arising in a desert land sparsely inhabited by a nomad race previously undistinguished in human annals, Islam sallied forth on its great adventure with the slenderest human backing and against the heaviest material odds. Yet Islam triumphed with seemingly miraculous ease, and a couple of generations saw the Fiery Crescent borne victorious from the Pyrenees to the Himalayas and from the deserts of Central Asia to the deserts of Central Africa.

This amazing success was due to a number of contributing factors, chief among them being the character of the Arab race, the nature of Mohammed's teaching, and the general state of the contemporary Eastern world. Undistinguished though the Arabs had hitherto been, they were a people of remarkable potentialities, which were at that moment patently seeking self-realization. For several generations before Mohammed, Arabia had been astir with exuberant vitality. The Arabs had outgrown their ancestral paganism and were instinctively yearning for better things. Athwart this seething ferment of mind and spirit Islam rang like a trumpet-call. Mohammed, an Arab of the Arabs, was the very incarnation of the soul of his race. Preaching a simple, austere monotheism, free from priestcraft or elaborate doctrinal trappings, he tapped the well-springs of religious zeal always present in the Semitic heart. Forgetting the chronic rivalries and blood-feuds which had consumed their energies in internecine strife, and welded into a glowing unity by the fire of their new-found faith, the Arabs poured forth from their deserts to conquer the earth for Allah, the One True God.

Thus Islam, like the resistless breath of the sirocco, the desert wind, swept out of Arabia and encountered—a spiritual vacuum. Those neighbouring Byzantine and Persian Empires, so imposing to the casual eye, were mere dried husks, devoid of real vitality. Their religions were a mockery and a sham. Persia's ancestral cult of Zoroaster had degenerated into "Magism"—a pompous priestcraft, tyrannical and persecuting, hated and secretly despised. As for Eastern Christianity, bedizened with the gewgaws of paganism and bedevilled by the maddening theological speculations of the decadent Greek mind, it had become a repellent caricature of the teachings of Christ. Both Magism and Byzantine Christendom were riven by great heresies which engendered savage persecutions and furious hates. Furthermore, both the Byzantine and Persian Empires were harsh despotisms which crushed their subjects to the dust and killed out all love of country or loyalty to the state. Lastly, the two empires had just fought a terrible war from which they had emerged mutually bled white and utterly exhausted.

1

Such was the world compelled to face the lava-flood of Islam. The result was inevitable. Once the disciplined strength of the East Roman legions and the Persian cuirassiers had broken before the fiery onslaught of the fanatic sons of the desert, it was all over. There was no patriotic resistance. The down-trodden populations passively accepted new masters, while the numerous heretics actually welcomed the overthrow of persecuting co-religionists whom they hated far worse than their alien conquerors. In a short time most of the subject peoples accepted the new faith, so refreshingly simple compared with their own degenerate cults. The Arabs, in their turn, knew how to consolidate their rule. They were no bloodthirsty savages, bent solely on loot and destruction. On the contrary, they were an innately gifted race, eager to learn and appreciative of the cultural gifts which older civilizations had to bestow. Intermarrying freely and professing a common belief, conquerors and conquered rapidly fused, and from this fusion arose a new civilization—the Saracenic civilization, in which the ancient cultures of Greece, Rome, and Persia were revitalized by Arab vigour and synthesized by the Arab genius and the Islamic spirit. For the first three centuries of its existence (circ. a.d. 650-1000) the realm of Islam was the most civilized and progressive portion of the world. Studded with splendid cities, gracious mosques, and quiet universities where the wisdom of the ancient world was preserved and appreciated, the Moslem East offered a striking contrast to the Christian West, then sunk in the night of the Dark Ages.

However, by the tenth century the Saracenic civilization began to display unmistakable symptoms of decline. This decline was at first gradual. Down to the terrible disasters of the thirteenth century it still displayed vigour and remained ahead of the Christian West. Still, by the year a.d. 1000 its golden age was over. For this there were several reasons. In the first place, that inveterate spirit of faction which has always been the bane of the Arab race soon reappeared once more. Rival clans strove for the headship of Islam, and their quarrels degenerated into bloody civil wars. In this fratricidal strife the fervour of the first days cooled, and saintly men like Abu Bekr and Omar, Islam's first standard-bearers, gave place to worldly minded leaders who regarded their position of "Khalifa"[1] as a means to despotic power and self-glorification. The seat of government was moved to Damascus in Syria, and afterward to Bagdad in Mesopotamia. The reason for this was obvious. In Mecca despotism was impossible. The fierce, free-born Arabs of the desert would tolerate no master, and their innate democracy had been sanctioned by the Prophet, who had explicitly declared that all Believers were brothers. The Meccan caliphate was a theocratic democracy. Abu Bekr and Omar were elected by the people, and held themselves responsible to public opinion, subject to the divine law as revealed by Mohammed in the Koran.

But in Damascus, and still more in Bagdad, things were different. There the pure-blooded Arabs were only a handful among swarms of Syrian and Persian converts and "Neo-Arab" mixed-bloods. These people were filled with traditions of despotism and were quite ready to yield the caliphs obsequious obedience. The caliphs, in their turn, leaned more and more upon these complaisant subjects, drawing from their ranks courtiers, officials, and ultimately soldiers. Shocked and angered, the proud Arabs gradually returned to the desert, while the government fell into the well-worn ruts of traditional Oriental despotism. When the caliphate was moved to Bagdad after the founding of the Abbaside dynasty (a.d. 750), Persian influence became preponderant. The famous Caliph Haroun-al-Rashid, the hero of the Arabian Nights, was a typical Persian monarch, a true successor of Xerxes and Chosroes, and as different from Abu Bekr or Omar as it is possible to conceive. And, in Bagdad, as elsewhere, despotic power was fatal to its possessors. Under its blight the "successors" of Mohammed became capricious tyrants or degenerate harem puppets, whose nerveless hands were wholly incapable of guiding the great Moslem Empire.

The empire, in fact, gradually went to pieces. Shaken by the civil wars, bereft of strong leaders, and deprived of the invigorating amalgam of the unspoiled desert Arabs, political unity could not endure. Everywhere there occurred revivals of suppressed racial or particularist tendencies. The very rapidity of Islam's expansion turned against it, now that the well-springs of that expansion were dried up. Islam had made millions of converts, of many sects and races, but it had digested them very imperfectly. Mohammed had really converted the Arabs, because he merely voiced ideas which were obscurely germinating in Arab minds and appealed to impulses innate in the Arab blood. When, however, Islam was accepted by non-Arab peoples, they instinctively interpreted the Prophet's message according to their particular racial tendencies and cultural backgrounds, the result being that primitive Islam was distorted or perverted. The most extreme example of this was in Persia, where the austere monotheism of Mohammed was transmuted into the elaborate mystical cult known as Shiism, which presently cut the Persians off from full communion with the orthodox Moslem world. The same transmutive tendency appears, in lesser degree, in the saint-worship of the North African Berbers and in the pantheism of the Hindu Moslems—both developments which Mohammed would have unquestionably execrated.

These doctrinal fissures in Islam were paralleled by the disruption of political unity. The first formal split occurred after the accession of the Abbasides. A member of the deposed Ommeyyad family fled to Spain, where he set up a rival caliphate at Cordova, recognized as lawful not only by the Spanish Moslems, but by the Berbers of North Africa. Later on another caliphate was set up in Egypt—the Fatimite caliphate, resting its title on descent from Mohammed's daughter Fatima. As for the Abbaside caliphs of Bagdad, they gradually declined in power, until they became mere puppets in the hands of a new racial element, the Turks.

Before describing that shift of power from Neo-Arab to Turkish hands which was so momentous for the history of the Islamic world, let us first consider the decline in cultural and intellectual vigour that set in concurrently with the disruption of political and religious unity during the later stages of the Neo-Arab period.

The Arabs of Mohammed's day were a fresh, unspoiled people in the full flush of pristine vigour, eager for adventure and inspired by a high ideal. They had their full share of Semitic fanaticism, but, though fanatical, they were not bigoted, that is to say, they possessed, not closed, but open minds. They held firmly to the tenets of their religion, but this religion was extremely simple. The core of Mohammed's teaching was theism plus certain practices. A strict belief in the unity of God, an equally strict belief in the divine mission[2] of Mohammed as set forth in the Koran, and certain clearly defined duties—prayer, ablutions, fasting, almsgiving, and pilgrimage—these, and these alone, constituted the Islam of the Arab conquerors of the Eastern world.

So simple a theology could not seriously fetter the Arab mind, alert, curious, eager to learn, and ready to adjust itself to conditions ampler and more complex than those prevailing in the parched environment of the desert. Now, not only did the Arabs relish the material advantages and luxuries of the more developed societies which they had conquered; they also appreciated the art, literature, science, and ideas of the older civilizations. The effect of these novel stimuli was the remarkable cultural and intellectual flowering which is the glory of Saracenic civilization. For a time thought was relatively free and produced a wealth of original ideas and daring speculations. These were the work not only of Arabs but also of subject Christians, Jews, and Persians, many of them being heretics previously depressed under the iron bands of persecuting Byzantine orthodoxy and Magism.

3

Gradually, however, this enlightened era passed away. Reactionary forces appeared and gained in strength. The liberals, who are usually known under the general title of "Motazelites," not only clung to the doctrinal simplicity of primitive Islam, but also contended that the test of all things should be reason. On the other hand, the conservative schools of thought asserted that the test should be precedent and authority. These men, many of them converted Christians imbued with the traditions of Byzantine orthodoxy, undertook an immense work of Koranic exegesis, combined with an equally elaborate codification and interpretation of the reputed sayings or "traditions" of Mohammed, as handed down by his immediate disciples and followers. As the result of these labours, there gradually arose a Moslem theology and scholastic philosophy as rigid, elaborate, and dogmatic as that of the mediæval Christian West.

Naturally, the struggle between the fundamentally opposed tendencies of traditionalism and rationalism was long and bitter. Yet the ultimate outcome was almost a foregone conclusion. Everything conspired to favour the triumph of dogma over reason. The whole historic tradition of the East (a tradition largely induced by racial and climatic factors[3]) was toward absolutism. This tradition had been interrupted by the inrush of the wild libertarianism of the desert. But the older tendency presently reasserted itself, stimulated as it was by the political transformation of the caliphate from theocratic, democracy to despotism.

This triumph of absolutism in the field of government in fact assured its eventual triumph in all other fields as well. For, in the long run, despotism can no more tolerate liberty of thought than it can liberty of action. Some of the Damascus caliphs, to be sure, toyed with Motazelism, the Ommeyyads being mainly secular-minded men to whom freethinking was intellectually attractive. But presently the caliphs became aware of liberalism's political implications. The Motazelites did not confine themselves to the realm of pure philosophic speculation. They also trespassed on more dangerous ground. Motazelite voices were heard recalling the democratic days of the Meccan caliphate, when the Commander of the Faithful, instead of being an hereditary monarch, was elected by the people and responsible to public opinion. Some bold spirits even entered into relations with the fierce fanatic sects of inner Arabia, like the Kharijites, who, upholding the old desert freedom, refused to recognize the caliphate and proclaimed theories of advanced republicanism.

The upshot was that the caliphs turned more and more toward the conservative theologians as against the liberals, just as they favoured the monarchist Neo-Arabs in preference to the intractable pure-blooded Arabs of the desert. Under the Abbasides the government came out frankly for religious absolutism. Standards of dogmatic orthodoxy were established, Motazelites were persecuted and put to death, and by the twelfth century a.d. the last vestiges of Saracenic liberalism were extirpated. The canons of Moslem thought were fixed. All creative activity ceased. The very memory of the great Motazelite doctors faded away. The Moslem mind was closed, not to be re-opened until our own day.

By the beginning of the eleventh century the decline of Saracenic civilization had become so pronounced that change was clearly in the air. Having lost their early vigour, the Neo-Arabs were to see their political power pass into other hands. These political heirs of the Neo-Arabs were the Turks. The Turks were a western branch of that congeries of nomadic tribes which, from time immemorial, have roamed over the limitless steppes of eastern and central Asia, and which are known collectively under the titles of "Uralo-Altaic" or "Turanian" peoples. The Arabs had been in contact with the Turkish nomads ever since the Islamic conquest of Persia, when the Moslem generals found the Turks beating restlessly against Persia's north-eastern frontiers. In the caliphate's palmy days the Turks were not feared. In fact, they were presently found to be very useful. A dull-witted folk with few ideas, the Turks could do two things superlatively well—obey orders and fight like devils. In other words, they made ideal mercenary soldiers. The caliphs were delighted, and enlisted ever larger numbers of them for their armies and their body-guards.

This was all very well while the caliphate was strong, but when it grew weak the situation altered. Rising everywhere to positions of authority, the Turkish mercenaries began to act like masters. Opening the eastern frontiers, they let in fresh swarms of their countrymen, who now came, not as individuals, but in tribes or "hordes" under their hereditary chiefs, wandering about at their own sweet will, settling where they pleased, and despoiling or evicting the local inhabitants.

The Turks soon renounced their ancestral paganism for Islam, but Islam made little change in their natures. In judging these Turkish newcomers we must not consider them the same as the present-day Ottoman Turks of Constantinople and Asia Minor. The modern Osmanli are so saturated with European and Near Eastern blood, and have been so leavened by Western and Saracenic ideas, they that are a very different people from their remote immigrant ancestors. Yet, even as it is, the modern Osmanli display enough of those unlovely Turanian traits which characterize the unmodified Turks of central Asia, often called "Turkomans," to distinguish them from their Ottoman kinsfolk to the west.

Now, what was the primitive Turkish nature? First and foremost, it was that of the professional soldier. Discipline was the Turk's watchword. No originality of thought, and but little curiosity. Few ideas ever penetrated the Turk's slow mind, and the few that did penetrate were received as military orders, to be obeyed without question and adhered to without reflection. Such was the being who took over the leadership of Islam from the Saracen's failing grasp.

No greater misfortune could have occurred both for Islam and for the world at large. For Islam it meant the rule of dull-witted bigots under which enlightened progress was impossible. Of course Islam did gain a great accession of warlike strength, but this new power was so wantonly misused as to bring down disastrous repercussions upon Islam itself. The first notable exploits of the immigrant Turkish hordes were their conquest of Asia Minor and their capture of Jerusalem, both events taking place toward the close of the eleventh century[4]. Up to this time Asia Minor had remained part of the Christian world. The original Arab flood of the seventh century, after overrunning Syria, had been stopped by the barrier of the Taurus Mountains; the Byzantine Empire had pulled itself together; and thenceforth, despite border bickerings, the Byzantine-Saracen frontier had remained substantially unaltered. Now, however, the Turks broke the Byzantine barrier, overran Asia Minor, and threatened even Constantinople, the eastern bulwark of Christendom. As for Jerusalem, it had, of course, been in Moslem hands since the Arab conquest of a.d. 637, but the caliph Omar had carefully respected the Christian "Holy Places," and his successors had neither persecuted the local Christians nor maltreated the numerous pilgrims who flocked perennially to Jerusalem from every part of the Christian world. But the Turks changed all this. Avid for loot, and filled with bigoted hatred of the "Misbelievers," they sacked the holy places, persecuted the Christians, and rendered pilgrimage impossible.

The effect of these twin disasters upon Christendom, occurring as they did almost simultaneously, was tremendous. The Christian West, then at the height of its religious fervour, quivered with mingled fear and wrath. Myriads of zealots, like Peter the Hermit, roused all Europe to frenzy. Fanaticism begat fanaticism, and the Christian West poured upon the Moslem East vast hosts of warriors in those extraordinary expeditions, the Crusades.

The Turkish conquest of Islam and its counterblast, the Crusades, were an immense misfortune for the world. They permanently worsened the relations between East and West. In the year a.d. 1000 Christian-Moslem relations were fairly good, and showed every prospect of becoming better. The hatreds engendered by Islam's first irruption were dying away. The frontiers of Islam and Christendom had become apparently fixed, and neither side showed much desire to encroach upon the other. The only serious debatable ground was Spain, where Moslem and Christian were continually at hand-grips; but, after all, Spain was mutually regarded as a frontier episode. Between Islam and Christendom, as a whole, intercourse was becoming steadily more friendly and more frequent. This friendly intercourse, if continued, might ultimately have produced momentous results for human progress. The Moslem world was at that time still well ahead of western Europe in knowledge and culture, but Saracenic civilization was ossifying, whereas the Christian West, despite its ignorance, rudeness, and barbarism, was bursting with lusty life and patently aspiring to better things. Had the nascent amity of East and West in the eleventh century continued to develop, both would have greatly profited. In the West the influence of Saracenic culture, containing, as it did, the ancient learning of Greece and Rome, might have awakened our Renaissance much earlier, while in the East the influence of the mediæval West, with its abounding vigour, might have saved Moslem civilization from the creeping paralysis which was overtaking it.

But it was not to be. In Islam the refined, easygoing Saracen gave place to the bigoted, brutal Turk. Islam became once more aggressive—not, as in its early days, for an ideal, but for sheer blood-lust, plunder, and destruction. Henceforth it was war to the knife between the only possible civilization and the most brutal and hopeless barbarism. Furthermore, this war was destined to last for centuries. The Crusades were merely Western counter-attacks against a Turkish assault on Christendom which continued for six hundred years and was definitely broken only under the walls of Vienna in 1683. Naturally, from these centuries of unrelenting strife furious hatreds and fanaticisms were engendered which still envenom the relations of Islam and Christendom. The atrocities of Mustapha Kemal's Turkish "Nationalists" and the atrocities of the Greek troops in Asia Minor, of which we read in our morning papers, are in no small degree a "carrying on" of the mutual atrocities of Turks and Crusaders in Palestine eight hundred years ago.

With the details of those old wars between Turks and Christians this book has no direct concern. The wars themselves should simply be noted as a chronic barrier between East and West. As for the Moslem East, with its declining Saracenic civilization bowed beneath the brutal Turkish yoke, it was presently exposed to even more terrible misfortunes. These misfortunes were also of Turanian origin. Toward the close of the twelfth century the eastern branches of the Turanian race were welded into a temporary unity by the genius of a mighty chieftain named Jenghiz Khan. Taking the sinister title of "The Inflexible Emperor," this arch-savage started out to loot the world. He first overran northern China, which he hideously ravaged, then turned his devastating course toward the west. Such was the rise of the terrible "Mongols," whose name still stinks in the nostrils of civilized mankind. Carrying with them skilled Chinese engineers using gunpowder for the reduction of fortified cities, Jenghiz Khan and his mounted hosts proved everywhere irresistible. The Mongols were the most appalling barbarians whom the world has ever seen. Their object was not conquest for settlement, not even loot, but in great part a sheer satanic lust for blood and destruction. They revelled in butchering whole populations, destroying cities, laying waste countrysides—and then passing on to fresh fields.

Jenghiz Khan died after a few years of his westward progress, but his successors continued his work with unabated zeal. Both Christendom and Islam were smitten by the Mongol scourge. All eastern Europe was ravaged and re-barbarized, the Russians showing ugly traces of the Mongol imprint to this day. But the woes of Christendom were as nothing to the woes of Islam. The Mongols never penetrated beyond Poland, and western Europe, the seat of Western civilization, was left unscathed. Not so Islam. Pouring down from the north-east, the Mongol hosts whirled like a cyclone over the Moslem world from India to Egypt, pillaging, murdering, and destroying. The nascent civilization of mediæval Persia, just struggling into the light beneath the incubus of Turkish harryings, was stamped flat under the Mongol hoofs, and the Mongols then proceeded to deal with the Moslem culture-centre—Bagdad. Bagdad had declined considerably from the gorgeous days of Haroun-al-Rashid, with its legendary million souls. However, it was still a great city, the seat of the caliphate and the unquestioned centre of Saracenic civilization. The Mongols stormed it (a.d. 1258), butchered its entire population, and literally wiped Bagdad off the face of the earth. And even this was not the worst. Bagdad was the capital of Mesopotamia. This "Land between the Rivers" had, in the very dawn of history, been reclaimed from swamp and desert by the patient labours of half-forgotten peoples who, with infinite toil, built up a marvellous system of irrigation that made Mesopotamia the perennial garden and granary of the world. Ages had passed and Mesopotamia had known many masters, but all these conquerors had respected, even cherished, the irrigation works which were the source of all prosperity. These works the Mongols wantonly, methodically destroyed. The oldest civilization in the world, the cradle of human culture, was hopelessly ruined; at least eight thousand years of continuous human effort went for naught, and Mesopotamia became the noisome land it still remains to-day, parched during the droughts of low water, soaked to fever-stricken marsh in the season of river-floods, tenanted only by a few mongrel fellahs inhabiting wretched mud villages, and cowed by nomad Bedouin browsing their flocks on the sites of ancient fields.

The destruction of Bagdad was a fatal blow to Saracenic civilization, especially in the East. And even before that dreadful disaster it had received a terrible blow in the West. Traversing North Africa in its early days, Islam had taken firm root in Spain, and had so flourished there that Spanish Moslem culture was fully abreast of that in the Moslem East. The capital of Spanish Islam was Cordova, the seat of the Western caliphate, a mighty city, perhaps more wonderful than Bagdad itself. For centuries Spanish Islam lived secure, confining the Christians to the mountainous regions of the north. As Saracen vigour declined, however, the Christians pressed the Moslems southward. In 1213 Spanish Islam was hopelessly broken at the tremendous battle of Las Navas de Tolosa. Thenceforth, for the victorious Christians it was a case of picking up the pieces. Cordova itself soon fell, and with it the glory of Spanish Islam, for the fanatical Christian Spaniards extirpated Saracenic civilization as effectually as the pagan Mongols were at that time doing. To be sure, a remnant of the Spanish Moslems held their ground at Granada, in the extreme south, until the year Columbus discovered America, but this was merely an episode. The Saracen civilization of the West was virtually destroyed.

Meanwhile the Moslem East continued to bleed under the Mongol scourge. Wave after wave of Mongol raiders passed over the land, the last notable invasion being that headed by the famous (or rather infamous) Tamerlane, early in the fifteenth century. By this time the western Mongols had accepted Islam, but that made little difference in their conduct. To show that Tamerlane was a true scion of his ancestor Jenghiz Khan, it may be remarked that his foible was pyramids of human skulls, his prize effort being one of 70,000 erected after the storming of the Persian city of Ispahan. After the cessation of the Mongol incursions, the ravaged and depopulated Moslem East fell under the sway of the Ottoman Turks.

The Ottoman Turks, or "Osmanli," were originally merely one of the many Turkish hordes which entered Asia Minor after the downfall of Byzantine rule. They owed their greatness mainly to a long line of able sultans, who gradually absorbed the neighbouring Turkish tribes and used this consolidated strength for ambitious conquests both to east and west. In 1453 the Osmanli extinguished the old Byzantine Empire by taking Constantinople, and within a century thereafter they had conquered the Moslem East from Persia to Morocco, had subjugated the whole Balkan Peninsula, and had advanced through Hungary to the walls of Vienna. Unlike their Mongol cousins, the Ottoman Turks built up a durable empire. It was a barbarous sort of empire, for the Turks understood very little about culture. The only things they could appreciate were military improvements. These, however, they thoroughly appreciated and kept fully abreast of the times. In their palmy days the Turks had the best artillery and the steadiest infantry in the world, and were the terror of Europe.

Meantime Europe was awakening to true progress and higher civilization. While the Moslem East was sinking under Mongol harryings and Turkish militarism, the Christian West was thrilling to the Renaissance and the discoveries of America and the water route to India. The effect of these discoveries simply cannot be over-estimated. When Columbus and Vasco da Gama made their memorable voyages at the end of the fifteenth century, Western civilization was pent up closely within the restricted bounds of west-central Europe, and was waging a defensive and none-too-hopeful struggle with the forces of Turanian barbarism. Russia lay under the heel of the Mongol Tartars, while the Turks, then in the full flush of their martial vigour, were marching triumphantly up from the south-east and threatening Europe's very heart. So strong were these Turanian barbarians, with Asia, North Africa, and eastern Europe in their grasp, that Western civilization was hard put to it to hold its own. Western civilization was, in fact, fighting with its back to the wall—the wall of a boundless ocean. We can hardly conceive how our mediæval forefathers viewed the ocean. To them it was a numbing, constricting presence; the abode of darkness and horror. No wonder mediæval Europe was static, since it faced on ruthless, aggressive Asia, and backed on nowhere. Then, in the twinkling of an eye, the sea-wall became a highway, and dead-end Europe became mistress of the ocean—and thereby mistress of the world.

The greatest strategic shift of fortune in all human history had taken place. Instead of fronting hopelessly on the fiercest of Asiatics, against whom victory by direct attack seemed impossible, the Europeans could now flank them at will. Furthermore, the balance of resources shifted in Europe's favour. Whole new worlds were unmasked whence Europe could draw limitless wealth to quicken its home life and initiate a progress that would soon place it immeasurably above its once-dreaded Asiatic assailants. What were the resources of the stagnant Moslem East compared with those of the Americas and the Indies? So Western civilization, quickened, energized, progressed with giant strides, shook off its mediæval fetters, grasped the talisman of science, and strode into the light of modern times.

Yet all this left Islam unmoved. Wrapping itself in the tatters of Saracenic civilization, the Moslem East continued to fall behind. Even its military power presently vanished, for the Turk sank into lethargy and ceased to cultivate the art of war. For a time the West, busied with internal conflicts, hesitated to attack the East, so great was the prestige of the Ottoman name. But the crushing defeat of the Turks in their rash attack upon Vienna in 1683 showed the West that the Ottoman Empire was far gone in decrepitude. Thenceforth, the empire was harried mercilessly by Western assaults and was saved from collapse only by the mutual jealousies of Western Powers, quarrelling over the Turkish spoils.

However, not until the nineteenth century did the Moslem world, as a whole, feel the weight of Western attack. Throughout the eighteenth century the West assailed the ends of the Moslem battle-line in eastern Europe and the Indies, but the bulk of Islam, from Morocco to Central Asia, remained almost immune. The Moslem world failed to profit by this respite. Plunged in lethargy, contemptuous of the European "Misbelievers," and accepting defeats as

8

the inscrutable will of Allah, Islam continued to live its old life, neither knowing nor caring to know anything about Western ideas or Western progress.

Such was the decrepit Moslem world which faced nineteenth-century Europe, energized by the Industrial Revolution, armed as never before by modern science and invention which had unlocked nature's secrets and placed hitherto-undreamed-of weapons in its aggressive hands. The result was a foregone conclusion. One by one, the decrepit Moslem states fell before the Western attack, and the whole Islamic world was rapidly partitioned among the European Powers. England took India and Egypt, Russia crossed the Caucasus and mastered Central Asia, France conquered North Africa, while other European nations grasped minor portions of the Moslem heritage. The Great War witnessed the final stage in this process of subjugation. By the terms of the treaties which marked its close, Turkey was extinguished and not a single Mohammedan state retained genuine independence. The subjection of the Moslem world was complete—on paper.

On paper! For, in its very hour of apparent triumph, Western domination was challenged as never before. During those hundred years of Western conquest a mighty internal change had been coming over the Moslem world. The swelling tide of Western aggression had at last moved the "immovable" East. At last Islam became conscious of its decrepitude, and with that consciousness a vast ferment, obscure yet profound, began to leaven the 250,000,000 followers of the Prophet from Morocco to China and from Turkestan to the Congo. The first spark was fittingly struck in the Arabian desert, the cradle of Islam. Here at the opening of the nineteenth century, arose the Wahabi movement for the reform of Islam, which presently kindled the far-flung "Mohammedan Revival," which in its turn begat the movement known as "Pan-Islamism." Furthermore, athwart these essentially internal movements there came pouring a flood of external stimuli from the West—ideas such as parliamentary government, nationalism, scientific education, industrialism, and even ultra-modern concepts like feminism, socialism, Bolshevism. Stirred by the interaction of all these novel forces and spurred by the ceaseless pressure of European aggression, the Moslem world roused more and more to life and action. The Great War was a shock of terrific potency, and to-day Islam is seething with mighty forces fashioning a new Moslem world. What are those forces moulding the Islam of the future? To their analysis and appraisal the body of this book is devoted.

FOOTNOTES:

[1] I. e. "Successor"; anglicized into the word "Caliph."

[2] To be carefully distinguished from divinity. Mohammed not only did not make any pretensions to divinity, but specifically disclaimed any such attributes. He regarded himself as the last of a series of divinely inspired prophets, beginning with Adam and extending through Moses and Jesus to himself, the mouthpiece of God's last and most perfect revelation.

[3] The influence of environment and heredity on human evolution in general and on the history of the East in particular, though of great importance, cannot be treated in a summary such as this. The influence of climatic and other environmental factors has been ably treated by Prof. Ellsworth Huntington in his various works, such as The Pulse of Asia (Boston, 1907); Civilization and Climate (Yale Univ. Press, 1915), and World-Power and Evolution (Yale Univ. Press, 1919). See also Chap. III. in Arminius Vambéry—Der Islam im neunzehnten Jahrhundert. Eine culturgeschichtliche Studie (Leipzig, 1875). For a summary of racial influences in Eastern history, see Madison Grant—The Passing of the Great Race (N.Y., 1916).

[4] The Turkish overrunning of Asia Minor took place after the destruction of the Byzantine army in the great battle of Manzikert, a.d. 1071. The Turks captured Jerusalem in 1076.


CHAPTER I

THE MOHAMMEDAN REVIVAL

By the eighteenth century the Moslem world had sunk to the lowest depth of its decrepitude. Nowhere were there any signs of healthy vigour, everywhere were stagnation and decay. Manners and morals were alike execrable. The last vestiges of Saracenic culture had vanished in a barbarous luxury of the few and an equally barbarous degradation of the multitude. Learning was virtually dead, the few universities which survived fallen into dreary decay and languishing in poverty and neglect. Government had become despotism tempered by anarchy and assassination. Here and there a major despot like the Sultan of Turkey or the Indian "Great Mogul" maintained some semblance of state authority, albeit provincial pashas were for ever striving to erect independent governments based, like their masters', on tyranny and extortion. The pashas, in turn, strove ceaselessly against unruly local chiefs and swarms of brigands who infested the countryside. Beneath this sinister hierarchy groaned the people, robbed, bullied, and ground into the dust. Peasant and townsman had alike lost all incentive to labour or initiative, and both agriculture and trade had fallen to the lowest level compatible with bare survival.

As for religion, it was as decadent as everything else. The austere monotheism of Mohammed had become overlaid with a rank growth of superstition and puerile mysticism. The mosques stood unfrequented and ruinous, deserted by the ignorant multitude, which, decked out in amulets, charms, and rosaries, listened to squalid fakirs or ecstatic dervishes, and went on pilgrimages to the tombs of "holy men," worshipped as saints and "intercessors" with that Allah who had become too remote a being for the direct devotion of these benighted souls. As for the moral precepts of the Koran, they were ignored or defied. Wine-drinking and opium-eating were well-nigh universal, prostitution was rampant, and the most degrading vices flaunted naked and unashamed. Even the holy cities, Mecca and Medina, were sink-holes of iniquity, while the "Hajj," or pilgrimage ordained by the Prophet, had become a scandal through its abuses. In fine: the life had apparently gone out of Islam, leaving naught but a dry husk of soulless ritual and degrading superstition behind. Could Mohammed have returned to earth, he would unquestionably have anathematized his followers as apostates and idolaters.

Yet, in this darkest hour, a voice came crying out of the vast Arabian desert, the cradle of Islam, calling the faithful back to the true path. This puritan reformer, the famous Abd-el-Wahab, kindled a fire which presently spread to the remotest corners of the Moslem world, purging Islam of its sloth and reviving the fervour of olden days. The great Mohammedan Revival had begun.

Mahommed ibn Abd-el-Wahab was born about the year a.d. 1700 in the heart of the Arabian desert, the region known as the Nejd. The Nejd was the one clean spot in the decadent Moslem world. We have already seen how, with the transformation of the caliphate from a theocratic democracy to an Oriental despotism, the free-spirited Arabs had returned scornfully to their deserts. Here they had maintained their wild freedom. Neither caliph nor sultan dared venture far into those vast solitudes of burning sand and choking thirst, where the rash invader was lured to sudden death in a whirl of stabbing spears. The Arabs recognized no master, wandering at will with their flocks and camels, or settled here and there in green oases hidden in the desert's heart. And in the desert they retained their primitive political and religious virtues. The nomad Bedouin lived under the sway of patriarchal "sheiks"; the settled dwellers in the oases usually acknowledged the authority of some leading family. But these rulers possessed the slenderest authority, narrowly circumscribed by well-established custom and a jealous public opinion which they transgressed at their peril. The Turks, to be sure, had managed to acquire a precarious authority over the holy cities and the Red Sea littoral, but the Nejd, the vast interior, was free. And, in religion, as in politics, the desert Arabs kept the faith of their fathers. Scornfully rejecting the corruptions of decadent Islam, they held fast to the simple theology of primitive Islam, so congenial to their Arab natures.

Into this atmosphere of an older and better age, Abd-el-Wahab was born. Displaying from the first a studious and religious bent, he soon acquired a reputation for learning and sanctity. Making the Meccan pilgrimage while still a young man, he studied at Medina and travelled as far as Persia, returning ultimately to the Nejd. He returned burning with holy wrath at what he had seen, and determined to preach a puritan reformation. For years he wandered up and down Arabia, and at last he converted Mahommed, head of the great clan of Saud, the most powerful chieftain in all the Nejd. This gave Abd-el-Wahab both moral prestige and material strength, and he made the most of his opportunities. Gradually, the desert Arabs were welded into a politico-religious unity like that effected by the Prophet. Abd-el-Wahab was, in truth, a faithful counterpart of the first caliphs, Abu Bekr and Omar. When he died in 1787 his disciple, Saud, proved a worthy successor. The new Wahabi state was a close counterpart of the Meccan caliphate. Though possessing great military power, Saud always considered himself responsible to public opinion and never encroached upon the legitimate freedom of his subjects. Government, though stern, was able and just. The Wahabi judges were competent and honest. Robbery, became almost unknown, so well was the public peace maintained. Education was sedulously fostered. Every oasis had its school, while teachers were sent to the Bedouin tribes.

Having consolidated the Nejd, Saud was now ready to undertake the greater task of subduing and purifying the Moslem world. His first objective was of course the holy cities. This objective was attained in the opening years of the nineteenth century. Nothing could stand against the rush of the Wahabi hosts burning with fanatic hatred against the Turks, who were loathed both as apostate Moslems and as usurpers of that supremacy in Islam which all Arabs believed should rest in Arab hands. When Saud died in 1814 he was preparing to invade Syria. It looked for a moment as though the Wahabis were to sweep the East and puritanize all Islam at a blow.

But it was not to be. Unable to stem the Wahabi flood, the Sultan of Turkey called on his powerful vassal, the famous Mehemet Ali. This able Albanian adventurer had by that time made himself master of Egypt. Frankly recognizing the superiority of the West, he had called in numerous European officers who rapidly fashioned a formidable army, composed largely of hard-fighting Albanian highlanders, and disciplined and equipped after European models. Mehemet Ali gladly answered the Sultan's summons, and it soon became clear that even Wahabi fanaticism was no match for European muskets and artillery handled by seasoned veterans. In a short time the holy cities were recaptured and the Wahabis were driven back into the desert. The nascent Wahabi empire had vanished like a mirage. Wahabism's political rôle was ended.[5]

11

However, Wahabism's spiritual rôle had only just begun. The Nejd remained a focus of puritan zeal whence the new spirit radiated in all directions. Even in the holy cities Wahabism continued to set the religious tone, and the numberless "Hajjis," or pilgrims, who came annually from every part of the Moslem world returned to their homes zealous reformers. Soon the Wahabi leaven began to produce profound disturbances in the most distant quarters. For example, in northern India a Wahabi fanatic, Seyid Ahmed,[6] so roused the Punjabi Mohammedans that he actually built up a theocratic state, and only his chance death prevented a possible Wahabi conquest of northern India. This state was shattered by the Sikhs, about 1830, but when the English conquered the country they had infinite trouble with the smouldering embers of Wahabi feeling, which, in fact, lived on, contributed to the Indian mutiny, and permanently fanaticized Afghanistan and the wild tribes of the Indian North-West Frontier.[7] It was during these years that the famous Seyid Mahommed ben Sennussi came from his Algerian home to Mecca and there imbibed those Wahabi principles which led to the founding of the great Pan-Islamic fraternity that bears his name. Even the Babbist movement in Persia, far removed though it was doctrinally from Wahabi teaching, was indubitably a secondary reflex of the Wahabi urge.[8] In fact, within a generation, the strictly Wahabi movement had broadened into the larger development known as the Mohammedan Revival, and this in turn was developing numerous phases, chief among them being the movement usually termed Pan-Islamism. That movement, particularly on its political side, I shall treat in the next chapter. At present let us examine the other aspects of the Mohammedan Revival, with special reference to its religious and cultural phases.

The Wahabi movement was a strictly puritan reformation. Its aim was the reform of abuses, the abolition of superstitious practices, and a return to primitive Islam. All later accretions— the writings and interpretations of the mediæval theologians, ceremonial or mystical innovations, saint worship, in fact every sort of change, were condemned. The austere monotheism of Mohammed was preached in all its uncompromising simplicity, and the Koran, literally interpreted, was taken as the sole guide for human action. This doctrinal simplification was accompanied by a most rigid code of morals. The prayers, fastings, and other practices enjoined by Mohammed were scrupulously observed. The most austere manner of living was enforced. Silken clothing, rich food, wine, opium, tobacco, coffee, and all other indulgences were sternly proscribed. Even religious architecture was practically tabooed, the Wahabis pulling down the Prophet's tomb at Medina and demolishing the minarets of mosques as godless innovations. The Wahabis were thus, despite their moral earnestness, excessively narrow-minded, and it was very fortunate for Islam that they soon lost their political power and were compelled thenceforth to confine their efforts to moral teaching.

Many critics of Islam point to the Wahabi movement as a proof that Islam is essentially retrograde and innately incapable of evolutionary development. These criticisms, however, appear to be unwarranted. The initial stage of every religious reformation is an uncritical return to the primitive cult. To the religious reformer the only way of salvation is a denial of all subsequent innovations, regardless of their character. Our own Protestant Reformation began in just this way, and Humanists like Erasmus, repelled and disgusted by Protestantism's puritanical narrowness, could see no good in the movement, declaring that it menaced all true culture and merely replaced an infallible Pope by an infallible Bible.

As a matter of fact, the puritan beginnings of the Mohammedan Revival presently broadened along more constructive lines, some of these becoming tinged with undoubted liberalism. The Moslem reformers of the early nineteenth century had not dug very deeply into their religious past before they discovered—Motazelism. We have already reviewed the great struggle which had raged between reason and dogma in Islam's early days, in which dogma had triumphed so completely that the very memory of Motazelism had faded away. Now, however, those memories were revived, and the liberal-minded reformers were delighted to find such striking confirmation of their ideas, both in the writings of the Motazelite doctors and in the sacred texts themselves. The principle that reason and not blind prescription was to be the test opened the door to the possibility of all those reforms which they had most at heart. For example, the reformers found that in the traditional writings Mohammed was reported to have said: "I am no more than a man; when I order you anything respecting religion, receive it; when I order you about the affairs of the world, then I am nothing more than man." And, again, as though foreseeing the day when sweeping changes would be necessary. "Ye are in an age in which, if ye abandon one-tenth of that which is ordered, ye will be ruined. After this, a time will come when he who shall observe one-tenth of what is now ordered will be redeemed."[9]

Before discussing the ideas and efforts of the modern Moslem reformers, it might be well to examine the assertions made by numerous Western critics, that Islam is by its very nature incapable of reform and progressive adaptation to the expansion of human knowledge. Such is the contention not only of Christian polemicists,[10] but also of rationalists like Renan and European administrators of Moslem populations like Lord Cromer. Lord Cromer, in fact, pithily summarizes this critical attitude in his statement: "Islam cannot be reformed; that is to say, reformed Islam is Islam no longer; it is something else."[11]

Now these criticisms, coming as they do from close students of Islam often possessing intimate personal acquaintance with Moslems, deserve respectful consideration. And yet an historical survey of religions, and especially a survey of the thoughts and accomplishments of Moslem reformers during the past century, seem to refute these pessimistic charges.

In the first place, it should be remembered that Islam to-day stands just about where Christendom stood in the fifteenth century, at the beginning of the Reformation. There is the same supremacy of dogma over reason, the same blind adherence to prescription and authority, the same suspicion and hostility to freedom of thought or scientific knowledge. There is no doubt that a study of the Mohammedan sacred texts, particularly of the "sheriat" or canon law, together with a glance over Moslem history for the last thousand years, reveal an attitude on the whole quite incompatible with modern progress and civilization. But was not precisely the same thing true of Christendom at the beginning of the fifteenth century? Compare the sheriat with the Christian canon law. The spirit is the same. Take, for example, the sheriat's prohibition on the lending of money at interest; a prohibition which, if obeyed, renders impossible anything like business or industry in the modern sense. This is the example oftenest cited to prove Islam's innate incompatibility with modern civilization. But the Christian canon law equally forbade interest, and enforced that prohibition so strictly, that for centuries the Jews had a monopoly of business in Europe, while the first Christians who dared to lend money (the Lombards) were regarded almost as heretics, were universally hated, and were frequently persecuted. Again, take the matter of Moslem hostility to freedom of thought and scientific investigation. Can Islam show anything more revolting than that scene in Christian history when, less than three hundred years ago,[12] the great Galileo was haled before the Papal Inquisition and forced, under threat of torture, to recant the damnable heresy that the earth went round the sun?

As a matter of fact, Mohammed reverenced knowledge. His own words are eloquent testimony to that. Here are some of his sayings:

"Seek knowledge, even, if need be, on the borders of China."

"Seek knowledge from the cradle to the grave."

"One word of knowledge is of more value than the reciting of a hundred prayers."

"The ink of sages is more precious than the blood of martyrs."

"One word of wisdom, learned and communicated to a Moslem brother, outweighs the prayers of a whole year."

"Wise men are the successors of the Prophet."

"God has created nothing better than reason."

"In truth, a man may have prayed, fasted, given alms, made pilgrimage, and all other good works; nevertheless, he shall be rewarded only in the measure that he has used his common sense."

These citations (and there are others of the same tenor) prove that the modern Moslem reformers have good scriptural backing for their liberal attitude. Of course I do not imply that the reform movement in Islam, just because it is liberal and progressive, is thereby ipso facto assured of success. History reveals too many melancholy instances to the contrary. Indeed, we have already seen how, in Islam itself, the promising liberal movement of its early days passed utterly away. What history does show, however, is that when the times favour progress, religions are adapted to that progress by being reformed and liberalized. No human society once fairly on the march was ever turned back by a creed. Halted it may be, but if the progressive urge persists, the doctrinal barrier is either surmounted, undermined, flanked, or swept aside. Now there is no possibility that the Moslem world will henceforth lack progressive influences. It is in close contact with Western civilization, and is being increasingly permeated with Western ideas. Islam cannot break away and isolate itself if it would. Everything therefore portends its profound modification. Of course critics like Lord Cromer contend that this modified Islam will be Islam no longer. But why not? If the people continue to call themselves Mohammedans and continue to draw spiritual sustenance from the message of Mohammed, why should they be denied the name? Modern Christianity is certainly vastly different from mediæval Christianity, while among the various Christian churches there exist the widest doctrinal variations. Yet all who consider themselves Christians are considered Christians by all except bigots out of step with the times.

Let us now scrutinize the Moslem reformers, judging them, not by texts and chronicles, but by their words and deeds; since, as one of their number, an Algerian, very pertinently remarks, "men should be judged, not by the letter of their sacred books, but by what they actually do."[13]

Modern Moslem liberalism, as we have seen, received its first encouragement from the discovery of the old Motazelite literature of nearly a thousand years before. To be sure, Islam had never been quite destitute of liberal minds. Even in its darkest days a few voices had been raised against the prevailing obscurantism. For example, in the sixteenth century the celebrated El-Gharani had written: "It is not at all impossible that God may hold in reserve for men of the future perceptions that have not been vouchsafed to the men of the past. Divine munificence never ceases to pour benefits and enlightenment into the hearts of wise men of every age."[14] These isolated voices from Islam's Dark Time helped to encourage the modern reformers, and by the middle of the nineteenth century every Moslem land had its group of forward-looking men. At first their numbers were, of course, insignificant, and of course they drew down upon themselves the anathemas of the fanatic Mollahs[15] and the hatred of the ignorant multitude. The first country where the reformers made their influence definitely felt was in India. Here a group headed by the famous Sir Syed Ahmed Khan started an important liberal movement, founding associations, publishing books and newspapers, and establishing the well-known college of Aligarh. Sir Syed Ahmed is a good type of the early liberal reformers. Conservative in temperament and perfectly orthodox in his theology, he yet denounced the current decadence of Islam with truly Wahabi fervour. He also was frankly appreciative of Western ideas and eager to assimilate the many good things which the West had to offer. As he wrote in 1867: "We must study European scientific works, even though they are not written by Moslems and though we may find in them things contrary to the teachings of the Koran. We should imitate the Arabs of olden days, who did not fear to shake their faith by studying Pythagoras."[16]

This nucleus of Indian Moslem liberals rapidly grew in strength, producing able leaders like Moulvie Cheragh Ali and Syed Amir Ali, whose scholarly works in faultless English are known throughout the world.[17] These men called themselves "Neo-Motazelites" and boldly advocated reforms such as a thorough overhauling of the sheriat and a general modernization of Islam. Their view-point is well set forth by another of their leading figures, S. Khuda Bukhsh. "Nothing was more distant from the Prophet's thought," he writes, "than to fetter the mind or to lay down fixed, immutable, unchanging laws for his followers. The Quran is a book of guidance to the faithful, and not an obstacle in the path, of their social, moral, legal, and intellectual progress." He laments Islam's present backwardness, for he continues: "Modern Islam, with its hierarchy of priesthood, gross fanaticism, appalling ignorance, and superstitious practices is, indeed, a discredit to the Islam of the Prophet Mohammed." He concludes with the following liberal confession of faith: "Is Islam hostile to progress? I will emphatically answer this question in the negative. Islam, stripped of its theology, is a perfectly simple religion. Its cardinal principle is belief in one God and belief in Mohammed as his apostle. The rest is mere accretion, superfluity."[18]

Meanwhile, the liberals were making themselves felt in other parts of the Moslem world. In Turkey liberals actually headed the government during much of the generation between the Crimean War and the despotism of Abdul Hamid,[19] and Turkish liberal ministers like Reshid Pasha and Midhat Pasha made earnest though unavailing efforts to liberalize and modernize the Ottoman Empire. Even the dreadful Hamidian tyranny could not kill Turkish liberalism. It went underground or into exile, and in 1908 put through the revolution which deposed the tyrant and brought the "Young Turks" to power. In Egypt liberalism took firm root, represented by men like Sheikh Mohammed Abdou, Rector of El Azhar University and respected friend of Lord Cromer. Even outlying fragments of Islam like the Russian Tartars awoke to the new spirit and produced liberal-minded, forward-looking men.[20]

The liberal reformers, whom I have been describing, of course form the part of evolutionary progress in Islam. They are in the best sense of the word conservatives, receptive to healthy change, yet maintaining their hereditary poise. Sincerely religious men, they have faith in Islam as a living, moral force, and from it they continue to draw their spiritual sustenance.

There are, however, other groups in the Moslem world who have so far succumbed to Western influences that they have more or less lost touch with both their spiritual and cultural pasts. In all the more civilized portions of the Moslem world, especially in countries long under European control like India, Egypt, and Algeria, there are many Moslems, Western educated and Western culture-veneered, who have drifted into an attitude varying from easygoing religious indifference to avowed agnosticism. From their minds the old Moslem zeal has entirely departed. The Algerian Ismael Hamet well describes the attitude of this class of his fellow-countrymen when he writes: "European scepticism is not without influence upon the Algerian Moslems, who, if they have kept some attachment for the external forms of their religion, usually ignore the unhealthy excesses of the religious sentiment. They do not give up their religion, but they no longer dream of converting all those who do not practise it; they want to hand it on to their children, but they do not worry about other men's salvation. This is not belief; it is not even free thought; but it is lukewarmness."[21]

Beyond these tepid latitudinarians are still other groups of a very different character. Here we find combined the most contradictory sentiments: young men whose brains are seething with radical Western ideas—atheism, socialism, Bolshevism, and what not. Yet, curiously enough, these fanatic radicals tend to join hands with the fanatic reactionaries of Islam in a common hatred of the West. Considering themselves the born leaders (and exploiters) of the ignorant masses, the radicals hunger for political power and rage against that Western domination which vetoes their ambitious pretensions. Hence, they are mostly extreme "Nationalists," while they are also deep in Pan-Islamic reactionary schemes. Indeed, we often witness the strange spectacle of atheists posing as Moslem fanatics and affecting a truly dervish zeal. Mr. Bukhsh well describes this type when he writes: "I know a gentleman, a Mohammedan by profession, who owes his success in life to his faith. Though, outwardly, he conforms to all the precepts of Islam and occasionally stands up in public as the champion and spokesman of his co-religionists; yet, to my utter horror, I found that he held opinions about his religion and its founder which even Voltaire would have rejected with indignation and Gibbon with commiserating contempt."[22]

Later on we shall examine more fully the activities of these gentry in the chapters devoted to Pan-Islamism and Nationalism. What I desire to emphasize here is their pernicious influence on the prospects of a genuine Mohammedan reformation as visualized by the true reformers whom I have described. Their malevolent desire to stir up the fanatic passions of the ignorant masses and their equally malevolent hatred of everything Western except military improvements are revealed by outbursts like the following from the pen of a prominent "Young Turk." "Yes, the Mohammedan religion is in open hostility to all your world of progress. Learn, ye European observers, that a Christian, whatever his position, by the mere fact that he is a Christian, is in our eyes a being devoid of all human dignity. Our reasoning is simple and definitive. We say: the man whose judgment is so perverted as to deny the evidence of the One God and to fabricate gods of different kinds, cannot be other than the most ignoble expression of human stupidity. To speak to him would be a humiliation to our reason and an offence to the grandeur of the Master of the Universe. The worshipper of false gods is a monster of ingratitude; he is the execration of the universe; to combat him, convert him, or annihilate him is the holiest task of the Faithful. These are the eternal commands of our One God. For us there are in this world only Believers and Misbelievers; love, charity, fraternity to Believers; disgust, hatred, and war to Misbelievers. Among Misbelievers, the most odious and criminal are those who, while recognizing God, create Him of earthly parents, give Him a son, a mother; so monstrous an aberration surpasses, in our eyes, all bounds of iniquity; the presence of such miscreants among us is the bane of our existence; their doctrine is a direct insult to the purity of our faith; their contact a pollution for our bodies; any relation with them a torture for our souls.

"While detesting you, we have been studying your political institutions and your military organizations. Besides the new arms which Providence procures for us by your own means, you yourselves have rekindled the inextinguishable faith of our heroic martyrs. Our Young Turks, our Babis, our new fraternities, all are sects in their varied forms, are inspired by the same thought, the same purpose. Toward what end? Christian civilization? Never!"[23]

Such harangues unfortunately find ready hearers among the Moslem masses. Although the liberal reformers are a growing power in Islam, it must not be forgotten that they are as yet only a minority, an élite, below whom lie the ignorant masses, still suffering from the blight of age-long obscurantism, wrapped in admiration of their own world, which they regard as the highest ideal of human existence, and fanatically hating everything outside as wicked, despicable, and deceptive. Even when compelled to admit the superior power of the West, they hate it none the less. They rebel blindly against the spirit of change which is forcing them out of their old ruts, and their anger is still further heightened by that ubiquitous Western domination which is pressing upon them from all sides. Such persons are as clay in the hands of the Pan-Islamic and Nationalist leaders who mould the multitude to their own sinister ends.

Islam is, in fact, to-day torn between the forces of liberal reform and chauvinistic reaction. The liberals are not only the hope of an evolutionary reformation, they are also favoured by the trend of the times, since the Moslem world is being continually permeated by Western progress and must continue to be thus permeated unless Western civilization itself collapses in ruin. Yet, though the ultimate triumph of the liberals appears probable, what delays, what setbacks, what fresh barriers of warfare and fanaticism may not the chauvinist reactionaries bring about! Neither the reform of Islam nor the relations between East and West are free from perils whose ominous possibilities we shall later discuss.

Meanwhile, there remains the hopeful fact that throughout the Moslem world a numerous and powerful minority, composed not merely of Westernized persons but also of orthodox conservatives, are aware of Islam's decadence and are convinced that a thoroughgoing reformation along liberal, progressive lines is at once a practical necessity and a sacred duty. Exactly how this reformation shall be legally effected has not yet been determined, nor is a detailed discussion of technical machinery necessary for our consideration.[24] History teaches us that where the will to reform is vitally present, reformation will somehow or other be accomplished.

One thing is certain: the reforming spirit, in its various manifestations, has already produced profound changes throughout Islam. The Moslem world of to-day is vastly different from the Moslem world of a century ago. The Wahabi leaven has destroyed abuses and has rekindled a purer religious faith. Even its fanatical zeal has not been without moral compensations. The spread of liberal principles and Western progress goes on apace. If there is much to fear for the future, there is also much to hope.

FOOTNOTES:

[5] On the Wahabi movement, see A. Le Chatelier, L'Islam au dix-neuvième Siècle (Paris, 1888); W. G. Palgrave, Essays on Eastern Questions (London, 1872); D. B. Macdonald, Muslim Theology (London, 1903); J. L. Burckhardt, Notes on the Bedouins and Wahabys (2 vols., London, 1831); A. Chodzko, "Le Déisme des Wahhabis," Journal Asiatique, IV., Vol. II., pp. 168 et seq.

[6] Not to be confused with Sir Syed Ahmed of Aligarh, the Indian Moslem liberal of the mid-nineteenth century.

[7] For English alarm at the latent fanaticism of the North Indian Moslems, down through the middle of the nineteenth century, see Sir W. W. Hunter, The Indian Musalmans (London, 1872).

[8] For the Babbist movement, see Clément Huart, La Réligion de Bab (Paris, 1889); Comte Arthur de Gobineau, Trois Ans en Perse (Paris, 1867). A good summary of all these early movements of the Mohammedan revival is found in Le Chatelier, op. cit.

[9] Mishkat-el-Masabih, I., 46, 51.

[10] The best recent examples of this polemical literature are the writings of the Rev. S. M. Zwemer, the well known missionary to the Arabs; especially his Arabia, the Cradle of Islam (Edinburgh, 1900), and The Reproach of Islam (London, 1915). Also see volume entitled The Mohammedan World of To-day, being a collection of the papers read at the Protestant Missionary Conference held at Cairo, Egypt, in 1906.

[11] Cromer, Modern Egypt, Vol. II., p. 229 (London, 1908). For Renan's attitude, see his L'Islamisme et la Science (Paris, 1883).

[12] In the year 1633.

[13] Ismael Hamet, Les Musulmans français du Nord de l'Afrique (Paris, 1906).

[14] Quoted by Dr. Perron in his work L'Islamisme (Paris, 1877).

[15] The Mollahs are the Moslem clergy, though they do not exactly correspond to the clergy of Christendom. Mohammed was averse to anything like a priesthood, and Islam makes no legal provision for an ordained priestly class or caste, as is the case in Christianity, Judaism, Brahmanism, and other religions. Theoretically any Moslem can conduct religious services. As time passed, however, a class of men developed who were learned in Moslem theology and law. These ultimately became practically priests, though theoretically they should be regarded as theological lawyers. There also developed religious orders of dervishes, etc.; but primitive Islam knew nothing of them.

[16] From the article by Léon Cahun in Lavisse et Rambeaud, Histoire Générale, Vol. XII., p. 498. This article gives an excellent general survey of the intellectual development of the Moslem world in the nineteenth century.

[17] Especially his best-known book, The Spirit of Islam (London, 1891).

[18] S. Khuda Bukhsh, Essays: Indian and Islamic, pp. 20, 24, 284. (London, 1912).

[19] 1856 to 1878.

[20] For the liberal movement among the Russian Tartars, see Arminius Vambéry, Western Culture in Eastern Lands (London, 1906).

[21] Ismael Hamet, Les Musulmans français du Nord de l'Afrique, p. 268 (Paris, 1906).

[22] S. Khuda Bukhsh, op. cit., p. 241.

[23] Sheikh Abd-ul-Haak, in Sherif Pasha's organ, Mecheroutiette, of August, 1921. Quoted from A. Servier, Le Nationalisme musulman, Constantine, Algeria, 1913.

[24] For such discussion of legal methods, see W. S. Blunt, The Future of Islam (London, 1882); A. Le Chatelier, L'Islam au dix-neuvième Siècle (Paris, 1888); Dr. Perron, L'Islamisme

(Paris, 1877); H. N. Brailsford "Modernism in Islam," The Fortnightly Review, September, 1908; Sir Theodore Morison, "Can Islam be Reformed?" The Nineteenth Century and After, October, 1908; M. Pickthall, "La Morale islamique," Revue Politique Internationale, July, 1916; XX, "L'Islam après la Guerre," Revue de Paris, 15 January, 1916.

CHAPTER II

PAN-ISLAMISM

Like all great movements, the Mohammedan Revival is highly complex. Starting with the simple, puritan protest of Wahabism, it has developed many phases, widely diverse and sometimes almost antithetical. In the previous chapter we examined the phase looking toward an evolutionary reformation of Islam and a genuine assimilation of the progressive spirit as well as the external forms of Western civilization. At the same time we saw that these liberal reformers are as yet only a minority, an élite; while the Moslem masses, still plunged in ignorance and imperfectly awakened from their age-long torpor, are influenced by other leaders of a very different character—men inclined to militant rather than pacific courses, and hostile rather than receptive to the West. These militant forces are, in their turn, complex. They may be grouped roughly under the general concepts known as "Pan-Islamism" and "Nationalism." It is to a consideration of the first of these two concepts, to Pan-Islamism, that this chapter is devoted.

Pan-Islamism, which in its broadest sense is the feeling of solidarity between all "True Believers," is as old as the Prophet, when Mohammed and his few followers were bound together by the tie of faith against their pagan compatriots who sought their destruction. To Mohammed the principle of fraternal solidarity among Moslems was of transcendent importance, and he succeeded in implanting this so deeply in Moslem hearts that thirteen centuries have not sensibly weakened it. The bond between Moslem and Moslem is to-day much stronger than that between Christian and Christian. Of course Moslems fight bitterly among themselves, but these conflicts never quite lose the aspect of family quarrels and tend to be adjourned in presence of infidel aggression. Islam's profound sense of solidarity probably explains in large part its extraordinary hold upon its followers. No other religion has such a grip on its votaries. Islam has won vast territories from Christianity and Brahmanism,[25] and has driven Magism from the face of the earth;[26] yet there has been no single instance where a people, once become Moslem, has ever abandoned the faith. Extirpated they may have been, like the Moors of Spain, but extirpation is not apostasy.

Islam's solidarity is powerfully buttressed by two of its fundamental institutions: the "Hajj," or pilgrimage to Mecca, and the caliphate. Contrary to the general opinion in the West, it is the Hajj rather than the caliphate which has exerted the more consistently unifying influence. Mohammed ordained the Hajj as a supreme act of faith, and every year fully 100,000 pilgrims arrive, drawn from every quarter of the Moslem world. There, before the sacred Kaaba of Mecca, men of all races, tongues, and cultures meet and mingle in an ecstasy of common devotion, returning to their homes bearing the proud title of "Hajjis," or Pilgrims—a title which insures them the reverent homage of their fellow Moslems for all the rest of their days. The political implications of the Hajj are obvious. It is in reality a perennial Pan-Islamic congress, where all the interests of the faith are discussed by delegates from every part of the Mohammedan world, and where plans are elaborated for Islam's defence and propagation. Here nearly all the militant leaders of the Mohammedan Revival (Abd-el-Wahab, Mahommed ben Sennussi, Djemal-ed-Din el-Afghani, and many more) felt the imperious summons to their task.[27]

As for the caliphate, it has played a great historic rôle, especially in its early days, and we have already studied its varying fortunes. Reduced to a mere shadow after the Mongol destruction of Bagdad, it was revived by the Turkish sultans, who assumed the title and were recognized as caliphs by the orthodox Moslem world.[28] However, these sultan-caliphs of Stambul[29] never succeeded in winning the religious homage accorded their predecessors of Mecca and Bagdad. In Arab eyes, especially, the spectacle of Turkish caliphs was an anachronism to which they could never be truly reconciled. Sultan Abdul Hamid, to be sure, made an ambitious attempt to revive the caliphate's pristine greatness, but such success as he attained was due more to the general tide of Pan-Islamic feeling than to the inherent potency of the caliphal name. The real leaders of modern Pan-Islamism either gave Abdul Hamid a merely qualified allegiance or were, like El Sennussi, definitely hostile. This was not realized in Europe, which came to fear Abdul Hamid as a sort of Mohammedan pope. Even to-day most Western observers seem to think that Pan-Islamism centres in the caliphate, and we see European publicists hopefully discussing whether the caliphate's retention by the discredited Turkish sultans, its transference to the Shereef of Mecca, or its total suppression, will best clip Pan-Islam's wings. This, however, is a distinctly short-sighted view. The caliphal institution is still undoubtedly venerated in Islam. But the shrewd leaders of the modern Pan-Islamic movement have long been working on a much broader basis. They realize that Pan-Islamism's real driving-power to-day lies not in the caliphate but in institutions like the Hajj and the great Pan-Islamic fraternities such as the Sennussiya, of which I shall presently speak.[30]

Let us now trace the fortunes of modern Pan-Islamism. Its first stage was of course the Wahabi movement. The Wahabi state founded by Abd-el-Wahab in the Nejd was modelled on the theocratic democracy of the Meccan caliphs, and when Abd-el-Wahab's princely disciple, Saud, loosed his fanatic hosts upon the holy cities, he dreamed that this was but the first step in a puritan conquest and consolidation of the whole Moslem world. Foiled in this grandiose design, Wahabism, nevertheless, soon produced profound political disturbances in distant regions like northern India and Afghanistan, as I have already narrated. They were, however, all integral parts of the Wahabi phase, being essentially protests against the political decadence of Moslem states and the moral decadence of Moslem rulers. These outbreaks were not inspired by any special fear or hatred of the West, since Europe was not yet seriously assailing Islam except in outlying regions like European Turkey or the Indies, and the impending peril was consequently not appreciated.

By the middle of the nineteenth century, however, the situation had radically altered. The French conquest of Algeria, the Russian acquisition of Transcaucasia, and the English mastery of virtually all India, convinced thoughtful Moslems everywhere that Islam was in deadly peril of falling under Western domination. It was at this time that Pan-Islamism assumed that essentially anti-Western character which it has ever since retained. At first resistance to Western encroachment was sporadic and unco-ordinated. Here and there heroic figures like Abd-el-Kader in Algeria and Shamyl in the Caucasus fought brilliantly against the European invaders. But though these paladins of the faith were accorded widespread sympathy from Moslems, they received no tangible assistance and, unaided, fell.

Fear and hatred of the West, however, steadily grew in intensity, and the seventies saw the Moslem world swept from end to end by a wave of militant fanaticism. In Algeria there was the Kabyle insurrection of 1871, while all over North Africa arose fanatical "Holy Men" preaching holy wars, the greatest of these being the Mahdist insurrection in the Egyptian

Sudan, which maintained itself against England's best efforts down to Kitchener's capture of Khartum at the very end of the century. In Afghanistan there was an intense exacerbation of fanaticism awakening sympathetic echoes among the Indian Moslems, both of which gave the British much trouble. In Central Asia there was a similar access of fanaticism, centring in the powerful Nakechabendiya fraternity, spreading eastward into Chinese territory and culminating in the great revolts of the Chinese Mohammedans both in Chinese Turkestan and Yunnan. In the Dutch East Indies there was a whole series of revolts, the most serious of these being the Atchin War, which dragged on interminably, not being quite stamped out even to-day.

The salient characteristic of this period of militant unrest is its lack of co-ordination. These risings were all spontaneous outbursts of local populations; animated, to be sure, by the same spirit of fear and hatred, and inflamed by the same fanatical hopes, but with no evidence of a central authority laying settled plans and moving in accordance with a definite programme. The risings were inspired largely by the mystical doctrine known as "Mahdism." Mahdism was unknown to primitive Islam, no trace of it occurring in the Koran. But in the "traditions," or reputed sayings of Mohammed, there occurs the statement that the Prophet predicted the coming of one bearing the title of "El Mahdi"[31] who would fill the earth with equity and justice. From this arose the widespread mystical hope in the appearance of a divinely inspired personage who would effect the universal triumph of Islam, purge the world of infidels, and assure the lasting happiness of all Moslems. This doctrine has profoundly influenced Moslem history. At various times fanatic leaders have arisen claiming to be El Mahdi, "The Master of the Hour," and have won the frenzied devotion of the Moslem masses; just as certain "Messiahs" have similarly excited the Jews. It was thus natural that, in their growing apprehension and impotent rage at Western aggression, the Moslem masses should turn to the messianic hope of Mahdism. Yet Mahdism, by its very nature, could effect nothing constructive or permanent. It was a mere straw fire; flaring up fiercely here and there, then dying down, leaving the disillusioned masses more discouraged and apathetic than before.

Now all this was recognized by the wiser supporters of the Pan-Islamic idea. The impotence of the wildest outbursts of local fanaticism against the methodical might of Europe convinced thinking Moslems that long preparation and complete co-ordination of effort were necessary if Islam was to have any chance of throwing off the European yoke. Such men also realized that they must study Western methods and adopt much of the Western technique of power. Above all, they felt that the political liberation of Islam from Western domination must be preceded by a profound spiritual regeneration, thereby engendering the moral forces necessary both for the war of liberation and for the fruitful reconstruction which should follow thereafter. At this point the ideals of Pan-Islamists and liberals approach each other. Both recognize Islam's present decadence; both desire its spiritual regeneration. It is on the nature of that regeneration that the two parties are opposed. The liberals believe that Islam should really assimilate Western ideas. The Pan-Islamists, on the other hand, believe that primitive Islam contains all that is necessary for regeneration, and contend that only Western methods and material achievements should be adopted by the Moslem world.

The beginnings of self-conscious, systematic Pan-Islamism date from about the middle of the nineteenth century. The movement crystallizes about two foci: the new-type religious fraternities like the Sennussiya, and the propaganda of the group of thinkers headed by Djemal-ed-Din. Let us first consider the fraternities.

Religious fraternities have existed in Islam for centuries. They all possess the same general type of organization, being divided into lodges ("Zawias") headed by Masters known as "Mokaddem," who exercise a more or less extensive authority over the "Khouan" or

Brethren. Until the foundation of the new-type organizations like the Sennussi, however, the fraternities exerted little practical influence upon mundane affairs. Their interests were almost wholly religious, of a mystical, devotional nature, often characterized by great austerities or by fanatical excesses like those practised by the whirling and howling dervishes. Such political influence as they did exert was casual and local. Anything like joint action was impossible, owing to their mutual rivalries and jealousies. These old-type fraternities still exist in great numbers, but they are without political importance except as they have been leavened by the new-type fraternities.

The new-type organizations date from about the middle of the nineteenth century, the most important in every way being the Sennussiya. Its founder, Seyid Mahommed ben Sennussi, was born near Mostaganem, Algeria, about the year 1800. As his title "Seyid" indicates, he was a descendant of the Prophet, and was thus born to a position of honour and importance.[32] He early displayed a strong bent for learning and piety, studying theology at the Moorish University of Fez and afterwards travelling widely over North Africa preaching a reform of the prevailing religious abuses. He then made the pilgrimage to Mecca, and there his reformist zeal was still further quickened by the Wahabi teachers. It was at that time that he appears to have definitely formulated his plan of a great puritan order, and in 1843 he returned to North Africa, settling in Tripoli, where he built his first Zawia, known as the "Zawia Baida," or White Monastery, in the mountains near Derna. So impressive was his personality and so great his organizing ability that converts flocked to him from all over North Africa. Indeed, his power soon alarmed the Turkish authorities in Tripoli, and relations became so strained that Seyid Mahommed presently moved his headquarters to the oasis of Jarabub, far to the south in the Lybian desert. When he died in 1859, his organization had spread over the greater part of North Africa.

Seyid Mahommed's work was carried on uninterruptedly by his son, usually known as Sennussi-el-Mahdi. The manner in which this son gained his succession typifies the Sennussi spirit. Seyid Mahommed had two sons, El Mahdi being the younger. While they were still mere lads, their father determined to put them to a test, to discover which of them had the stronger faith. In presence of the entire Zawia he bade both sons climb a tall palm-tree, and then adjured them by Allah and his Prophet to leap to the ground. The younger lad leaped at once and reached the ground unharmed; the elder boy refused to spring. To El Mahdi, "who feared not to commit himself to the will of God," passed the right to rule. Throughout his long life Sennussi-el-Mahdi justified his father's choice, displaying wisdom and piety of a high order, and further extending the power of the fraternity. During the latter part of his reign he removed his headquarters to the oasis of Jowf, still farther into the Lybian desert, where he died in 1902, and was succeeded by his nephew, Ahmed-el-Sherif, the present head of the Order, who also appears to possess marked ability.

With nearly eighty years of successful activity behind it, the Sennussi Order is to-day one of the vital factors in Islam. It counts its adherents in every quarter of the Moslem world. In Arabia its followers are very numerous, and it profoundly influences the spiritual life of the holy cities, Mecca and Medina. North Africa, however, still remains the focus of Sennussism. The whole of northern Africa, from Morocco to Somaliland, is dotted with its Zawias, or lodges, all absolutely dependent upon the Grand Lodge, headed by The Master, El Sennussi. The Sennussi stronghold of Jowf lies in the very heart of the Lybian Sahara. Only one European eye[33] has ever seen this mysterious spot. Surrounded by absolute desert, with wells many leagues apart, and the routes of approach known only to experienced Sennussi guides, every one of whom would suffer a thousand deaths rather than betray him, El Sennussi, The Master, sits serenely apart, sending his orders throughout North Africa.

The influence exerted by the Sennussiya is profound. The local Zawias are more than mere "lodges." Besides the Mokaddem, or Master, there is also a "Wekil," or civil governor, and these officers have discretionary authority not merely over the Zawia members but also over the community at large—at least, so great is the awe inspired by the Sennussiya throughout North Africa, that a word from Wekil or Mokaddem is always listened to and obeyed. Thus, besides the various European colonial authorities, British, French, or Italian, as the case may be, there exists an occult government with which the colonial authorities are careful not to come into conflict.

On their part, the Sennussi are equally careful to avoid a downright breach with the European Powers. Their long-headed, cautious policy is truly astonishing. For more than half a century the order has been a great force, yet it has never risked the supreme adventure. In many of the fanatic risings which have occurred in various parts of Africa, local Sennussi have undoubtedly taken part, and the same was true during the Italian campaign in Tripoli and in the late war, but the order itself has never officially entered the lists.

In fact, this attitude of mingled cautious reserve and haughty aloofness is maintained not only towards Christians but also towards the other powers that be in Islam. The Sennussiya has always kept its absolute freedom of action. Its relations with the Turks have never been cordial. Even the wily Abdul Hamid, at the height of his prestige as the champion of Pan-Islamism, could never get from El Sennussi more than coldly platonic expressions of approval, and one of Sennussi-el-Mahdi's favourite remarks was said to have been: "Turks and Christians: I will break both of them with one and the same stroke." Equally characteristic was his attitude toward Mahommed Ahmed, the leader of the "Mahdist" uprising in the Egyptian Sudan. Flushed with victory, Mahommed Ahmed sent emissaries to El Sennussi, asking his aid. El Sennussi refused, remarking haughtily: "What have I to do with this fakir from Dongola? Am I not myself Mahdi if I choose?"

These Fabian tactics do not mean that the Sennussi are idle. Far from it. On the contrary, they are ceaselessly at work with the spiritual arms of teaching, discipline, and conversion. The Sennussi programme is the welding, first, of Moslem Africa and, later, of the whole Moslem world into the revived "Imâmât" of Islam's early days; into a great theocracy, embracing all True Believers—in other words, Pan-Islamism. But they believe that the political liberation of Islam from Christian domination must be preceded by a profound spiritual regeneration. Toward this end they strive ceaselessly to improve the manners and morals of the populations under their influence, while they also strive to improve material conditions by encouraging the better cultivation of oases, digging new wells, building rest-houses along the caravan routes, and promoting trade. The slaughter and rapine practised by the Sudanese Mahdists disgusted the Sennussi and drew from their chief words of scathing condemnation.

All this explains the Order's unprecedented self-restraint. This is the reason why, year after year and decade after decade, the Sennussi advance slowly, calmly, coldly; gathering great latent power, but avoiding the temptation to expend it one instant before the proper time. Meanwhile they are covering North Africa with their lodges and schools, disciplining the people to the voice of their Mokaddems and Wekils; and, to the southward, converting millions of pagan negroes to the faith of Islam.[34]

Nothing better shows modern Islam's quickened vitality than the revival of missionary fervour during the past hundred years. Of course Islam has always displayed strong proselytizing power. Its missionary successes in its early days were extraordinary, and even in its period of decline it never wholly lost its propagating vigour. Throughout the Middle Ages

Islam continued to gain ground in India and China; the Turks planted it firmly in the Balkans; while between the fourteenth and sixteenth centuries Moslem missionaries won notable triumphs in such distant regions as West Africa, the Dutch Indies, and the Philippines. Nevertheless, taking the Moslem world as a whole, religious zeal undoubtedly declined, reaching low-water mark during the eighteenth century.

The first breath of the Mohammedan Revival, however, blew the smouldering embers of proselytism into a new flame, and everywhere except in Europe Islam began once more advancing portentously along all its far-flung frontiers. Every Moslem is, to some extent, a born missionary and instinctively propagates his faith among his non-Moslem neighbours, so the work was carried on not only by priestly specialists but also by multitudes of travellers, traders, and humble migratory workers.[35] Of course numerous zealots consecrated their lives to the task. This was particularly true of the religious fraternities. The Sennussi have especially distinguished themselves by their apostolic fervour, and from those natural monasteries, the oases of the Sahara, thousands of "Marabouts" have gone forth with flashing eyes and swelling breasts to preach the marvels of Islam, devoured with a zeal like that of the Christian mendicant friars of the Middle Ages. Islam's missionary triumphs among the negroes of West and Central Africa during the past century have been extraordinary. Every candid European observer tells the same story. As an Englishman very justly remarked some twenty years ago: "Mohammedanism is making marvellous progress in the interior of Africa. It is crushing paganism out. Against it the Christian propaganda is a myth."[36] And a French Protestant missionary remarks in similar vein: "We see Islam on its march, sometimes slowed down but never stopped, towards the heart of Africa. Despite all obstacles encountered, it tirelessly pursues its way. It fears nothing. Even Christianity, its most serious rival, Islam regards without hate, so sure is it of victory. While Christians dream of the conquest of Africa, the Mohammedans do it."[37]

The way in which Islam is marching southward is dramatically shown by a recent incident. A few years ago the British authorities suddenly discovered that Mohammedanism was pervading Nyassaland. An investigation brought out the fact that it was the work of Zanzibar Arabs. They began their propaganda about 1900. Ten years later almost every village in southern Nyassaland had its Moslem teacher and its mosque hut. Although the movement was frankly anti-European, the British authorities did not dare to check it for fear of repercussions elsewhere. Many European observers fear that it is only a question of time when Islam will cross the Zambezi and enter South Africa.

And these gains are not made solely against paganism. They are being won at the expense of African Christianity as well. In West Africa the European missions lose many of their converts to Islam, while across the continent the ancient Abyssinian Church, so long an outpost against Islam, seems in danger of submersion by the rising Moslem tide. Not by warlike incursions, but by peaceful penetration, the Abyssinians are being Islamized. "Tribes which, fifty or sixty years ago, counted hardly a Mohammedan among them, to-day live partly or wholly according to the precepts of Islam."[38]

Islam's triumphs in Africa are perhaps its most noteworthy missionary victories, but they by no means tell the whole story, as a few instances drawn from other quarters of the Moslem world will show. In the previous chapter I mentioned the liberal movement among the Russian Tartars. That, however, was only one phase of the Mohammedan Revival in that region, another phase being a marked resurgence of proselyting zeal. These Tartars had long been under Russian rule, and the Orthodox Church had made persistent efforts to convert them, in some instances with apparent success. But when the Mohammedan Revival reached the Tartars early in the nineteenth century, they immediately began labouring with their christianized brethren, and in a short time most of these reverted to Islam despite the best efforts of the Orthodox Church and the punitive measures of the Russian governmental authorities. Tartar missionaries also began converting the heathen Turko-Finnish tribes to the northward, in defiance of every hindrance from their Russian masters.[39]

In China, likewise, the nineteenth century witnessed an extraordinary development of Moslem energy. Islam had reached China in very early times, brought in by Arab traders and bands of Arab mercenary soldiers. Despite centuries of intermarriage with Chinese women, their descendants still differ perceptibly from the general Chinese population, and regard themselves as a separate and superior people. The Chinese Mohammedans are mainly concentrated in the southern province of Yunnan and the inland provinces beyond. Besides these racially Chinese Moslems, another centre of Mohammedan population is found in the Chinese dependency of Eastern or Chinese Turkestan, inhabited by Turkish stocks and conquered by the Chinese only in the eighteenth century. Until comparatively recent times the Chinese Moslems were well treated, but gradually their proud-spirited attitude alarmed the Chinese Government, which withdrew their privileges and persecuted them. Early in the nineteenth century the breath of the Mohammedan Revival reached China, as it did every other part of the Moslem world, and the Chinese Mohammedans, inflamed by resurgent fanaticism, began a series of revolts culminating in the great rebellions which took place about the year 1870, both in Yunnan and in Eastern Turkestan. As usual, these fanaticized Moslems displayed fierce fighting power. The Turkestan rebels found an able leader, one Yakub Beg, and for some years both Turkestan and Yunnan were virtually independent. To many European observers at that time it looked as though the rebels might join hands, erect a permanent Mohammedan state in western China, and even overrun the whole empire. The fame of Yakub Beg spread through the Moslem world, the Sultan of Turkey honouring him with the high title of Commander of the Faithful. After years of bitter fighting, accompanied by frightful massacres, the Chinese Government subdued the rebels. The Chinese Moslems, greatly reduced in numbers, have not yet recovered their former strength; but their spirit is still unbroken, and to-day they number fully 10,000,000. Thus, Chinese Islam, despite its setbacks, is a factor to be reckoned with in the future.[40]

The above instances do not exhaust the list of Islam's activities during the past century. In India, for example, Islam has continued to gain ground rapidly, while in the Dutch Indies it is the same story.[41] European domination actually favours rather than retards the spread of Islam, for the Moslem finds in Western improvements, like the railroad, the post-office, and the printing-press, useful adjuncts to Islamic propaganda.

Let us now consider the second originating centre of modern Pan-Islamism—the movement especially associated with the personality of Djemal-ed-Din.

Seyid Djemal-ed-Din el-Afghani was born early in the nineteenth century at Asadabad, near Hamadan, in Persia, albeit, as his name shows, he was of Afghan rather than Iranian descent, while his title "Seyid," meaning descendant of the Prophet, implies a strain of Arab blood. Endowed with a keen intelligence, great personal magnetism, and abounding vigour, Djemal-ed-Din had a stormy and chequered career. He was a great traveller, knowing intimately not only most of the Moslem world but western Europe as well. From these travels, supplemented by wide reading, he gained a notable fund of information which he employed effectively in his manifold activities. A born propagandist, Djemal-ed-Din attracted wide attention, and wherever he went in Islam his strong personality started an intellectual ferment. Unlike El Sennussi, he concerned himself very little with theology, devoting himself to politics. Djemal-ed-Din was the first Mohammedan who fully grasped the impending peril of Western domination, and he devoted his life to warning the Islamic world of the danger and attempting to elaborate measures of defence. By European colonial authorities he was soon singled out as a dangerous agitator. The English, in particular, feared and persecuted him. Imprisoned for a while in India, he went to Egypt about 1880, and had a hand in the anti-European movement of Arabi Pasha. When the English occupied Egypt in 1882 they promptly expelled Djemal, who continued his wanderings, finally reaching Constantinople. Here he found a generous patron in Abdul-Hamid, then evolving his Pan-Islamic policy. Naturally, the Sultan was enchanted with Djemal, and promptly made him the head of his Pan-Islamic propaganda bureau. In fact, it is probable that the success of the Sultan's Pan-Islamic policy was largely due to Djemal's ability and zeal. Djemal died in 1896 at an advanced age, active to the last.

Djemal-ed-Din's teachings may be summarized as follows:

"The Christian world, despite its internal differences of race and nationality, is, as against the East and especially as against Islam, united for the destruction of all Mohammedan states.

"The Crusades still subsist, as well as the fanatical spirit of Peter the Hermit. At heart, Christendom still regards Islam with fanatical hatred and contempt. This is shown in many ways, as in international law, before which Moslem nations are not treated as the equals of Christian nations.

"Christian governments excuse the attacks and humiliations inflicted upon Moslem states by citing the latter's backward and barbarous condition; yet these same governments stifle by a thousand means, even by war, every attempted effort of reform and revival in Moslem lands.

"Hatred of Islam is common to all Christian peoples, not merely to some of them, and the result of this spirit is a tacit, persistent effort for Islam's destruction.

"Every Moslem feeling and aspiration is caricatured and calumniated by Christendom. 'The Europeans call in the Orient "fanaticism" what at home they call "nationalism" and "patriotism." And what in the West they call "self-respect," "pride," "national honour," in the East they call "chauvinism." What in the West they esteem as national sentiment, in the East they consider xenophobia.'[42]

"From all this, it is plain that the whole Moslem world must unite in a great defensive alliance, to preserve itself from destruction; and, to do this, it must acquire the technique of Western progress and learn the secrets of European power."

Such, in brief, are the teachings of Djemal-ed-Din, propagated with eloquence and authority for many years. Given the state of mingled fear and hatred of Western encroachment that was steadily spreading throughout the Moslem world, it is easy to see how great Djemal's influence must have been. And of course Djemal was not alone in his preaching. Other influential Moslems were agitating along much the same lines as early as the middle of the nineteenth century. One of these pioneers was the Turkish notable Aali Pasha, who was said to remark: "What we want is rather an increase of fanaticism than a diminution of it."[43] Arminius Vambéry, the eminent Hungarian Oriental scholar, states that shortly after the Crimean War he was present at a militant Pan-Islamic gathering, attended by emissaries from far parts of the Moslem world, held at Aali Pasha's palace.[44]

Such were the foundations upon which Sultan Abdul Hamid built his ambitious Pan-Islamic structure. Abdul Hamid is one of the strangest personalities of modern times. A man of unusual intelligence, his mind was yet warped by strange twists which went to the verge of insanity. Nursing ambitious, grandiose projects, he tried to carry them out by dark and tortuous methods which, though often cleverly Macchiavellian, were sometimes absurdly puerile. An autocrat by nature, he strove to keep the smallest decisions dependent on his arbitrary will, albeit he was frequently guided by clever sycophants who knew how to play upon his superstitions and his prejudices.

Abdul Hamid ascended the throne in 1876 under very difficult circumstances. The country was on the verge of a disastrous Russian war, while the government was in the hands of statesmen who were endeavouring to transform Turkey into a modern state and who had introduced all sorts of Western political innovations, including a parliament. Abdul Hamid, however, soon changed all this. Taking advantage of the confusion which marked the close of the Russian war, he abolished parliament and made himself as absolute a despot as any of his ancestors had ever been. Secure in his autocratic power, Abdul Hamid now began to evolve his own peculiar policy, which, from the first, had a distinctly Pan-Islamic trend[45]. Unlike his immediate predecessors, Abdul Hamid determined to use his position as caliph for far-reaching political ends. Emphasizing his spiritual headship of the Mohammedan world rather than his political headship of the Turkish state, he endeavoured to win the active support of all Moslems and, by that support, to intimidate European Powers who might be formulating aggressive measures against the Ottoman Empire. Before long Abdul Hamid had built up an elaborate Pan-Islamic propaganda organization, working mainly by secretive, tortuous methods. Constantinople became the Mecca of all the fanatics and anti-Western agitators like Djemal-ed-Din. And from Constantinople there went forth swarms of picked emissaries, bearing to the most distant parts of Islam the Caliph's message of hope and impending deliverance from the menace of infidel rule.

Abdul Hamid's Pan-Islamic propaganda went on uninterruptedly for nearly thirty years. Precisely what this propaganda accomplished is very difficult to estimate. In the first place, it was cut short, and to some extent reversed, by the Young-Turk resolution of 1908 which drove Abdul Hamid from the throne. It certainly was never put to the test of a war between Turkey and a first-class European Power. This is what renders any theoretical appraisal so inconclusive. Abdul Hamid did succeed in gaining the respectful acknowledgment of his spiritual authority by most Moslem princes and notables, and he certainly won the pious veneration of the Moslem masses. In the most distant regions men came to regard the mighty Caliph in Stambul as, in very truth, the Defender of the Faith, and to consider his empire as the bulwark of Islam. On the other hand, it is a far cry from pious enthusiasm to practical performance. Furthermore, Abdul Hamid did not succeed in winning over powerful Pan-Islamic leaders like El Sennussi, who suspected his motives and questioned his judgment; while Moslem liberals everywhere disliked him for his despotic, reactionary, inefficient rule. It is thus a very debatable question whether, if Abdul Hamid had ever called upon the Moslem world for armed assistance in a "holy war," he would have been generally supported.

Yet Abdul Hamid undoubtedly furthered the general spread of Pan-Islamic sentiment throughout the Moslem world. In this larger sense he succeeded; albeit not so much from his position as caliph as because he incarnated the growing fear and hatred of the West. Thus we may conclude that Abdul Hamid's Pan-Islamic propaganda did produce profound and lasting effects which will have to be seriously reckoned with.

The Young-Turk revolution of 1908 greatly complicated the situation. It was soon followed by the Persian revolution and by kindred symptoms in other parts of the East. These events brought into sudden prominence new forces, such as constitutionalism, nationalism, and even social unrest, which had long been obscurely germinating in Islam but which had been previously denied expression. We shall later consider these new forces in detail. The point to be here noted is their complicating effect on the Pan-Islamic movement. Pan-Islamism was, in fact, cross-cut and deflected from its previous course, and a period of confusion and mental uncertainty supervened.

This interim period was short. By 1912 Pan-Islamism had recovered its poise and was moving forward once more. The reason was renewed pressure from the West. In 1911 came Italy's barefaced raid on Turkey's African dependency of Tripoli, while in 1912 the allied Christian Balkan states attacked Turkey in the Balkan War, which sheared away Turkey's European provinces to the very walls of Constantinople and left her crippled and discredited. Moreover, in those same fateful years Russia and England strangled the Persian revolution, while France, as a result of the Agadir crisis, closed her grip on Morocco. Thus, in a scant two years, the Moslem world had suffered at European hands assaults not only unprecedented in gravity but, in Moslem eyes, quite without provocation.

The effect upon Islam was tremendous. A flood of mingled despair and rage swept the Moslem world from end to end. And, of course, the Pan-Islamic implication was obvious. This was precisely what Pan-Islam's agitators had been preaching for fifty years—the Crusade of the West for Islam's destruction. What could be better confirmation of the warnings of Djemal-ed-Din?

The results were soon seen. In Tripoli, where Turks and Arabs had been on the worst of terms, both races clasped hands in a sudden access of Pan-Islamic fervour, and the Italian invaders were met with a fanatical fury that roused Islam to wild applause and inspired Western observers with grave disquietude. "Why has Italy found 'defenceless' Tripoli such a hornets' nest?" queried Gabriel Hanotaux, a former French minister of foreign affairs. "It is because she has to do, not merely with Turkey, but with Islam as well. Italy has set the ball rolling—so much the worse for her—and for us all."[46] The Anglo-Russian man-handling of Persia likewise roused much wrathful comment throughout Islam,[47] while the impending extinction of Moroccan independence at French hands was discussed with mournful indignation.

But with the coming of the Balkan War the wrath of Islam knew no bounds. From China to the Congo, pious Moslems watched with bated breath the swaying battle-lines in the far-off Balkans, and when the news of Turkish disaster came, Islam's cry of wrathful anguish rose hoarse and high. A prominent Indian Mohammedan well expressed the feelings of his co-religionists everywhere when he wrote: "The King of Greece orders a new Crusade. From the London Chancelleries rise calls to Christian fanaticism, and Saint Petersburg already speaks of the planting of the Cross on the dome of Sant' Sophia. To-day they speak thus; to-morrow they will thus speak of Jerusalem and the Mosque of Omar. Brothers! Be ye of one mind, that it is the duty of every True Believer to hasten beneath the Khalifa's banner and to sacrifice his life for the safety of the faith."[48] And another Indian Moslem leader thus adjured the British authorities: "I appeal to the present government to change its anti-Turkish attitude before the fury of millions of Moslem fellow-subjects is kindled to a blaze and brings disaster."[49]

Most significant of all were the appeals made at this time by Moslems to non-Mohammedan Asiatics for sympathy and solidarity against the hated West. This was a development as unprecedented as it was startling. Mohammed, revering as he did the Old and New Testaments, and regarding himself as the successor of the divinely inspired prophets Moses and Jesus, had enjoined upon his followers relative respect for Christians and Jews ("Peoples of the Book") in contrast with other non-Moslems, whom he stigmatized as "Idolaters." These injunctions of the Prophet had always been heeded, and down to our own days the hatred of Moslems for Christians, however bitter, had been as nothing compared with their loathing and contempt for "Idolaters" like the Brahmanist Hindus or the Buddhists and Confucianists of the Far East.

The first symptom of a change in attitude appeared during the Russo-Japanese War of 1904. So great had Islam's fear and hatred of the Christian West then become, that the triumph of an Asiatic people over Europeans was enthusiastically hailed by many Moslems, even though the victors were "Idolaters." It was quite in keeping with Pan-Islamism's strong missionary bent that many pious Moslems should have dreamed of bringing these heroes within the Islamic fold. Efforts to get in touch with Japan were made. Propagandist papers were founded, missionaries were selected, and the Sultan sent a warship to Japan with a Pan-Islamic delegation aboard. Throughout Islam the projected conversion of Japan was widely discussed. Said an Egyptian journal in the year 1906: "England, with her sixty million Indian Moslems, dreads this conversion. With a Mohammedan Japan, Mussulman policy would change entirely."[50] And, at the other end of the Moslem world, a Chinese Mohammedan sheikh wrote: "If Japan thinks of becoming some day a very great power and making Asia the dominator of the other continents, it will be only by adopting the blessed religion of Islam."[51]

Of course it soon became plain to these enthusiasts that while Japan received Islam's emissaries with smiling courtesy, she had not the faintest intention of turning Mohammedan. Nevertheless, the first step had been taken towards friendly relations with non-Moslem Asia, and the Balkan War drove Moslems much further in this direction. The change in Moslem sentiment can be gauged by the numerous appeals made by the Indian Mohammedans at this time to Hindus, as may be seen from the following sample entitled significantly "The Message of the East." "Spirit of the East," reads this noteworthy document, "arise and repel the swelling flood of Western aggression! Children of Hindustan, aid us with your wisdom, culture, and wealth; lend us your power, the birthright and heritage of the Hindu! Let the Spirit Powers hidden in the Himalayan mountain-peaks arise. Let prayers to the god of battles float upward; prayers that right may triumph over might; and call to your myriad gods to annihilate the armies of the foe!"[52]

To any one who realizes the traditional Moslem attitude towards "Idolaters" such words are simply amazing. They betoken a veritable revolution in outlook. And such sentiments were not confined to Indian Moslems; they were equally evident among Chinese Moslems as well. Said a Mohammedan newspaper of Chinese Turkestan, advocating a fraternal union of all Chinese against Western aggression: "Europe has grown too presumptuous. It will deprive us of our liberty; it will destroy us altogether if we do not bestir ourselves promptly and prepare for a powerful resistance."[53] During the troublous first stages of the Chinese revolution, the Mohammedans, emerging from their sulky aloofness, co-operated so loyally with their Buddhist and Confucian fellow-patriots that Dr. Sun-Yat-Sen, the Republican leader, announced gratefully: "The Chinese will never forget the assistance which their Moslem fellow-countrymen have rendered in the interest of order and liberty."[54]

The Great War thus found Islam everywhere deeply stirred against European aggression, keenly conscious of its own solidarity, and frankly reaching out for Asiatic allies in the projected struggle against European domination.

Under these circumstances it may at first sight appear strange that no general Islamic explosion occurred when Turkey entered the lists at the close of 1914 and the Sultan Caliph issued a formal summons to the Holy War. Of course this summons was not the flat failure which Allied reports led the West to believe at the time. As a matter of fact, there was trouble in practically every Mohammedan land under Allied control. To name only a few of many instances: Egypt broke into a tumult smothered only by overwhelming British reinforcements, Tripoli burst into a flame of insurrection that drove the Italians headlong to the coast, Persia was prevented from joining Turkey only by prompt Russo-British intervention, while the Indian North-West Frontier was the scene of fighting that required the presence of a quarter of a million Anglo-Indian troops. The British Government has officially admitted that during 1915 the Allies' Asiatic and African possessions stood within a hand's breadth of a cataclysmic insurrection.

That insurrection would certainly have taken place if Islam's leaders had everywhere spoken the fateful word. But the word was not spoken. Instead, influential Moslems outside of Turkey generally condemned the latter's action and did all in their power to calm the passions of the fanatic multitude.

The attitude of these leaders does credit to their discernment. They recognized that this was neither the time nor the occasion for a decisive struggle with the West. They were not yet materially prepared, and they had not perfected their understandings either among themselves or with their prospective non-Moslem allies. Above all, the moral urge was lacking. They knew that athwart the Khalifa's writ was stencilled "Made in Germany." They knew that the "Young-Turk" clique which had engineered the coup was made up of Europeanized renegades, many of them not even nominal Moslems, but atheistic Jews. Far-sighted Moslems had no intention of pulling Germany's chestnuts out of the fire, nor did they wish to further Prussian schemes of world-dominion which for themselves would have meant a mere change of masters. Far better to let the West fight out its desperate feud, weaken itself, and reveal fully its future intentions. Meanwhile Islam could bide its time, grow in strength, and await the morrow.

The Versailles peace conference was just such a revelation of European intentions as the Pan-Islamic leaders had been waiting for in order to perfect their programmes and enlist the moral solidarity of their followers. At Versailles the European Powers showed unequivocally that they had no intention of relaxing their hold upon the Near and Middle East. By a number of secret treaties negotiated during the war, the Ottoman Empire had been virtually partitioned between the victorious Allies, and these secret treaties formed the basis of the Versailles settlement. Furthermore, Egypt had been declared a British protectorate at the very beginning of the war, while the Versailles conference had scarcely adjourned before England announced an "agreement" with Persia which made that country another British protectorate in fact if not in name. The upshot was, as already stated, that the Near and Middle East were subjected to European political domination as never before.

But there was another side to the shield. During the war years the Allied statesmen had officially proclaimed times without number that the war was being fought to establish a new world-order based on such principles as the rights of small nations and the liberty of all peoples. These pronouncements had been treasured and memorized throughout the East. When, therefore, the East saw a peace settlement based, not upon these high professions, but upon the imperialistic secret treaties, it was fired with a moral indignation and sense of outraged justice never known before. A tide of impassioned determination began rising which has set already the entire East in tumultuous ferment, and which seems merely the premonitory ground-swell of a greater storm. So ominous were the portents that even before the Versailles conference had adjourned many European students of Eastern affairs expressed grave alarm. Here, for example, is the judgment of Leone Caetani, Duke of Sermoneta, an Italian authority on Mohammedan questions. Speaking in the spring of 1919 on the war's effect on the East, he said: "The convulsion has shaken Islamic and Oriental civilization to its foundations. The entire Oriental world, from China to the Mediterranean, is in ferment. Everywhere the hidden fire of anti-European hatred is burning. Riots in Morocco, risings in Algiers, discontent in Tripoli, so-called Nationalist attempts in Egypt, Arabia, and Lybia are all different manifestations of the same deep sentiment, and have as their object the rebellion of the Oriental world against European civilization."[55]

Those words are a prophetic forecast of what has since occurred in the Moslem world. Because recent events are perhaps even more involved with the nationalistic aspirations of the Moslem peoples than they are with the strictly Pan-Islamic movement, I propose to defer their detailed discussion till the chapter on Nationalism. We should, however, remember that Moslem nationalism and Pan-Islamism, whatever their internal differences, tend to unite against the external pressure of European domination and equally desire Islam's liberation from European political control. Remembering these facts, let us survey the present condition of the Pan-Islamic movement.

Pan-Islamism has been tremendously stimulated by Western pressure, especially by the late war and the recent peace settlements. However, Pan-Islamism must not be considered as merely a defensive political reaction against external aggression. It springs primarily from that deep sentiment of unity which links Moslem to Moslem by bonds much stronger than those which unite the members of the Christian world. These bonds are not merely religious, in the technical sense; they are social and cultural as well. Throughout the Moslem world, despite wide differences in local customs and regulations, the basic laws of family and social conduct are everywhere the same. "The truth is that Islam is more than a creed, it is a complete social system; it is a civilization with a philosophy, a culture, and an art of its own; in its long struggle against the rival civilization of Christendom it has become an organic unit conscious of itself."[56]

To this Islamic civilization all Moslems are deeply attached. In this larger sense, Pan-Islamism is universal. Even the most liberal-minded Moslems, however much they may welcome Western ideas, and however strongly they may condemn the fanatical, reactionary aspects of the political Pan-Islamic movement, believe fervently in Islam's essential solidarity. As a leading Indian Moslem liberal, The Aga Khan, remarks: "There is a right and legitimate Pan-Islamism to which every sincere and believing Mohammedan belongs—that is, the theory of the spiritual brotherhood and unity of the children of the Prophet. The real spiritual and cultural unity of Islam must ever grow, for to the follower of the Prophet it is the foundation of the life and the soul."[57]

If such is the attitude of Moslem liberals, thoroughly conversant with Western culture and receptive to Western progress, what must be the feelings of the Moslem masses, ignorant, reactionary, and fanatical? Besides perfectly understandable fear and hatred due to Western aggression, there is, among the Moslem masses, a great deal of genuine fanaticism caused, not by European political domination, but by religious bigotry and blind hatred of Western civilization.[58] But this fanaticism has, of course, been greatly inflamed by the political events of the past decade, until to-day religious, cultural, and political hatred of the West have coalesced in a state of mind decidedly ominous for the peace of the world. We should not delude ourselves into minimizing the dangerous possibilities of the present situation. Just because the fake "Holy War" proclaimed by the Young-Turks at German instigation in 1914 did not come off is no reason for believing that a real holy war is impossible. As a German staff-officer in Turkish service during the late struggle very candidly says: "The Holy War was an absolute fiasco just because it was not a Holy War."[59] I have already explained how most Moslems saw through the trick and refused to budge.

However, the long series of European aggressions, culminating in the recent peace settlements which subjected virtually the entire Moslem world to European domination, have been steadily rousing in Moslem hearts a spirit of despairing rage that may have disastrous consequences. Certainly, the materials for a holy war have long been heaping high. More than twenty years ago Arminius Vambéry, who knew the Moslem world as few Europeans have ever known it, warned the West of the perils engendered by recklessly imperialistic policies. "As time passes," he wrote in 1898, "the danger of a general war becomes ever greater. We should not forget that time has considerably augmented the adversary's force of resistance. I mean by this the sentiment of solidarity which is becoming livelier of late years among the peoples of Islam, and which in our age of rapid communication is no longer a negligible quantity, as it was even ten or twenty years ago.

"It may not be superfluous to draw the attention of our nineteenth-century Crusaders to the importance of the Moslem press, whose ramifications extend all over Asia and Africa, and whose exhortations sink more profoundly than they do with us into the souls of their readers. In Turkey, India, Persia, Central Asia, Java, Egypt, and Algeria, native organs, daily and periodical, begin to exert a profound influence. Everything that Europe thinks, decides, and executes against Islam spreads through those countries with the rapidity of lightning. Caravans carry the news to the heart of China and to the equator, where the tidings are commented upon in very singular fashion. Certain sparks struck at our meetings and banquets kindle, little by little, menacing flames. Hence, it would be an unpardonable legerity to close our eyes to the dangers lurking beneath an apparent passivity. What the Terdjuman of Crimea says between the lines is repeated by the Constantinople Ikdam, and is commented on and exaggerated at Calcutta by The Moslem Chronicle.

"Of course, at present, the bond of Pan-Islamism is composed of tenuous and dispersed strands. But Western aggression might easily unite those strands into a solid whole, bringing about a general war".[60]

In the decades which have elapsed since Vambéry wrote those lines the situation has become much more tense. Moslem resentment at European dominance has increased, has been reinforced by nationalistic aspirations almost unknown during the last century, and possesses methods of highly efficient propaganda. For example, the Pan-Islamic press, to which Vambéry refers, has developed in truly extraordinary fashion. In 1900 there were in the whole Islamic world not more than 200 propagandist journals. By 1906 there were 500, while in 1914 there were well over 1000.[61] Moslems fully appreciate the post-office, the railroad, and other modern methods of rapidly interchanging ideas. "Every Moslem country is in communication with every other Moslem country: directly, by means of special emissaries, pilgrims, travellers, traders, and postal exchanges; indirectly, by means of Mohammedan newspapers, books, pamphlets, leaflets, and periodicals. I have met with Cairo newspapers in Bagdad, Teheran, and Peshawar; Constantinople newspapers in Basra and Bombay; Calcutta newspapers in Mohammerah, Kerbela, and Port Said."[62] As for the professional Pan-Islamic propagandists, more particularly those of the religious fraternities, they swarm everywhere, rousing the fanaticism of the people: "Travelling under a thousand disguises— as merchants, preachers, students, doctors, workmen, beggars, fakirs, mountebanks, pretended fools or rhapsodists, these emissaries are everywhere well received by the Faithful and are efficaciously protected against the suspicious investigations of the European colonial authorities."[63]

Furthermore, there is to-day in the Moslem world a widespread conviction, held by liberals and chauvinists alike (albeit for very different reasons), that Islam is entering on a period of Renaissance and renewed glory. Says Sir Theodore Morison: "No Mohammedan believes that

Islamic civilization is dead or incapable of further development. They recognize that it has fallen on evil days; that it has suffered from an excessive veneration of the past, from prejudice and bigotry and narrow scholasticism not unlike that which obscured European thought in the Middle Ages; but they believe that Islam too is about to have its Renaissance, that it is receiving from Western learning a stimulus which will quicken it into fresh activity, and that the evidences of this new life are everywhere manifest."[64]

Sir Theodore Morison describes the attitude of Moslem liberals. How Pan-Islamists with anti-Western sentiments feel is well set forth by an Egyptian, Yahya Siddyk, in his well-known book, The Awakening of the Islamic Peoples in the Fourteenth Century of the Hegira.[65] The book is doubly interesting because the author has a thorough Western education, holding a law degree from the French university of Toulouse, and is a judge on the Egyptian bench. Although, writing nearly a decade before the cataclysm, Yahya Siddyk clearly foresaw the imminence of the European War. "Behold," he writes, "these Great Powers ruining themselves in terrifying armaments; measuring each other's strength with defiant glances; menacing each other; contracting alliances which continually break and which presage those terrible shocks which overturn the world and cover it with ruins, fire, and blood! The future is God's, and nothing is lasting save His Will."

Yahya Siddyk considers the Western world degenerate. "Does this mean," he asks, "that Europe, our 'enlightened guide,' has already reached the summit of its evolution? Has it already exhausted its vital force by two or three centuries of hyperexertion? In other words: is it already stricken with senility, and will it see itself soon obliged to yield its civilizing rôle to other peoples less degenerate, less neurasthenic, that is to say, younger, more robust, more healthy, than itself? In my opinion, the present marks Europe's apogee, and its immoderate colonial expansion means, not strength, but weakness. Despite the aureole of so much grandeur, power, and glory, Europe is to-day more divided and more fragile than ever, and ill conceals its malaise, its sufferings, and its anguish. Its destiny is inexorably working out!...

"The contact of Europe on the East has caused us both much good and much evil: good, in the material and intellectual sense; evil, from the moral and political point of view. Exhausted by long struggles, enervated by a brilliant civilization, the Moslem peoples inevitably fell into a malaise; but they are not stricken, they are not dead! These peoples, conquered by the force of cannon, have not in the least lost their unity, even under the oppressive régimes to which the Europeans have long subjected them....

"I have said that the European contact has been salutary to us from both the material and intellectual point of view. What reforming Moslem princes wished to impose by force on their Moslem subjects is to-day realized a hundredfold. So great has been our progress in the last twenty-five years in science, letters, and art that we may well hope to be in all these things the equals of Europe in less than half a century....

"A new era opens for us with the fourteenth century of the Hegira, and this happy century will mark our Renaissance and our great future! A new breath animates the Mohammedan peoples of all races; all Moslems are penetrated with the necessity of work and instruction! We all wish to travel, do business, tempt fortune, brave dangers. There is in the East, among the Mohammedans, a surprising activity, an animation, unknown twenty-five years ago. There is to-day a real public opinion throughout the East."

The author concludes: "Let us hold firm, each for all, and let us hope, hope, hope! We are fairly launched on the path of progress: let us profit by it! It is Europe's very tyranny which has wrought our transformation! It is our continued contact with Europe that favours our

33

evolution and inevitably hastens our revival! It is simply history repeating itself; the Will of God fulfilling itself despite all opposition and all resistance.... Europe's tutelage over Asiatics is becoming more and more nominal—the gates of Asia are closing against the European! Surely we glimpse before us a revolution without parallel in the world's annals. A new age is at hand!"

If this was the way Pan-Islamists were thinking in the opening years of the century, it is clear that their views must have been confirmed and intensified by the Great War.[66] The material power of the West was thereby greatly reduced, while its prestige was equally sapped by the character of the peace settlement and by the attendant disputes which broke out among the victors. The mutual rivalries and jealousies of England, France, Italy, and their satellites in the East have given Moslems much food for hopeful thought, and have caused corresponding disquietude in European minds. A French publicist recently admonished his fellow Europeans that "Islam does not recognize our colonial frontiers," and added warningly, "the great movement of Islamic union inaugurated by Djemal-ed-Din el-Afghani is going on."[67]

The menacing temper of Islam is shown by the furious agitation which has been going on for the last three years among India's 70,000,000 Moslems against the dismemberment of the Ottoman Empire. This agitation is not confined to India. It is general throughout Islam, and Sir Theodore Morison does not overstate the case when he says: "It is time the British public realized the gravity of what is happening in the East. The Mohammedan world is ablaze with anger from end to end at the partition of Turkey. The outbreaks of violence in centres so far remote as Kabul and Cairo are symptoms only of this widespread resentment. I have been in close touch with Mohammedans of India for close upon thirty years and I think it is my duty to warn the British public of the passionate resentment which Moslems feel at the proposed dismemberment of the Turkish Empire. The diplomats at Versailles apparently thought that outside the Turkish homelands there is no sympathy for Turkey. This is a disastrous blunder. You have but to meet the Mohammedan now in London to realize the white heat to which their anger is rising. In India itself the whole of the Mohammedan community from Peshawar to Arcot is seething with passion upon this subject. Women inside the Zenanas are weeping over it. Merchants who usually take no interest in public affairs are leaving their shops and counting-houses to organize remonstrances and petitions; even the mediæval theologians of Deoband and the Nadwatul-Ulama, whose detachment from the modern world is proverbial, are coming from their cloisters to protest against the destruction of Islam."[68]

Possibly the most serious aspect of the situation is that the Moslem liberals are being driven into the camp of political Pan-Islamism. Receptive though the liberals are to Western ideas, and averse though they are to Pan-Islamism's chauvinistic, reactionary tendencies, Europe's intransigence is forcing them to make at least a temporary alliance with the Pan-Islamic and Nationalist groups, even though the liberals know that anything like a holy war would dig a gulf between East and West, stop the influx of Western stimuli, favour reactionary fanaticism, and perhaps postpone for generations a modernist reformation of Islam.

Perhaps it is symptomatic of a more bellicose temper in Islam that the last few years have witnessed the rapid spread of two new puritan, fanatic movements—the Ikhwan and the Salafiya. The Ikhwan movement began obscurely about ten years ago in inner Arabia—the Nejd. It is a direct outgrowth of Wahabism, from which it differs in no essential respect. So rapid has been Ikhwanism's progress that it to-day absolutely dominates the entire Nejd, and it is headed by desert Arabia's most powerful chieftain, Bin Saud, a descendant of the Saud who headed the Wahabi movement a hundred years ago. The fanaticism of the Ikhwans is said to be extraordinary, while their programme is the old Wahabi dream of a puritan conversion of the whole Islamic world.[69] As for the Salafi movement, it started in India even more obscurely than Ikhwanism did in Arabia, but during the past few years it has spread widely through Islam. Like Ikhwanism, it is puritanical and fanatical in spirit, its adherents being found especially among dervish organizations.[70] Such phenomena, taken with everything else, do not augur well for the peace of the East.

So much for Pan-Islamism's religious and political sides. Now let us glance at its commercial and industrial aspects—at what may be called economic Pan-Islamism.

Economic Pan-Islamism is the direct result of the permeation of Western ideas. Half a century ago the Moslem world was economically still in the Middle Ages. The provisions of the sheriat, or Moslem canon law, such as the prohibition of interest rendered economic life in the modern sense impossible. What little trade and industry did exist was largely in the hands of native Christians or Jews. Furthermore, the whole economic life of the East was being disorganized by the aggressive competition of the West. Europe's political conquest of the Moslem world was, in fact, paralleled by an economic conquest even more complete. Everywhere percolated the flood of cheap, abundant European machine-made goods, while close behind came European capital, temptingly offering itself in return for loans and concessions which, once granted, paved the way for European political domination.

Yet in economics as in politics the very completeness of Europe's triumph provoked resistance. Angered and alarmed by Western exploitation, Islam frankly recognized its economic inferiority and sought to escape from its subjection. Far-sighted Moslems began casting about for a modus vivendi with modern life that would put Islam economically abreast of the times. Western methods were studied and copied. The prohibitions of the sheriat were evaded or quietly ignored.

The upshot has been a marked evolution toward Western economic standards. This evolution is of course still in its early stages, and is most noticeable in lands most exposed to Western influences like India, Egypt, and Algeria. Yet everywhere in the Moslem world the trend is the same. The details of this economic transformation will be discussed in the chapter devoted to economic change. What we are here concerned with is its Pan-Islamic aspect. And that aspect is very strong. Nowhere does Islam's innate solidarity come out better than in the economic field. The religious, cultural, and customary ties which bind Moslem to Moslem enable Mohammedans to feel more or less at home in every part of the Islamic world, while Western methods of transit and communication enable Mohammedans to travel and keep in touch as they never could before. New types of Moslems—wholesale merchants, steamship owners, business men, bankers, even factory industrialists and brokers—are rapidly evolving; types which would have been simply unthinkable a century, or even half a century, ago.

And these new men understand each other perfectly. Bound together both by the ties of Islamic fraternity and by the pressure of Western competition, they co-ordinate their efforts much more easily than politicals have succeeded in doing. Here liberals, Pan-Islamists, and nationalists can meet on common ground. Here is no question of political conspiracies, revolts, or holy wars, challenging the armed might of Europe and risking bloody repression or blind reaction. On the contrary, here is merely a working together of fellow Moslems for economic ends by business methods which the West cannot declare unlawful and dare not repress.

What, then, is the specific programme of economic Pan-Islamism? It is easily stated: the wealth of Islam for Moslems. The profits of trade and industry for Moslem instead of Christian hands. The eviction of Western capital by Moslem capital. Above all, the breaking of Europe's grip on Islam's natural resources by the termination of concessions in lands, mines, forests, railways, custom-houses, by which the wealth of Islamic lands is to-day drained away to foreign shores.

Such are the aspirations of economic Pan-Islamism. They are wholly modern concepts, the outgrowth of those Western ideas whose influence upon the Moslem world I shall now discuss.[71]

FOOTNOTES:

[25] Islam has not only won much ground in India, Brahmanism's homeland, but has also converted virtually the entire populations of the great islands of Java and Sumatra, where Brahmanism was formerly ascendant.

[26] The small Parsi communities of India, centring in Bombay, are the sole surviving representatives of Zoroastrianism. They were founded by Zoroastrian refugees after the Mohammedan conquest of Persia in the seventh century a.d.

[27] Though Mecca is forbidden to non-Moslems, a few Europeans have managed to make the Hajj in disguise, and have written their impressions. Of these, Snouck Hurgronje's Mekka (2 vols., The Hague, 1888) and Het Mekkaansche Feest (Leiden, 1889) are the most recent good works. Also see Burton and Burckhardt. A recent account of value from the pen of a Mohammedan liberal is: Gazanfar Ali Khan, With the Pilgrims to Mecca; The Great Pilgrimage of A. H. 1319 (A.D. 1902), with an Introduction by Arminius Vambéry (London, 1905).

[28] The Shiite Persians of course refused to recognize any Sunnite or orthodox caliphate; while the Moors pay spiritual allegiance to their own Shereefian sultans.

[29] The Turkish name for Constantinople.

[30] On the caliphate, see Sir W. Muir, The Caliphate: Its Rise, Decline, and Fall (Edinburgh, 1915); Sir Mark Sykes, The Caliph's Last Heritage (London, 1915); XX, "L'Islam après la Guerre," Revue de Paris, 15 January, 1916; "The Indian Khilafat Delegation," Foreign Affairs, July, 1920 (Special Supplement).

[31] Literally, "he who is guided aright."

[32] "Seyid" means "Lord." This title is borne only by descendants of the Prophet.

[33] The explorer Dr. Nachtigal.

[34] On the Islamic fraternities in general and the Sennussiya in particular see W. S. Blunt, The Future of Islam (London, 1882); O. Depont and X. Coppolani, Les Confréries réligieuses musulmanes (Paris, 1897); H. Duveyrier, La Confrérie musulmane de Sidi Mohammed ben Ali es Sénoussi (Paris, 1884); A. Le Chatelier, Les Confréries musulmanes du Hedjaz (Paris, 1887); L. Petit, Confréries musulmanes (Paris, 1899); L. Rinn, Marabouts et Khouan (Algiers, 1884); A. Servier, Le Nationalisme musulman (Constantine, Algeria, 1913); Simian, Les Confréries islamiques en Algérie (Algiers, 1910); Achmed Abdullah (himself a Sennussi), "The Sennussiyehs," The Forum, May, 1914; A. R. Colquhoun, "Pan-Islam," North American Review, June, 1906; T. R. Threlfall, "Senussi and His Threatened Holy War," Nineteenth Century, March, 1900; Captain H. A. Wilson, "The Moslem Menace," Nineteenth Century and After, September, 1907; ... "La Puissance de l'Islam: Ses Confréries Réligieuses," Le

Correspondant, 25 November and 10 December, 1909. The above judgments, particularly regarding the Sennussiya, vary greatly, some being highly alarmist, others minimizing its importance. A full balancing of the entire subject is that of Commandant Binger, "Le Péril de l'Islam," Bulletin du Comité de l'Afrique française, 1902. Personal interviews of educated Moslems with El Sennussi are Si Mohammed el Hechaish, "Chez les Senoussia et les Touareg," L'Expansion Coloniale française, 1900; Muhammad ibn Utman, Voyage au Pays des Sénoussia à travers la Tripolitaine (translated from the Arabic), Paris, 1903.

[35] On Moslem missionary activity in general, see Jansen, Verbreitung des Islams (Berlin, 1897); M. Townsend, Asia and Europe, pp. 46-49, 60-61, 81; A. Le Chatelier, L'Islam au dix-neuvième Siècle (Paris, 1888); various papers in The Mohammedan World To-day (London, 1906).

[36] T. R. Threlfall, "Senussi and His Threatened Holy War," Nineteenth Century, March, 1900.

[37] D. A. Forget, L'Islam et le Christianisme dans l'Afrique centrale, p. 65 (Paris, 1900). For other statements regarding Moslem missionary activity in Africa, see G. Bonet-Maury, L'Islamisme et le Christianisme en Afrique (Paris, 1906); E. W. Blyden, Christianity, Islam, and the Negro Race (London, 1887); Forget, op. cit.

[38] A. Guérinot, "L'Islam et l'Abyssinie," Revue du Monde musulman, 1918. Also see similar opinion of the Protestant missionary K. Cederquist, "Islam and Christianity in Abyssinia," The Moslem World, April, 1921.

[39] S. Brobovnikov, "Moslems in Russia," The Moslem World, January, 1911.

[40] Broomhall, Islam in China (London, 1910); Nigârèndé, "Notes sur les Musulmans Chinois," Revue du Monde musulman, January, 1907; paper on Islam in China in The Mohammedan World To-day (London, 1906).

[41] See papers on Islam in Java and Sumatra in The Mohammedan World To-day (London, 1906); A. Cabaton, Java, Sumatra, and the Dutch East Indies (translated from the Dutch), New York, 1916.

[42] Quoted from article by "X," "Le Pan-Islamisme et le Pan-Turquisme," Revue du Monde musulman, March, 1913. This authoritative article is, so the editor informs us, from the pen of an eminent Mohammedan—"un homme d'étât musulman." For other activities of Djemal-ed-Din, see A. Servier, Le Nationalisme musulman, pp. 10-13.

[43] Quoted from W. G. Palgrave, Essays on Eastern Questions, p. 111 (London, 1872).

[44] A. Vambéry, Western Culture in Eastern Lands, p. 351 (London, 1906).

[45] Abdul Hamid's Pan-Islamic schemes were first clearly discerned by the French publicist Gabriel Charmes as early as 1881, and his warnings were published in his prophetic book L'Avenir de la Turquie—Le Panislamisme (Paris, 1883).

[46] Gabriel Hanotaux, "La Crise méditerranéenne et l'Islam," Revue Hebdomadaire, April 13, 1912.

[47] See "X," "La Situation politique de la Perse," Revue du Monde musulman, June, 1914; B. Temple, "The Place of Persia in World-Politics," Proceedings of the Central Asian Society, May 4, 1910; W. M. Shuster, The Strangling of Persia (New York, 1912).

[48] Quoted from A. Vambéry, "Die türkische Katastrophe und die Islamwelt," Deutsche Revue, July, 1913.

[49] Shah Mohammed Naimatullah, "Recent Turkish Events and Moslem India," Asiatic Review, October, 1913.

[50] Quoted by F. Farjanel, "Le Japon et l'Islam," Revue du Monde musulman, November, 1906.

[51] Farjanel, supra.

[52] Quoted by Vambéry, supra.

[53] Vambéry, "An Approach between Moslems and Buddhists," Nineteenth Century and After, April, 1912.

[54] Vambéry, "An Approach between Moslems and Buddhists," Nineteenth Century and After, April, 1912.

[55] Special cable to the New York Times, dated Rome, May 28, 1919.

[56] Sir T. Morison, "England and Islam," Nineteenth Century and After, July, 1919.

[57] H. H. The Aga Khan, India in Transition, p. 158 (London, 1918).

[58] This hatred of Western civilization, as such, will be discussed in the next chapter.

[59] Ernst Paraquin, formerly Ottoman lieutenant-colonel and chief of general staff, in the Berliner Tageblatt, January 24, 1920.

[60] A. Vambéry, La Turquie d'aujourd'hui et d'avant Quarante Ans, pp. 71, 72 (Paris, 1898).

[61] A. Servier, Le Nationalisme musulman, p. 182.

[62] B. Temple, "The Place of Persia in World-Politics," Proceedings of the Central Asian Society, May, 1910.

[63] L. Rinn, Marabouts et Khouan, p. vi.

[64] Sir T. Morison, "England and Islam," op. cit.

[65] Yahya Siddyk, Le Reveil des Peuples islamiques au quatorzième Siècle de l'Hégire (Cairo, 1907). Also published in Arabic.

[66] For a full discussion of the effect of the Great War upon Asiatic and African peoples, see my book The Rising Tide of Colour against White World-Supremacy (New York and London, 1920).

[67] L. Massignon, "L'Islam et la Politique des Alliés," Revue des Sciences politiques, June, 1920.

[68] Sir T. Morison, "England and Islam," op. cit.

[69] For the Ikhwan movement, see P. W. Harrison, "The Situation in Arabia," Atlantic Monthly, December, 1920; S. Mylrea, "The Politico-Religious Situation in Arabia," The Moslem World, July, 1919.

[70] For the Salafi movement, see "Wahhabisme—Son Avenir sociale et le Mouvement salafi," Revue du Monde musulman, 1919.

[71] On the general subject of economic Pan-Islamism, see A. Le Chatelier, "Le Reveil de l'Islam—Sa Situation économique," Revue Économique internationale, July, 1910; also his article "Politique musulmane," Revue du Monde musulman, September, 1910; M. Pickthall, "La Morale islamique," Revue Politique internationale, July, 1916; S. Khuda Bukhsh, Essays: Indian and Islamic (London, 1912).

CHAPTER III

THE INFLUENCE OF THE WEST

The influence of the West is the great dynamic in the modern transformation of the East. The ubiquitous impact of Westernism is modifying not merely the Islamic world but all non-Moslem Asia and Africa,[72] and in subsequent pages we shall examine the effects of Western influence upon the non-Moslem elements of India. Of course Western influence does not entirely account for Islam's recent evolution. We have already seen that, for the last hundred years, Islam itself has been engendering forces which, however quickened by external Western stimuli, are essentially internal in their nature, arising spontaneously and working toward distinctive, original goals. It is not a mere copying of the West that is to-day going on in the Moslem world, but an attempt at a new synthesis—an assimilation of Western methods to Eastern ends. We must always remember that the Asiatic stocks which constitute the bulk of Islam's followers are not primitive savages like the African negroes or the Australoids, but are mainly peoples with genuine civilizations built up by their own efforts from the remote past. In view of their historic achievements, therefore, it seems safe to conclude that in the great ferment now stirring the Moslem world we behold a real Renaissance, whose genuineness is best attested by the fact that there have been similar movements in former times.

The modern influence of the West on the East is quite unprecedented in both intensity and scope. The far more local, partial influence of Greece and Rome cannot be compared to it. Another point to be noted is that this modern influence of the West upon the East is a very recent thing. The full impact of Westernism upon the Orient as a whole dates only from about the middle of the nineteenth century. Since then, however, the process has been going on by leaps and bounds. Roads and railways, posts and telegraphs, books and papers, methods and ideas, have penetrated, or are in process of penetrating, every nook and cranny of the East. Steamships sail the remotest seas. Commerce drives forth and scatters the multitudinous products of Western industry among the remotest peoples. Nations which only half a century ago lived the life of thirty centuries ago, to-day read newspapers and go to business in electric tram-cars. Both the habits and thoughts of Orientals are being revolutionized. To a discussion of the influence of the West upon the Moslem world the remainder of this book will be devoted. The chief elements will be separately analysed in subsequent chapters, the present chapter being a general survey of an introductory character.

The permeation of Westernism is naturally most advanced in those parts of Islam which have been longest under Western political control. The penetration of the British "Raj" into the remotest Indian jungles, for example, is an extraordinary phenomenon. By the coinage, the post-office, the railroads, the administration of justice, the encouragement of education, the relief of famine, and a thousand other ways, the great organization has penetrated all India. But even in regions where European control is still nominal, the permeation of Westernism has gone on apace. The customs and habits of the people have been distinctly modified. Western material improvements and comforts like the kerosene-oil lamp and the sewing-machine are to-day part and parcel of the daily life of the people. New economic wants have been created; standards of living have been raised; canons of taste have been altered.[73]

In the intellectual and spiritual fields, likewise, the leaven of Westernism is clearly apparent. We have already seen how profoundly Moslem liberal reformers have been influenced by Western ideas and the spirit of Western progress. Of course in these fields Westernism has progressed more slowly and has awakened much stronger opposition than it has on the material plane. Material innovations, especially mechanical improvements, comforts, and luxuries, make their way much faster than novel customs or ideas, which usually shock established beliefs or ancestral prejudices. Tobacco was taken up with extraordinary rapidity by every race and clime, and the kerosene-lamp has in half a century penetrated the recesses of Central Asia and of China; whereas customs like Western dress and ideas like Western education encounter many setbacks and are often adopted with such modifications that their original spirit is denatured or perverted. The superior strength and skill of the West are to-day generally admitted throughout the East, but in many quarters the first receptivity to Western progress and zeal for Western ideas have cooled or have actually given place to a reactionary hatred of the very spirit of Western civilization.[74]

Western influences are most apparent in the upper and middle classes, especially in the Western-educated intelligentsia which to-day exists in every Eastern land. These élites of course vary greatly in numbers and influence, but they all possess a more or less definite grasp of Western ideas. In their reactions to Westernism they are sharply differentiated. Some, while retaining the fundamentals of their ancestral philosophy of life, attempt a genuine assimilation of Western ideals and envisage a higher synthesis of the spirits of East and West. Others break with their traditional pasts, steep themselves in Westernism, and become more or less genuinely Westernized. Still others conceal behind their Western veneer disillusionment and detestation.[75]

Of course it is in externals that Westernization is most pronounced. The Indian or Turkish "intellectual," holding Western university degrees and speaking fluently several European languages, and the wealthy prince or pasha, with his motor-cars, his racing-stables, and his annual "cure" at European watering-places, appear very Occidental to the casual eye. Such men wear European clothes, eat European food, and live in houses partly or wholly furnished in European style. Behind this façade exists every possible variation of inner life, from earnest enthusiasm for Western ideals to inveterate reaction.

These varied attitudes toward Westernism are not parked off by groups or localities, they co-exist among the individuals of every class and every land in the East. The entire Orient is, in fact, undergoing a prodigious transformation, far more sudden and intense than anything the West has ever known. Our civilization is mainly self-evolved; a natural growth developing by normal, logical, and relatively gradual stages. The East, on the contrary, is undergoing a concentrated process of adaptation which, with us, was spread over centuries, and the result is not so much evolution as revolution—political, economic, social, idealistic, religious, and much more besides. The upshot is confusion, uncertainty, grotesque anachronism, and glaring contradiction. Single generations are sundered by unbridgeable mental and spiritual gulfs. Fathers do not understand sons; sons despise their fathers. Everywhere the old and the new struggle fiercely, often within the brain or spirit of the same individual. The infinite complexity of this struggle as it appears in India is well summarized by Sir Valentine Chirol when he speaks of the many "currents and cross-currents of the confused movement which is stirring the stagnant waters of Indian life—the steady impact of alien ideas on an ancient and obsolescent civilization; the more or less imperfect assimilation of those ideas by the few; the dread and resentment of them by those whose traditional ascendancy they threaten; the disintegration of old beliefs, and then again their aggressive revival; the careless diffusion of an artificial system of education, based none too firmly on mere intellectualism, and bereft of all moral or religious sanction; the application of Western theories of administration and of jurisprudence to a social formation stratified on lines of singular rigidity; the play of modern economic forces upon primitive conditions of industry and trade; the constant and unconscious but inevitable friction between subject races and their alien rulers; the reverberation of distant wars and distant racial conflicts; the exaltation of an Oriental people in the Far East."[76] These lines, though written about India, apply with fair exactitude to every other portion of the Near and Middle East to-day. As a French writer remarks with special reference to the Levant: "The truth is that the Orient is in transformation, and the Mohammedan mentality as well—though not perhaps exactly as we might wish. It is undergoing a period of crisis, wherein the past struggles everywhere against the present; where ancient customs, impaired by modern innovations, present a hybrid and disconcerting spectacle."[77]

To this is largely due the unlovely traits displayed by most of the so-called "Westernized" Orientals; the "stucco civilization"[78] of the Indian Babu, and the boulevardier "culture" of the Turkish "Effendi"—syphilized rather than civilized. Any profound transformation must engender many worthless by-products, and the contemporary Westernization of the Orient has its dark as well as its bright side. The very process of reform, however necessary and inevitable, lends fresh virulence to old ills and imports new evils previously unknown. As Lord Cromer says: "It is doubtful whether the price which is being paid for introducing European civilization into these backward Eastern societies is always recognized as fully as it should be. The material benefits derived from European civilization are unquestionably great, but as regards the ultimate effect on public and private morality the future is altogether uncertain."[79]

The good and the evil of Westernization are alike mostly clearly evident among the ranks of the educated élites. Some of these men show the happiest effects of the Western spirit, but an even larger number fall into the gulf between old and new, and there miserably perish. Lord Cromer characterized many of the "Europeanized" Egyptians as "at the same time de-Moslemized Moslems and invertebrate Europeans";[80] while another British writer thus pessimistically describes the superficial Europeanism prevalent in India: "Beautiful Mogul palaces furnished with cracked furniture from Tottenham Court Road. That is what we have done to the Indian mind. We have not only made it despise its own culture and throw it out; we have asked it to fill up the vacant spaces with furniture which will not stand the climate. The mental Eurasianism of India is appalling. Such minds are nomad. They belong to no civilization, no country, and no history. They create a craving that cannot be satisfied, and ideals that are unreal. They falsify life. They deprive men of the nourishment of their cultural past, and the substitutes they supply are unsubstantial.... We sought to give the Eastern mind

41

a Western content and environment; we have succeeded too well in establishing intellectual and moral anarchy in both."[81]

These patent evils of Westernization are a prime cause of that implacable hatred of everything Western which animates so many Orientals, including some well acquainted with the West. Such persons are precious auxiliaries to the ignorant reactionaries and to the rebels against Western political domination.

The political predominance of the West over the East is, indeed, the outstanding factor in the whole question of Western influence upon the Orient. We have already surveyed Europe's conquest of the Near and Middle East during the past century, and we have seen how helpless the backward, decrepit Moslem world was in face of the twofold tide of political and economic subjugation. In fact, the economic phase was perhaps the more important factor in the rapidity and completeness of Europe's success. To be sure, some Eastern lands were subjugated at a stroke by naked military force, as in the French expedition to Algiers, the Russian conquest of central Asia, and the Italian descent upon Tripoli. Much oftener, however, subjection began by the essentially economic process known as "pacific penetration"—the acquirement of a financial grip upon a hitherto independent Oriental country by Western capital in the form of loans and concessions, until the assumption of Western political control became little more than a formal registration of what already existed in fact. Such is the story of the subjection of Egypt, Morocco, and Persia, while England's Indian Empire started in a purely trading venture—the East India Company. The tremendous potency of "pacific penetration" is often not fully appreciated. Take the significance of one item alone—railway concessions. Says that keen student of Weltpolitik, Doctor Dillon: "Railways are the iron tentacles of latter-day expanding Powers. They are stretched out caressingly at first. But once the iron has, so to say, entered the soul of the weaker nation, the tentacles swell to the dimensions of brawny arms, and the embrace tightens to a crushing grip."[82]

On the question of the abstract rightness or wrongness of this subjection of the East by the West, I do not propose to enter. It has been exhaustively discussed, pro and con, and every reader of these pages is undoubtedly familiar with the stock arguments on both sides. The one thing certain is that this process of subjugation was, broadly speaking, inevitable. Given two worlds at such different levels as East and West at the beginning of the nineteenth century—the West overflowing with vitality and striding at the forefront of human progress, the East sunk in lethargy and decrepitude—and it was a foregone conclusion that the former would encroach upon the latter.

What does concern us in our present discussion is the effect of European political control upon the general process of Westernization in Eastern lands. And there can be no doubt that such Westernization was thereby greatly furthered. Once in control of an Oriental country, the European rulers were bound to favour its Westernization for a variety of reasons. Mere self-interest impelled them to make the country peaceful and prosperous, in order to extract profit for themselves and reconcile the inhabitants to their rule. This meant the replacement of inefficient and sanguinary native despotisms inhibiting progress and engendering anarchy by stable colonial governments, maintaining order, encouraging industry, and introducing improvements like the railway, the post, sanitation, and much more besides. In addition to these material innovations, practically all the Western governments endeavoured to better the social, intellectual, and spiritual condition of the peoples that had come under their control. The European Powers who built up colonial empires during the nineteenth century were actuated by a spirit far more enlightened than that of former times, when the early colonial empires of Spain, Portugal, Holland, and the English East India Company had been run on the brutal and short-sighted doctrine of sheer exploitation. In the nineteenth century all Western rule in the Orient was more or less impregnated with the ideal of "The White Man's Burden." The great empire-builders of the nineteenth century, actuated as they were not merely by self-interest and patriotic ambition but also by a profound sense of obligation to improve the populations which they had brought under their country's sway, felt themselves bearers of Western enlightenment and laboured to diffuse all the benefits of Western civilization. They honestly believed that the extension of Western political control was the best and quickest, perhaps the only, means of modernizing the backward portions of the world.

That standpoint is ably presented by a British "liberal imperialist," Professor Ramsay Muir, who writes: "It is an undeniable fact that the imperialism of the European peoples has been the means whereby European civilization has been in some degree extended to the whole world, so that to-day the whole world has become a single economic unit, and all its members are parts of a single political system. And this achievement brings us in sight of the creation of a world-order such as the wildest dreamers of the past could never have anticipated. Without the imperialism of the European peoples North and South America, Australia, South Africa, must have remained wildernesses, peopled by scattered bands of savages. Without it India and other lands of ancient civilization must have remained, for all we can see, externally subject to that endless succession of wars and arbitrary despotisms which have formed the substance of their history through untold centuries, and under which neither rational and equal law nor political liberty, as we conceive them, were practicable conceptions. Without it the backward peoples of the earth must have continued to stagnate under the dominance of an unchanging primitive customary régime, which has been their state throughout recorded time. If to-day the most fruitful political ideas of the West—the ideas of nationality and self-government—which are purely products of Western civilization, are beginning to produce a healthy fermentation in many parts of the non-European world, that result is due to European Imperialism."[83]

The ethics of modern imperialism have nowhere been better formulated than in an essay by Lord Cromer. "An imperial policy," he writes, "must, of course, be carried out with reasonable prudence, and the principles of government which guide our relations with whatsoever races are brought under our control must be politically and economically sound and morally defensible. This is, in fact, the keystone of the imperial arch. The main justification of imperialism is to be found in the use which is made of imperial power. If we make good use of our power, we may face the future without fear that we shall be overtaken by the Nemesis which attended Roman misrule. If the reverse is the case, the British Empire will deserve to fall, and of a surety it will ultimately fall."[84]

Such are the basic sanctions of Western imperialism as evolved during the nineteenth century. Whether or not it is destined to endure, there can be no question that this prodigious extension of European political control greatly favoured the spread of Western influences of every kind. It is, of course, arguable that the East would have voluntarily adopted Western methods and ideas even if no sort of Western pressure had been applied. But they would have been adopted much more slowly, and this vital element of time renders such arguments mere academic speculation. For the vital, expanding nineteenth-century West to have deliberately restrained itself while the backward East blunderingly experimented with Westernism, accepting and rejecting, buying goods and refusing to pay for them, negotiating loans and then squandering and repudiating them, inviting in Europeans and then expelling or massacring them, would have been against all history and human nature.

As a matter of fact, Western pressure was applied, as it was bound to be applied; and this constant, ubiquitous, unrelenting pressure, broke down the barriers of Oriental conservatism and inertia as nothing else could have done, forced the East out of its old ruts, and compelled it to take stock of things as they are in a world of hard facts instead of reminiscent dreams. In subsequent chapters we shall examine the manifold results of this process which has so profoundly transformed the Orient during the past hundred years. Here we will continue our general survey by examining the more recent aspects of Western control over the East and the reactions of the East thereto.

In my opinion, the chief fallacy involved in criticisms of Western control over Eastern lands arises from failure to discriminate between nineteenth-century and twentieth-century imperialism. Nineteenth-century imperialism was certainly inevitable, and was apparently beneficial in the main. Twentieth-century imperialism cannot be so favourably judged. By the year 1900 the Oriental peoples were no longer mere fanatical obscurantists neither knowing nor caring to know anything outside the closed circle of their ossified, decadent civilizations. The East had been going to school, and wanted to begin to apply what it had been taught by the West. It should have been obvious that these peoples, whose past history proved them capable of achievement and who were now showing an apparently genuine desire for new progress, needed to be treated differently from what they had been. In other words, a more liberal attitude on the part of the West had become advisable.

But no such change was made. On the contrary, in the West itself, the liberal idealism which had prevailed during most of the nineteenth century was giving way to that spirit of fierce political and economic rivalry which culminated in the Great War.[85] Never had Europe been so avid for colonies, for "spheres of influence," for concessions and preferential markets; in fine, so "imperialistic," in the unfavourable sense of the term. The result was that with the beginning of the twentieth century Western pressure on the East, instead of being relaxed, was redoubled; and the awakening Orient, far from being met with sympathetic consideration, was treated more ruthlessly than it had been for two hundred years. The way in which Eastern countries like Turkey and Persia, striving to reform themselves and protect their independence, were treated by Europe's new Realpolitik would have scandalized the liberal imperialists of a generation before. It certainly scandalized present-day liberals, as witness these scathing lines written in 1912 by the well-known British publicist Sidney Low:

"The conduct of the Most Christian Powers during the past few years has borne a striking resemblance to that of robber-bands descending upon an unarmed and helpless population of peasants. So far from respecting the rights of other nations, they have exhibited the most complete and cynical disregard for them. They have, in fact, asserted the claim of the strong to prey upon the weak, and the utter impotence of all ethical considerations in the face of armed force, with a crude nakedness which few Eastern military conquerors could well have surpassed.

"The great cosmic event in the history of the last quarter of a century has been the awakening of Asia after centuries of somnolence. The East has suddenly sprung to life, and endeavoured to throw itself vigorously into the full current of Western progress. Japan started the enterprise; and, fortunately for herself, she entered upon it before the new Western policy had fully developed itself, and while certain archaic ideals about the rights of peoples and the sanctity of treaties still prevailed. When the new era was inaugurated by the great Japanese statesmen of the nineteenth century, Europe did not feel called upon to interfere. We regarded the Japanese renaissance with interest and admiration, and left the people of Nippon to work out the difficulties of their own salvation, unobstructed. If that revolution had taken place thirty years later, there would probably have been a different story to tell; and New

44

Japan, in the throes of her travail, would have found the armed Great Powers at her bedside, each stretching forth a mailed fist to grab something worth taking. Other Eastern countries which have endeavoured to follow the example of Japan during the present century have had worse luck. During the past ten years a wave of sheer materialism and absolute contempt for international morality has swept across the Foreign Offices of Europe, and has reacted disastrously upon the various Eastern nations in their desperate struggles to reform a constitutional system. They have been attempting to carry out the suggestions made to them for generations by benevolent advisers in Christendom.

"Now, when they take these counsels to heart, and endeavour, with halting steps, and in the face of immense obstacles, to pursue the path of reform, one might suppose that their efforts would be regarded with sympathetic attention by the Governments of the West; and that, even if these offered no direct aid, they would at least allow a fair trial." But, on the contrary, "one Great Power after another has used the opportunity presented by the internal difficulties of the Eastern countries to set out upon a career of annexation."[86]

We have already seen how rapid was this career of annexation, extinguishing the independence of the last remaining Mohammedan states at the close of the Great War. We have also seen how it exacerbated Moslem fear and hatred of the West. And the West was already feared and hated for many reasons. In the preceding chapter we traced the growth of the Pan-Islamic movement, and in subsequent chapters we shall trace the development of Oriental nationalism. These politico-religious movements, however, by no means exhaust the list of Oriental reactions to Westernism. There are others, economic, social, racial in character. In view of the complex nature of the Orient's reaction against Westernism, let us briefly analyse the problem in its various constituent elements.

Anti-Western feeling has been waning in some quarters and waxing in others during the past hundred years. By temperamental reactionaries and fanatics things Western have, of course, always been abhorred. But, leaving aside this intransigeant minority, the attitude of other categories of Orientals has varied greatly according to times and circumstances. By liberal-minded persons Western influences were at first hailed with cordiality and even with enthusiasm. In the opening chapter we saw how the liberal reformers welcomed the Western concept of progress and made it one of the bases of their projected religious reformation. And the liberals displayed the same attitude in secular matters. The liberal statesmen who governed Turkey during the third quarter of the nineteenth century made earnest efforts to reform the Ottoman State, and it was the same in other parts of the Moslem world. An interesting example is the attempt made by General Kheir-ed-Din to modernize Tunis. This man, a Circassian by birth, had won the confidence of his master, the Bey, who made him vizier. In 1860 he toured Europe and returned greatly impressed with its civilization. Convinced of Europe's infinite superiority, he desired passionately to transplant Western ideas and methods to Tunis. This he believed quite feasible, and the result would, so he thought, be Tunis's rapid regeneration. Kheir-ed-Din was not in the least a hater of the West. He merely recognized clearly the Moslem world's peril of speedy subjection to the West if it did not set its house rapidly in order, and he therefore desired, in a perfectly legitimate feeling of patriotism, to press his country along the road of progress, that it might be able to stand alone and preserve its independence.

So greatly was the Bey impressed by Kheir-ed-Din's report that he gave him a free hand in his reforming endeavours. For a short time Kheir-ed-Din displayed great activity, though he encountered stubborn opposition from reactionary officials. His work was cut short by his untimely death, and Tunis, still unmodernized, fell twenty years later under the power of France. Kheir-ed-Din, however, worked for posterity. In order to rouse his compatriots to the realities of their situation he published a remarkable book, The Surest Means of Knowing the State of Nations. This book has profoundly influenced both liberals and nationalists throughout the Near East, especially in North Africa, where it has become the bible of Tunisian and Algerian nationalism. In his book Kheir-ed-Din shows his co-religionists the necessity of breaking with their attitude of blind admiration for the past and proud indifference to everything else, and of studying what is going on in the outer world. Europe's present prosperity is due, he asserts, not to natural advantages or to religion, but "to progress in the arts and sciences, which facilitate the circulation of wealth and exploit the treasures of the earth by an enlightened protection constantly given to agriculture, industry, and commerce: all natural consequences of justice and liberty—two things which, for Europeans, have become second nature." In past ages the Moslem world was great and progressive, because it was then liberal and open to progress. It declined through bigotry and obscurantism. But it can revive by reviving the spirit of its early days.

I have stressed the example of the Tunisian Kheir-ed-Din rather than the better-known Turkish instances because it illustrates the general receptivity of mid-nineteenth-century Moslem liberals to Western ideas and their freedom from anti-Western feeling.[87] As time passed, however, many of these erstwhile liberals, disillusioned with the West for various reasons, notably European aggression, became the bitterest enemies of the West, hating the very spirit of Western civilization.[88]

This anti-Western feeling has, of course, been greatly exacerbated since the beginning of the present century. As an influential Mohammedan wrote just before the Great War: "The events of these last ten years and the disasters which have stricken the Mohammedan world have awakened in its bosom a sentiment of mutual cordiality and devotion hitherto unknown, and a unanimous hatred against all its oppressors has been the ferment which to-day stirs the hearts of all Moslems."[89] The bitter rancour seething in many Moslem hearts shows in outbursts like the following, from the pen of a popular Turkish writer at the close of the Balkan Wars: "We have been defeated, we have been shown hostility by the outside world, because we have become too deliberative, too cultured, too refined in our conceptions of right and wrong, of humanity and civilization. The example of the Bulgarian army has taught us that every soldier facing the enemy must return to the days of barbarism, must have a thirst of blood, must be merciless in slaughtering children and women, old and weak, must disregard others' property, life, and honour. Let us spread blood, suffering, wrong, and mourning. Thus only may we become the favourites of the civilized world like King Ferdinand's army."[90]

The Great War itself was hailed by multitudes of Moslems as a well-merited Nemesis on Western arrogance and greed. Here is how a leading Turkish newspaper characterized the European Powers: "They would not look at the evils in their own countries or elsewhere, but interfered at the slightest incident in our borders; every day they would gnaw at some part of our rights and our sovereignty; they would perform vivisection on our quivering flesh and cut off great pieces of it. And we, with a forcibly controlled spirit of rebellion in our hearts and with clinched but powerless fists, silent and depressed, would murmur as the fire burned within: 'Oh, that they might fall out with one another! Oh, that they might eat one another up!' And lo! to-day they are eating each other up, just as the Turk wished they would."[91]

Such anti-Western sentiments are not confined to journalists or politicians, they are shared by all classes, from princes to peasants. Each class has its special reasons for hating European political control. The native princes, even when maintained upon their thrones and confirmed in their dignities and emoluments, bitterly resent their state of vassalage and their loss of limitless, despotic power. "Do you know, I can hardly buy a pen or a sword for myself without asking the Resident for permission?" remarked an Indian rajah bitterly. His attitude was precisely that of Khedive Tewfik Pasha, who, in the early days of the British occupation of Egypt, while watching a review of British troops, said to one of his ministers: "Do you suppose I like this? I tell you, I never see an English sentinel in my streets without longing to jump out of my carriage and strangle him with my own hands."[92] The upper classes feel much the same as their sovereigns. They regret their former monopoly of privilege and office. This is especially true of the Western-educated intelligentsia, who believe that they should hold all government posts and resent bitterly the reservation of high-salaried directive positions for Europeans. Of course many intelligent liberals realize so fully the educative effect of European control that they acquiesce in a temporary loss of independence in order to complete their modernization and ultimately be able to stand alone without fear of reaction or anarchy. However, these liberals are only a small minority, hated by their upper-class fellows as time-servers and renegades, and sundered by an immense gulf from the ignorant masses.

At first sight we might think that the masses would, on the whole, be favourably disposed toward European political control. Despite certain economic disadvantages that Westernization has imposed, the masses have unquestionably gained most by European rule. Formerly exploited ruthlessly by both princes and upper classes, the peasants and town workers are to-day assured peace, order, justice, and security for their landholdings and the fruits of their toil. Now it would be a mistake to think that the masses are insensible to all this. The fact is, they do recognize the benefits of European rule. Nevertheless, the new rulers, while tolerated and even respected, are never beloved. Furthermore, as the generation which knew the old régime dies off, its evils are forgotten, and the younger generation, taking present benefits for granted, murmurs at the flaws in the existing order, and lends a readier ear to native agitators extolling the glories of independence and idealizing the "good old times."

The truth of the matter is that, despite all its shortcomings, the average Oriental hankers after the old way of life. Even when he recognizes the good points of the new, he nevertheless yearns irrationally for the old. "A Moslem ruler though he oppress me and not a kafir[93] though he work me weal" is a Moslem proverb of long standing. Every colonial administration, no matter how enlightened, runs counter to this ineradicable aversion of Moslems for Christian rule. A Russian administrator in Central Asia voices the sentiments of European officials generally when he states: "Pious Moslems cannot accommodate themselves to the government of Giaours."[94]

Furthermore, it must be remembered that most Orientals either do not recognize much benefit in European rule, or, even though they do recognize considerable benefits, consider these more than offset by many points which, in their eyes, are maddening annoyances or burdens. The very things which we most pride ourselves on having given to the Orient— peace, order, justice, security—are not valued by the Oriental anywhere near as highly as we might expect. Of course he likes these things, but he would prefer to get less of them if what he did get was given by native rulers, sharing his prejudices and point of view. Take the single factor of justice. As an English writer remarks: "The Asiatic is not delighted with justice per se; indeed, the Asiatic really cares but little about it if he can get sympathy in the sense in which he understands that misunderstood word.... This is the real reason why every Asiatic in his heart of hearts prefers the rule of his own nationality, bad though it be, to the most ideal rule of aliens. For when he is ruled by his own countrymen, he is dealt with by people who understand his frailties, and who, though they may savagely punish him, are at least in sympathy with the motives which prompt his delinquencies."[95]

47

Take again the matter of order. The average Oriental not only does not appreciate, but detests, our well-regulated, systematic manner of life. Accustomed as he has been for centuries to a slipshod, easygoing existence, in which, if there was much injustice, there was also much favouritism, he instinctively hates things like sanitary measures and police regulations. Accustomed to a wide "personal liberty" in the anarchic sense, he is not willing to limit this liberty for the common weal. He wants his own way, even though it involves possible dangers to himself—dangers which may always be averted by bribery, favouritism, or violence. Said an American who had listened to a Filipino's glowing words on independence: "What could you do, if you were independent, that you cannot do now?" "I could build my house there in the middle of the street, if I wanted to." "But suppose your neighbour objected and interfered?" "I would 'get' him." "But suppose he 'got' you?" A shrug of the shoulders was the only answer.[96]

The fact is that the majority of Orientals, despite the considerable penetration of Western ideas and methods that has been going on for the last century, still love their old ruts and hate to be budged out of them. They realize that Western rule furthers more than anything else the Westernization of their social system, their traditional manner of life, and they therefore tend to react fanatically against it. Every innovation imposed by the colonial authorities is apt to rouse the most purblind resistance. For example, compulsory vaccination was bitterly opposed for years by the natives of Algeria. The French officials pointed out that smallpox, hitherto rampant, was being rapidly extirpated. The natives replied that, in their opinion, it was merely a crafty scheme for sterilizing them sexually and thus make room for French colonists. The officials thereupon pointed to the census figures, which showed that the natives were increasing at an unprecedented rate. The natives merely shrugged their shoulders and continued to inveigh against the innovation.

This whole matter has been well summarized by a French writer with a wide knowledge of Mohammedan lands. Says Louis Bertrand:

"In reality, all these peoples, indisposed as they are by their traditions, customs, and climates to live according to our social ideal, hate to endure the constraint of our police, of our administration—in a word, of any sort of regulated government, no matter how just and honest. Delivered from the most anarchic and vexatious of tyrannies, they remain in spirit more or less like our vagabonds, always hoping to escape from the gendarmes. In vain do we point out to the Arabs of North Africa that, thanks to the protection of France, they are no longer pillaged by Turkish despots nor massacred and tortured by rival tribes. They see only one thing: the necessity of paying taxes for matters that they do not understand. We shall never realize the rage, the fury, aroused in our Algerian towns by the simple health department ordinance requiring the emptying of a garbage-can at a fixed hour. At Cairo and elsewhere I have observed the same rebellious feelings among the donkey-boys and cab-drivers subjected to the regulations of the English policeman.

"But it is not merely our municipal and administrative regulations which they find insupportable; it is all our habits, taken en bloc—in a word, the order which regulates our civilized life. For instance: on the railway-line from Jaffa to Jerusalem the train stops at a station beside which stands the tomb of a holy man. The schedule calls for a stop of a minute at most. But no sooner had we arrived than what was my stupefaction to see all the Mohammedans on the train get off, spread their prayer-rugs, and tranquilly begin their devotions. The station-master blew his whistle, the conductor yelled at them that he was going to leave them behind; nobody budged. A squad of railway employees had to be mobilized, who, with blows and curses, finally bundled these pious persons back into the train again. The business lasted a good quarter of an hour, and was not easy. The more vigorous of the worshippers put up an energetic resistance.

"The above is only a casual instance, chosen at random. What is certain is that these peoples do not yet understand what we mean by exactitude, and that the concept of a well-regulated existence has not yet penetrated their heads."[97]

What has just been written of course applies primarily to the ignorant masses. But this attitude of mind is more or less common to all classes of Oriental peoples. The habits of centuries are not easily transformed. In fact, it must not be forgotten that the upper classes were able to enjoy most fully the capricious personal liberty of the unmodified East, and that, therefore, though they may be better able to understand the value of Westernization, they have in one sense the most to lose.[98]

In fact, for all Orientals, high and low alike, the "good old times" had charms which they mournfully regret. For the prince, the pasha, the courtier, existence was truly an Oriental paradise. To be sure, the prince might at any moment be defeated and slain by a rival monarch; the pasha strangled at his master's order; the courtier tortured through a superior's whim. But, meanwhile, it was "life," rich and full. "Each of these men had his own character and his own renown among his countrymen, and each enjoyed a position such as is now unattainable in Europe, in which he was released from laws, could indulge his own fancies, bad or good, and was fed every day and all day with the special flattery of Asia—that willing submissiveness to mere volition which is so like adoration, and which is to its recipients the most intoxicating of delights. Each, too, had his court of followers, and every courtier shared in the power, the luxury, and the adulation accruing to his lord. The power was that of life and death; the luxury included possession of every woman he desired; the adulation was, as I have said, almost religious worship."[99]

But, it may be asked, what about the poor man, exploited by this hierarchy of capricious despots? What had he to gain from all this? Well, in most cases, he got nothing at all; but he might gain a great deal. Life in the old Orient was a gigantic lottery. Any one, however humble, who chanced to please a great man, might rise to fame and fortune at a bound. And this is just what pleases the Eastern temperament; for in the East, "luck" and caprice are more prized than the "security" cherished in the West. In the Orient the favourite stories are those narrating sudden and amazing shifts of fortune—beggars become viziers or viziers become beggars, and all in a single night. To the majority of Orientals it is still the uncertainties of life, and the capricious favour of the powerful, which make it most worth living; not the sure reward of honesty and well-regulated labour. All these things made the life of the Orient infinitely interesting to all. And it is precisely this gambler's interest which Westernization has more or less destroyed. As an English writer very justly remarks à propos of modern Egypt: "Our rule may be perfect, but the East finds it dull. The old order was a ragged garment, but it was gay. Its very vicissitude had a charm. 'Ah! yes,' said an Egyptian to a champion of English rule, 'but in the old days a beggar might sit at the gate, and if he were found pleasing in the eyes of a great lady, he might be a great man on the morrow.' There is a natural and inevitable regret for the gorgeous and perilous past, when favour took the place of justice, and life had great heights and depths—for the Egypt of Joseph, Haroun-al-Rashid, and Ismail Pasha. We have spread the coat of broadcloth over the radiant garment."[100]

Saddened and irritated by the threatened loss of so much that they hold dear, it is not strange that many Eastern conservatives glorify the past as a sort of Golden Age, infinitely superior to anything the West can produce, and in this they are joined by many quondam liberals, disillusioned with Westernism and flying into the arms of reaction. The result is a spirit of hatred against everything Western, which sometimes assumes the most extravagant forms. Says Louis Bertrand: "During a lecture that I attended at Cairo the speaker contended that France owed Islam (1) its civilization and sciences; (2) half of its vocabulary; (3) all that was best in the character and mentality of its population, seeing that, from the Middle Ages to the Revolution of 1789, all the reformers who laboured for its enfranchisement—Albigensians, Vaudois, Calvinists, and Camisards—were probably descendants of the Saracens. It was nothing less than the total annexation of France to Morocco." Meanwhile, "it has become the fashion for fervent (Egyptian) nationalists to go to Spain and meditate in the gardens of the Alcazar of Seville or in the patios of the Alhambra of Granada on the defunct splendours of western Islam."[101]

Even more grotesque are the rhapsodies of the Hindu wing of this Golden Age school. These Hindu enthusiasts far outdo the wildest flights of their Moslem fellows. They solemnly assert that Hindustan is the nursery and home of all true religion, philosophy, culture, civilization, science, invention, and everything else; and they aver that when India's present regrettable eclipse is past (an eclipse of course caused entirely by English rule) she is again to shine forth in her glory for the salvation of the whole world. Employing to the full the old adage that there is nothing new under the sun, they have "discovered" in the Vedas and other Hindu sacred texts "irrefutable" evidence that the ancient Hindu sages anticipated all our modern ideas, including such up-to-date matters as bomb-dropping aeroplanes and the League of Nations.[102]

All this rhapsodical laudation of the past will, in the long run, prove futile. The East, like the West, has its peculiar virtues; but the East also has its special faults, and it is the faults which, for the last thousand years, have been gaining on the virtues, resulting in backwardness, stagnation, and inferiority. To-day the East is being penetrated—and quickened—by the West. The outcome will never be complete Westernization in the sense of a mere wholesale copying and absolute transformation; the East will always remain fundamentally itself. But it will be a new self, the result of a true assimilation of Western ideas. The reactionaries can only delay this process, and thereby prolong the Orient's inferiority and weakness.

Nevertheless, the reactionary attitude, though unintelligent, is intelligible. Westernization hurts too many cherished prejudices and vested interests not to arouse chronic resistance. This resistance would occur even if Western influences were all good and Westerners all angels of light. But of course Westernization has its dark side, while our Western culture-bearers are animated not merely by altruism, but also by far less worthy motives. This strengthens the hand of the Oriental reactionaries and lends them the cover of moral sanctions. In addition to the extremely painful nature of any transformative process, especially in economic and social matters, there are many incidental factors of an extremely irritating nature.

To begin with, the mere presence of the European, with his patent superiority of power and progress, is a constant annoyance and humiliation. This physical presence of the European is probably as necessary to the Orient's regeneration as it is inevitable in view of the Orient's present inferiority. But, however beneficial, it is none the less a source of profound irritation. These Europeans disturb everything, modify customs, raise living standards, erect separate "quarters" in the cities, where they form "extraterritorial" colonies exempt from native law and customary regulation. An English town rises in the heart of Cairo, a "Little Paris" eats into Arabesque Algiers, while European Pera flaunts itself opposite Turkish Stambul.

As for India, it is dotted with British "enclaves". "The great Presidency towns, Calcutta, Bombay, Madras, are European cities planted on Indian soil. All the prominent buildings are

European, though in some of the more recent ones an endeavour has been made to adopt what is known as the 'Indo-Saracenic' style of architecture. For the rest, the streets are called by English names, generally the names of bygone viceroys and governors, or of the soldiers who conquered the land and quelled the mutiny—heroes whose effigies meet you at every turn. The shops are English shops, where English or Eurasian assistants traffic in English goods. English carriages and motors bowl along the macadamized or tarred roads of Old England. On every hand there is evidence of the instinctive effort to reproduce, as nearly as the climate will permit, English conditions of life.... Almost the whole life of the people of India is relegated to the back streets, not to say the slums—frankly called in Madras the Black Town. There are a few points—clubs and gymkhanas specially established to that end—where Englishmen, and even women, meet Indian men, and even women, of the wealthier classes, on a basis of social equality. But few indeed are the points of contact between the Asian town and the European city which has been superimposed upon it. The missionary, the Salvation Army outpost, perhaps the curiosity-hunting tourist, may go forth into the bazaars; but the European community as a whole cares no more for the swarming brown multitudes around it than the dwellers on an island care for the fishes in the circumambient sea."[103] And what is true of the great towns holds good for scores of provincial centres, "stations," and cantonments. The scale may be smaller, but the type is the same.

The European in the Orient is thus everywhere profoundly an alien, living apart from the native life. And the European is not merely an aloof alien; he is a ruling alien as well. Always his attitude is that of the superior, the master. This attitude is not due to brutality or snobbery; it is inherent in the very essence of the situation. Of course many Europeans have bad manners, but that does not change the basic reality of the case. And this reality is that, whatever the future may bring, the European first established himself in the Orient because the West was then infinitely ahead of the East; and he is still there to-day because, despite all recent changes, the East is still behind the West. Therefore the European in the Orient is still the ruler, and so long as he stays there must continue to rule—justly, temperately, with politic regard for Eastern progress and liberal devolution of power as the East becomes ripe for its liberal exercise—but, nevertheless, rule. Wherever the Occidental has established his political control, there are but two alternatives: govern or go. Furthermore, in his governing, the Occidental must rule according to his own lights; despite all concessions to local feeling, he must, in the last analysis, act as a Western, not as an Eastern, ruler. Lord Cromer voices the heart of all true colonial government when he says: "In governing Oriental races the first thought must be what is good for them, but not necessarily what they think is good for them."[104]

Now all this is inevitable, and should be self-evident. Nevertheless, the fact remains that even the most enlightened Oriental can hardly regard it as other than a bitter though salutary medicine, while most Orientals feel it to be humiliating or intolerable. The very virtues of the European are prime causes of his unpopularity. For, as Meredith Townsend well says: "The European is, in Asia, the man who will insist on his neighbour doing business just after dinner, and being exact when he is half-asleep, and being 'prompt' just when he wants to enjoy,—and he rules in Asia and is loved in Asia accordingly."[105]

Furthermore, the European in the Orient is disliked not merely as a ruler and a disturber, but also as a man of widely different race. This matter of race is very complicated,[106] but it cuts deep and is of fundamental importance. Most of the peoples of the Near and Middle East with which our present discussion is concerned belong to what is known as the "brown" category of the human species. Of course, in strict anthropology, the term is inexact. Anthropologically, we cannot set off a sharply differentiated group of "brown" types as a "brown race," as we can set off the "white" types of Europe as a "white race" or the "yellow"

Mongoloid types of the Far East as a "yellow race." This is because the Near and Middle East have been racially a vast melting-pot, or series of melting-pots, wherein conquest and migration have continually poured new heterogeneous elements, producing the most diverse ethnic amalgamations. Thus to-day some of the Near and Middle Eastern peoples are largely white, like the Persians and Ottoman Turks; others, like the southern Indians and Yemenite Arabs, are largely black; while still others, like the Himalayan and Central Asian peoples, have much yellow blood. Again, as there is no brown racial type-norm, as there are white and yellow type-norms, so there is no generalized brown culture like those possessed by yellows and whites. The great brown spiritual bond is Islam, yet in India, the chief seat of brown population, Islam is professed by only one-fifth of the inhabitants. Lastly, while the spiritual frontiers of the Moslem world coincide mainly with the ethnic frontiers of the brown world, Islam overlaps at several points, including some pure whites in eastern Europe, many true yellows in the Far East, and multitudes of negroes in Africa.

Nevertheless, despite these partial modifications, the terms "brown race" and "brown world" do connote genuine realities which science and politics alike recognize to be essentially true. There certainly is a fundamental comity between the brown peoples. This comity is subtle and intangible in character; yet it exists, and under certain circumstances it is capable of momentous manifestations. Its salient feature is the instinctive recognition by all Near and Middle Eastern peoples that they are fellow "Asiatics," however bitter may be their internecine feuds. This instinctive "Asiatic" feeling has been noted by historians for more than two thousand years, and it is true to-day as in the past.

The great racial divisions of mankind are the most fundamental, the most permanent, the most ineradicable things in human experience. They are not mere diverse colorations of skin. Matters like complexion, stature, and hair-formation are merely the outward, visible symbols of correlative mental and spiritual differences which reveal themselves in sharply contrasted temperaments and view-points, and which translate themselves into the infinite phenomena of divergent group-life.

Now it is one of these basic racial lines of cleavage which runs between "East" and "West." Broadly speaking, the Near and Middle East is the "brown world," and this differentiates it from the "white world" of the West in a way which never can be really obliterated. Indeed, to attempt to obliterate the difference by racial fusion would be the maddest of follies. East and West can mutually quicken each other by a mutual exchange of ideas and ideals. They can only harm each other by transfusions of blood. To unite physically would be the greatest of disasters. East and West have both given much to the world in the past, and promise to give more in the future. But whatever of true value they are to give can be given only on condition that they remain essentially themselves. Ethnic fusion would destroy both their race-souls and would result in a dreary mongrelization from which would issue nothing but degeneration and decay.

Both East and West instinctively recognize the truth of this, and show it by their common contempt for the "Eurasian"—the mongrel offspring of unions between the two races. As Meredith Townsend well says: "The chasm between the brown man and the white is unfathomable, has existed in all ages, and exists still everywhere. No white man marries a brown wife, no brown man marries a white wife, without an inner sense of having been false to some unintelligible but irresistible command."[107]

The above summary of the political, economic, social, and racial differences between East and West gives us a fair idea of the numerous cross-currents which complicate the relations of the two worlds and which hinder Westernization. The Westernizing process is assuredly going on, and in subsequent chapters we shall see how far-reaching is its scope. But the factors just considered will indicate the possibilities of reaction and will roughly assign the limits to which Westernization may ultimately extend.

One thing is certain: Western political control in the Orient, however prolonged and however imposing in appearance, must ever rest on essentially fragile foundations. The Western rulers will always remain an alien caste; tolerated, even respected, perhaps, but never loved and never regarded as anything but foreigners. Furthermore, Western rule must necessarily become more precarious with the increasing enlightenment of the subject peoples, so that the acquiescence of one generation may be followed by the hostile protest of the next. It is indeed an unstable equilibrium, hard to maintain and easily upset.

The latent instability of European political control over the Near and Middle East was dramatically shown by the moral effect of the Russo-Japanese War. Down to that time the Orient had been so helpless in face of European aggression that most Orientals had come to regard Western supremacy with fatalistic resignation. But the defeat of a first-class European Power by an Asiatic people instantly broke the spell, and all Asia and Africa thrilled with a wild intoxication which we can scarcely conceive. A Scotch missionary thus describes the effect of the Japanese victories on northern India, where he was stationed at the time: "A stir of excitement passed over the north of India. Even the remote villagers talked over the victories of Japan as they sat in their circles and passed round the huqqa at night. One of the older men said to me, 'There has been nothing like it since the mutiny'. A Turkish consul of long experience in Western Asia told me that in the interior you could see everywhere the most ignorant peasants 'tingling' with the news. Asia was moved from end to end, and the sleep of the centuries was finally broken. It was a time when it was 'good to be alive,' for a new chapter was being written in the book of the world's history."[108]

Of course the Russo-Japanese War did not create this new spirit, whose roots lay in the previous epoch of subtle changes that had been going on. The Russo-Japanese War was thus rather the occasion than the cause of the wave of exultant self-confidence which swept over Asia and Africa in the year 1904. But it did dramatize and clarify ideas that had been germinating half-unconsciously in millions of Oriental minds, and was thus the sign manual of the whole nexus of forces making for a revivified Orient.

Furthermore, this new temper profoundly influenced the Orient's attitude toward the series of fresh European aggressions which then began. It is a curious fact that just when the Far East had successfully resisted European encroachment, the Near and Middle East should have been subjected to European aggressions of unparalleled severity. We have already noted the furious protests and the unwonted moral solidarity of the Moslem world at these manifestations of Western Realpolitik. It would be interesting to know exactly how much of this defiant temper was due to the heartening example of Japan. Certainly our ultra-imperialists of the West were playing a dangerous game during the decade between 1904 and 1914. As Arminius Vambéry remarked after the Italian raid on Tripoli: "The more the power and authority of the West gains ground in the Old World, the stronger becomes the bond of unity and mutual interest between the separate factions of Asiatics, and the deeper burns the fanatical hatred of Europe. Is it wise or expedient by useless provocation and unnecessary attacks to increase the feeling of animosity, to hurry on the struggle between the two worlds, and to nip in the bud the work of modern culture which is now going on in Asia?"[109]

The Great War of course immensely aggravated an already critical situation. The Orient suddenly saw the European peoples, who, in racial matters, had hitherto maintained something like solidarity, locked in an internecine death-grapple of unparalleled ferocity; it saw those same peoples put one another furiously to the ban as irreconcilable foes; it saw white race-unity cleft by moral and political gulfs which white men themselves continuously iterated would never be filled. The one redeeming feature of the struggle, in Oriental eyes, was the liberal programme which the Allied statesmen inscribed upon their banners. But when the war was over and the Allies had won, it promptly leaked out that at the very time when the Allied leaders were making their liberal speeches they had been negotiating a series of secret treaties partitioning the Near East between them in a spirit of the most cynical imperialism; and in the peace conferences that closed the war it was these secret treaties, not the liberal speeches, which determined the Oriental settlement, resulting (on paper at least) in the total subjugation of the Near and Middle East to European political control.

The wave of wrath which thereupon rolled over the East was not confined to furious remonstrance like the protests of pre-war days. There was a note of immediate resistance and rebellion not audible before. This rebellious temper has translated itself into warlike action which has already forced the European Powers to abate some of their extreme pretensions and which will undoubtedly make them abate others in the near future. The details of this post-war unrest will be discussed in later chapters. Suffice it to say here that the Great War has shattered European prestige in the East and has opened the eyes of Orientals to the weaknesses of the West. To the Orient the war was a gigantic course of education. For one thing, millions of Orientals and negroes were taken from the remotest jungles of Asia and Africa to serve as soldiers and labourers in the White Man's War. Though the bulk of these auxiliaries were used in colonial operations, more than a million of them were brought to Europe itself. Here they killed white men, raped white women, tasted white luxuries, learned white weaknesses—and went home to tell their people the whole story.[110] Asia and Africa to-day know Europe as they never knew it before, and we may be sure that they will make use of their knowledge. The most serious factor in the situation is that the Orient realizes that the famous Versailles "Peace" which purports to have pacified Europe is no peace, but rather an unconstructive, unstatesmanlike futility that left old sores unhealed and even dealt fresh wounds. Europe to-day lies debilitated and uncured, while Asia and Africa see in this a standing incitement to rash dreams and violent action.

Such is the situation to-day: an East, torn by the conflict between new and old, facing a West riven with dissension and sick from its mad follies. Probably never before have the relations between the two worlds contained so many incalculable, even cataclysmic, possibilities. The point to be here noted is that this strange new East which now faces us is mainly the result of Western influences permeating it in unprecedented fashion for the past hundred years. To the chief elements in that permeation let us now turn.

FOOTNOTES:

[72] For the larger aspects, see my book The Rising Tide of Colour against White World-Supremacy (New York and London, 1920).

[73] On these points, see Arminius Vambéry, Western Culture in Eastern Lands (London, 1906); also his La Turquie d'aujourd'hui et d'avant Quarante Ans (Paris, 1898); C. S. Cooper, The Modernizing of the Orient (New York, 1914); S. Khuda Bukhsh, Essays: Indian and Islamic (London, 1912); A. J. Brown, "Economic Changes in Asia," The Century, March, 1904.

[74] For the effect of the West intellectually and spiritually, see Vambéry, op. cit.; Sir Valentine Chirol, Indian Unrest (London, 1910); J. N. Farquhar, Modern Religious Movements in India (New York, 1915); Rev. J. Morrison, New Ideas in India: A Study of Social, Political, and

Religious Developments (Edinburgh, 1906); the Earl of Cromer, Modern Egypt, especially Vol. II., pp. 228-243 (London, 1908).

[75] For the Westernised élites, see L. Bertrand, Le Mirage Orientale (Paris, 1910); Cromer, op. cit.; A. Métin, L'Inde d'aujourd'hui: Étude Sociale (Paris, 1918); A. Le Chatelier, "Politique musulmane," Revue du Monde musulman, September, 1910.

[76] Chirol, op. cit., pp 321-322.

[77] Bertrand, op. cit., p 39. See also Bukhsh, op. cit.; Farquhar, op. cit.; Morrison, op. cit.; R. Mukerjee, The Foundations of Indian Economics (London, 1916); D. H. Dodwell, "Economic Transition in India," Economic Journal, December, 1910.

[78] W. S. Lilly, India and Its Problems, p. 243 (London, 1902).

[79] Cromer, op. cit., Vol. II., p. 231.

[80] Ibid., p. 228.

[81] J. Ramsay Macdonald, The Government of India, pp. 171-172 (London, 1920). On the evils of Westernization, see further: Bukhsh, Cromer, Dodwell, Mukerjee, already cited; Sir W. M. Ramsay, "The Turkish Peasantry of Anatolia," Quarterly Review, January, 1918; H. M. Hyndman, The Awakening of Asia (New York, 1919); T. Rothstein, Egypt's Ruin (London, 1910); Captain P. Azan, Recherche d'une Solution de la Question indigène en Algérie (Paris, 1903).

[82] E. J. Dillon, "Persia," Contemporary Review, June, 1910.

[83] Ramsay Muir, "Europe and the Non-European World," The New Europe, June 28, 1917.

[84] The Earl of Cromer, Political and Literary Essays, p. 5 (London, 1913).

[85] For a full discussion of these changes in Western ideas, see my Rising Tide of Colour against White World-Supremacy, especially chaps. vi. and vii.

[86] Sidney Low, "The Most Christian Powers," Fortnightly Review, March, 1912.

[87] On this point see also A. Vambéry, Western Culture in Eastern Lands (London, 1906); W. S. Blunt, The Future of Islam (London, 1882); also the two articles by Léon Cahun on intellectual and social developments in the Islamic world during the nineteenth century in Lavisse et Rambaud, Histoire Générale, Vol. XI., chap. xv.; Vol. XII., chap. xiv.

[88] See A. Vambéry, Der Islam im neunzehnten Jahrhundert, chap. vi. (Leipzig, 1875).

[89] "X," "La Situation politique de la Perse," Revue du Monde musulman, June, 1914. As already stated, the editor vouches for this anonymous writer as a distinguished Mohammedan official—"un homme d'état musulman."

[90] Ahmed Emin, The Development of Modern Turkey as Measured by Its Press, p. 108 (Columbia University Ph.D. Thesis, New York, 1914).

[91] The Constantinople Tanine. Quoted from The Literary Digest, October 24, 1914, p. 784. This attitude toward the Great War and the European Powers was not confined to Mohammedan peoples; it was common to non-white peoples everywhere. For a survey of this feeling throughout the world, see my Rising Tide of Colour against White World-Supremacy, pp. 13-16.

[92] Both the above instances are taken from C. S. Cooper, The Modernizing of the Orient, pp. 339-340 (New York, 1914).

[93] An "Unbeliever"—in other words, a Christian.

[94] Quoted by A. Woeikof, Le Turkestan russe (Paris, 1914).

[95] B. L. Putnam Weale, The Conflict of Colour, p. 193 (London, 1910).

[96] Quoted from H. H. Powers, The Great Peace, p. 82 (New York, 1918).

[97] L. Bertrand, Le Mirage oriental, pp. 441-442 (Paris, 1910).

[98] On this point see the very interesting essay by Meredith Townsend entitled "The Charm of Asia for Asiatics," in his book Asia and Europe, pp. 120-128.

[99] Townsend, op. cit., p. 104.

[100] H. Spender, "England, Egypt, and Turkey," Contemporary Review, October, 1906.

[101] Bertrand, pp. 209, 210.

[102] For discussion of this Hindu attitude see W. Archer, India and the Future (London, 1918); Young and Ferrers, India in Conflict (London, 1920). Also see Hindu writings of this nature: H. Maitra, Hinduism: The World-Ideal (London, 1916); A. Coomaraswamy, The Dance of Siva (New York, 1918); M. N. Chatterjee, "The World and the Next War," Journal of Race Development, April, 1916.

[103] Archer, pp. 11, 12.

[104] Cromer, Political and Literary Essays, p. 25.

[105] Townsend, Asia and Europe, p. 128.

[106] I have dealt with it at length in my Rising Tide of Colour against White World-Supremacy.

[107] Townsend, p. 97.

[108] Rev. C. F. Andrews, The Renaissance in India, p. 4 (London, 1911). For other similar accounts of the effect of the Russo-Japanese War upon Oriental peoples generally, see A. M. Low, "Egyptian Unrest," The Forum, October, 1906; F. Farjanel, "Le Japon et l'Islam," Revue du Monde musulman, November, 1906; "Oriental Ideals as Affected by the Russo-Japanese War," American Review of Reviews, February, 1905; A. Vambéry, "Japan and the Mahometan World," Nineteenth Century and After, April, 1905; Yahya Siddyk, op. cit., p. 42.

[109] A. Vambéry, "An Approach between Moslems and Buddhists," Nineteenth Century and After, April, 1912.

[110] For the effect of the war on Asia and Africa, see A. Demangeon, Le Déclin de l'Europe (Paris, 1920); H. M. Hyndman, The Awakening of Asia (New York, 1919); E. D. Morel, The Black Man's Burden (New York, 1920); F. B. Fisher, India's Silent Revolution (New York, 1919); also, my Rising Tide of Color against White World-Supremacy.

CHAPTER IV

POLITICAL CHANGE

The Orient's chief handicap has been its vicious political tradition. From earliest times the typical form of government in the East has been despotism—the arbitrary rule of an absolute monarch, whose subjects are slaves, holding their goods, their honours, their very lives, at his will and pleasure. The sole consistent check upon Oriental despotism has been religion. Some critics may add "custom"; but it amounts to the same thing, for in the East custom always acquires a religious sanction. The mantle of religion of course covers its ministers, the priests forming a privileged caste. But, with these exceptions, Oriental despotism has usually known no bounds; and the despot, so long as he respected religion and the priesthood, has been able to act pretty much as he chose. In the very dawn of history we see Pharaoh exhausting all Egypt to gratify his whim for a colossal pyramid tomb, and throughout history Oriental life has been cursed by this fatal political simplicity.

Now manifold human experience has conclusively proved that despotism is a bad form of government in the long run. Of course there is the legendary "benevolent despot"—the "father of his people," surrounded by wise counsellors and abolishing evils by a nod or a stroke of the pen. That is all very well in a fairy-tale. But in real life the "benevolent despot" rarely happens and still more rarely succeeds himself. The "father of his people" usually has a pompous son and a vicious grandson, who bring the people to ruin. The melancholy trinity—David, Solomon, Rehoboam—has reappeared with depressing regularity throughout history.

Furthermore, even the benevolent despot has his limitations. The trouble with all despots, good or bad, is that their rule is entirely personal. Everything, in the last analysis, depends on the despot's personal will. Nothing is fixed or certain. The benevolent despot himself may discard his benevolence overnight, and the fate of an empire may be jeopardized by the monarch's infatuation for a woman or by an upset in his digestion.

We Occidentals have, in fact, never known "despotism," in its Simon Pure, Oriental sense; not even under the Roman Empire. Indeed, we can hardly conceive what it means. When we speak of a benevolent despot we usually think of the "enlightened autocrats" of eighteenth-century Europe, such as Frederick the Great. But these monarchs were not "despots" as Orientals understand it. Take Frederick, for example. He was regarded as absolute. But his subjects were not slaves. Those proud Prussian officers, starched bureaucrats, stiff-necked burghers, and stubborn peasants each had his sense of personal dignity and legal status. The unquestioning obedience which they gave Frederick was given not merely because he was their king, but also because they knew that he was the hardest-working man in Prussia and tireless in his devotion to the state. If Frederick had suddenly changed into a lazy, depraved, capricious tyrant, his "obedient" Prussians would have soon showed him that there were limits to his power.

In the Orient it is quite otherwise. In the East "there lies upon the eyes and foreheads of all men a law which is not found in the European decalogue; and this law runs: 'Thou shalt honour and worship the man whom God shall set above thee for thy King: if he cherish thee, thou shalt love him; and if he plunder and oppress thee thou shalt still love him, for thou art his slave and his chattel.'"[111] The Eastern monarch may immure himself in his harem, casting the burdens of state upon the shoulders of a grand vizier. This vizier has thenceforth limitless power; the life of every subject is in his hands. Yet, any evening, at the pout of a dancing-girl, the monarch may send from his harem to the vizier's palace a negro "mute," armed with the bowstring. And when that black mute arrives, the vizier, doffing his robe of office, and with neither question nor remonstrance, will bare his neck to be strangled. That is real despotism—the despotism that the East has known.

Such is the political tradition of the Orient. And it is surely obvious that under such a tradition neither ordered government nor consistent progress is possible. Eastern history is, in fact, largely a record of sudden flowerings and equally sudden declines. A strong, able man cuts his way to power in a period of confusion and decay. He must be strong and able, or he would not win over other men of similar nature struggling for the coveted prize. His energy and ability soon work wonders. He knows the rough-and-ready way of getting things done. His vigour and resolution supply the driving-power required to compel his subordinates to act with reasonable efficiency, especially since incompetence or dishonesty are punished with the terrible severity of the Persian king who flayed an unjust satrap alive and made the skin into the seat of the official chair on which the new satrap sat to administer justice.

While the master lives, things may go well. But the master dies, and is succeeded by his son. This son, even assuming that he has inherited much of his father's ability, has had the worst possible upbringing. Raised in the harem, surrounded by obsequious slaves and designing women, neither his pride nor his passions have been effectively restrained, and he grows up a pompous tyrant and probably precociously depraved. Such a man will not be apt to look after things as his father did. And as soon as the master's eye shifts, things begin to go to pieces. How can it be otherwise? His father built up no governmental machine, functioning almost automatically, as in the West. His officers worked from fear or personal loyalty; not out of a patriotic sense of duty or impersonal esprit de corps. Under the grandson, matters get even worse, power slips from his incompetent hands and is parcelled out among many local despots, of whom the strongest cuts his way to power, assuming that the decadent state is not overrun by some foreign conqueror. In either eventuality, the old cycle—David, Solomon, Rehoboam—is finished, and a new cycle begins—with the same destined end.

That, in a nutshell, is the political history of the East. It has, however, been modified or temporarily interrupted by the impact of more liberal political influences, exerted sometimes from special Eastern regions and sometimes from the West. Not all the Orient has been given over to unrelieved despotism. Here and there have been peoples (mostly mountain or pastoral peoples) who abhorred despotism. Such a people have always been the Arabs. We have already seen how the Arabs, fired by Islam, established a mighty caliphate which, in its early days, was a theocratic democracy. Of course we have also seen how the older tradition of despotism reasserted itself over most of the Moslem world, how the democratic caliphate turned into a despotic sultanate, and how the liberty-loving Arabs retired sullenly to their deserts. Political liberalism, like religious liberalism, was crushed and almost forgotten. Almost—not quite; for memories of the Meccan caliphate, like memories of Motazelism, remained in the back of men's minds, ready to come forth again with better days. After all,

58

free Arabia still stood, with every Arab tribesman armed to the teeth to see that it kept free. And then, there was Islam. No court theologian could entirely explain away the fact that Mohammed had said things like "All Believers are brothers" and "All Moslems are free." No court chronicler could entirely expunge from Moslem annals the story of Islam's early days, known as the Wakti-Seadet, or "Age of Blessedness." Even in the darkest times Moslems of liberal tendencies must have been greatly interested to read that the first caliph, Abu Bekr, after his election by the people, said: "Oh nation! you have chosen me, the most unworthy among you, for your caliph. Support me as long as my actions are just. If otherwise, admonish me, rouse me to a sense of my duty. Truth alone is desirable, and lies are despicable.... As I am the guardian of the weak, obey me only so long as I obey the Sheriat [Divine Law]. But if you see that I deviate but in the minutest details from this law, you need obey me no more."[112]

In fine, no subsequent distortions could entirely obliterate the fact that primitive Islam was the supreme expression of a freedom-loving folk whose religion must necessarily contain many liberal tendencies. Even the sheriat, or canon law, is, as Professor Lybyer states, "fundamentally democratic and opposed in essence to absolutism."[113] Vambéry well summarizes this matter when he writes: "It is not Islam and its doctrines which have devastated the western portion of Asia and brought about the present sad state of things; but it is the tyranny of the Moslem princes, who have wilfully perverted the doctrines of the Prophet, and sought and found maxims in the Koran as a basis for their despotic rule. They have not allowed the faintest suspicion of doubt in matters of religion, and, efficaciously distorting and crushing all liberal principles, they have prevented the dawn of a Moslem Renaissance."[114]

In the opening chapter we saw how Oriental despotism reached its evil maximum in the eighteenth century, and how the Mohammedan Revival was not merely a puritan reformation of religion, but was also in part a political protest against the vicious and contemptible tyrants who misruled the Moslem world. This internal movement of political liberalism was soon cross-cut by another political current coming in from the West. Comparing the miserable decrepitude of the Moslem East with Europe's prosperity and vigour, thinking Moslems were beginning to recognize their shortcomings, and they could not avoid the conclusion that their woes were in large part due to their wretched governments. Indeed, a few even of the Moslem princes came to realize that there must be some adoption of Western political methods if their countries were to be saved from destruction. The most notable examples of this new type of Oriental sovereign were Sultan Mahmud II of Turkey and Mehemet Ali of Egypt, both of whom came to power about the beginning of the nineteenth century.

Of course none of these reforming princes had the slightest idea of granting their subjects constitutional liberties or of transforming themselves into limited monarchs. They intended to remain absolute, but absolute more in the sense of the "enlightened autocrat" of Europe and less in the sense of the purely Oriental despot. What they wanted were true organs of government—army, civil service, judiciary, etc.—which would function efficiently and semi-automatically as governmental machinery, and not as mere amorphous masses of individuals who had to be continuously prodded and punished by the sovereign in order to get anything done.

Mahmud II, Mehemet Ali, and their princely colleagues persisted in their new policies, but the outcome of these "reforms from above" was, on the whole, disappointing. The monarchs might build barracks and bureaux on European models and fill them with soldiers and bureaucrats in European clothes, but they did not get European results. Most of these "Western-type" officials knew almost nothing about the West, and were therefore incapable

59

of doing things in Western fashion. In fact, they had small heart for the business. Devoid of any sort of enthusiasm for ideas and institutions which they did not comprehend, they applied themselves to the work of reform with secret ill-will and repugnance, moved only by blind obedience to their sovereign's command. As time passed, the military branches did gain some modern efficiency, but the civil services made little progress, adopting many Western bureaucratic vices but few or none of the virtues.

Meanwhile reformers of quite a different sort began to appear: men demanding Western innovations like constitutions, parliaments, and other phenomena of modern political life. Their numbers were constantly recruited from the widening circles of men acquainted with Western ideas through the books, pamphlets, and newspapers which were being increasingly published, and through the education given by schools on the Western model which were springing up. The third quarter of the nineteenth century saw the formation of genuine political parties in Turkey, and in 1876 the liberal groups actually wrung from a weak sultan the grant of a parliament.

These early successes of Moslem political liberalism were, however, followed by a period of reaction. The Moslem princes had become increasingly alarmed at the growth of liberal agitation among their subjects and were determined to maintain their despotic authority. The new Sultan of Turkey, Abdul Hamid, promptly suppressed his parliament, savagely persecuted the liberals, and restored the most uncompromising despotism. In Persia the Shah repressed a nascent liberal movement with equal severity, while in Egypt the spendthrift rule of Khedive Ismail ended all native political life by provoking European intervention and the imposition of British rule. Down to the Young-Turk revolution of 1908 there were few overt signs of liberal agitation in those Moslem countries which still retained their independence. Nevertheless, the agitation was there, working underground. Hundreds of youthful patriots fled abroad, both to obtain an education and to conduct their liberal propaganda, and from havens of refuge like Switzerland these "Young-Turks," "Young-Persians," and others issued manifestoes and published revolutionary literature which was smuggled into their homelands and eagerly read by their oppressed brethren.[115]

As the years passed, the cry for liberty grew steadily in strength. A young Turkish poet wrote at this time: "All that we admire in European culture as the fruit of science and art is simply the outcome of liberty. Everything derives its light from the bright star of liberty. Without liberty a nation has no power, no prosperity; without liberty there is no happiness; and without happiness, existence, true life, eternal life, is impossible. Everlasting praise and glory to the shining light of freedom!"[116] By the close of the nineteenth century keen-sighted European observers noted the working of the liberal ferment under the surface calm of absolutist repression. Thus, Arminius Vambéry, revisiting Constantinople in 1896, was astounded by the liberal evolution that had taken place since his first sojourn in Turkey forty years before. Although Constantinople was subjected to the severest phase of Hamidian despotism, Vambéry wrote, "The old attachment of Turkey for the absolute régime is done for. We hear much in Europe of the 'Young-Turk' Party; we hear even of a constitutional movement, political emigrés, revolutionary pamphlets. But what we do not realize is the ferment which exists in the different social classes, and which gives us the conviction that the Turk is in progress and is no longer clay in the hands of his despotic potter. In Turkey, therefore, it is not a question of a Young-Turk Party, because every civilized Ottoman belongs to this party."[117]

In this connection we should note the stirrings of unrest that were now rapidly developing in the Eastern lands subject to European political control. By the close of the nineteenth century only four considerable Moslem states—Turkey, Persia, Morocco, and Afghanistan—retained anything like independence from European domination. Since Afghanistan and Morocco were so backward that they could hardly be reckoned as civilized countries, it was only in Turkey and Persia that genuine liberal movements against native despotism could arise. But in European-ruled countries like India, Egypt, and Algeria, the cultural level of the inhabitants was high enough to engender liberal political aspirations as well as that mere dislike of foreign rule which may be felt by savages as well as by civilized peoples.

These liberal aspirations were of course stimulated by the movements against native despotism in Turkey and Persia. Nevertheless, the two sets of phenomena must be sharply distinguished from each other. The Turkish and Persian agitations were essentially movements of liberal reform. The Indian, Egyptian, Algerian, and kindred agitations were essentially movements for independence, with no settled programme as to how that independence should be used after it had been attained. These latter movements are, in fact, "nationalist" rather than liberal in character, and it is in the chapters devoted to nationalism that they will be discussed. The point to be noted here is that they are really coalitions, against the foreign ruler, of men holding very diverse political ideas, embracing as these "nationalist" coalitions do not merely genuine liberals but also self-seeking demagogues and even stark reactionaries who would like to fasten upon their liberated countries the yoke of the blackest despotism. Of course all the nationalist groups use the familiar slogans "freedom" and "liberty"; nevertheless, what many of them mean is merely freedom and liberty from foreign tutelage—in other words, independence. We must always remember that patriotism has no essential connection with liberalism. The Spanish peasants, who shouted "liberty" as they rose against Napoleon's armies, greeted their contemptible tyrant-king with delirious enthusiasm and welcomed his glorification of absolutism with cries of "Long live chains!"

The period of despotic reaction which had afflicted Turkey and Persia since the beginning of the last quarter of the nineteenth century came dramatically to an end in the year 1908. Both countries exploded into revolution, the Turks deposing the tyrant Abdul Hamid, the Persians rising against their infamous ruler Muhammad Ali Shah, "perhaps the most perverted, cowardly, and vice-sodden monster that had disgraced the throne of Persia in many generations."[118] These revolutions released the pent-up liberal forces which had been slowly gathering strength under the repression of the previous generation, and the upshot was that Turkey and Persia alike blossomed out with constitutions, parliaments, and all the other political machinery of the West.

How the new régimes would have worked in normal times it is profitless to speculate, because, as a matter of fact, the times were abnormal to the highest degree. Unfortunately for the Turks and Persians, they had made their revolutions just when the world was entering that profound malaise which culminated in the Great War. Neither Turkey nor Persia were allowed time to attempt the difficult process of political transformation. Lynx-eyed Western chancelleries noted every blunder and, in the inevitable weakness of transition, pounced upon them to their undoing. The Great War merely completed a process of Western aggression and intervention which had begun some years before.

This virtual absence of specific fact-data renders largely academic any discussion of the much-debated question whether or not the peoples of the Near and Middle East are capable of "self-government"; that is, of establishing and maintaining ordered, constitutional political life. Opinions on this point are at absolute variance. Personally, I have not been able to make up my mind on the matter, so I shall content myself with stating the various arguments without attempting to draw any general conclusion. Before stating these contrasted view-points, however, I would draw attention to the distinction which should be made between the Mohammedan peoples and the non-Mohammedan Hindus of India. Moslems everywhere possess the democratic political example of Arabia as well as a religion which, as regards its own followers at least, contains many liberal tendencies. The Hindus have nothing like this. Their political tradition has been practically that of unrelieved Oriental despotism, the only exceptions being a few primitive self-governing communities in very early times, which never exerted any widespread influence and quickly faded away. As for Brahminism, the Hindu religion, it is perhaps the most illiberal cult which ever afflicted mankind, dividing society as it does into an infinity of rigid castes between which no real intercourse is possible; each caste regarding all those of lesser rank as unclean, polluting creatures, scarcely to be distinguished from animals. It is obvious that with such handicaps the establishment of true self-government will be apt to be more difficult for Hindus than for Mohammedans, and the reader should keep this point in mind in the discussion which follows.

Considering first the attitude of those who do not believe the peoples of the Near and Middle East capable of real self-government in the Western sense either now or in the immediate future, we find this thesis both ably and emphatically stated by Lord Cromer. Lord Cromer believed that the ancient tradition of despotism was far too strong to be overcome, at least in our time. "From the dawn of history," he asserts, "Eastern politics have been stricken with a fatal simplicity. Do not let us for one moment imagine that the fatally simple idea of despotic rule will readily give way to the far more complex conception of ordered liberty. The transformation, if it ever takes place at all, will probably be the work, not of generations, but of centuries.... Our primary duty, therefore, is, not to introduce a system which, under the specious cloak of free institutions, will enable a small minority of natives to misgovern their countrymen, but to establish one which will enable the mass of the population to be governed according to the code of Christian morality. A freely elected Egyptian parliament, supposing such a thing to be possible, would not improbably legislate for the protection of the slave-owner, if not the slave-dealer, and no assurance can be felt that the electors of Rajputana, if they had their own way, would not re-establish suttee. Good government has the merit of presenting a more or less attainable ideal. Before Orientals can attain anything approaching to the British ideal of self-government, they will have to undergo very numerous transmigrations of political thought." And Lord Cromer concludes pessimistically: "It will probably never be possible to make a Western silk purse out of an Eastern sow's ear."[119]

In similar vein, the veteran English publicist Doctor Dillon, writing after the Turkish and Persian revolutions, had little hope in their success, and ridiculed the current "faith in the sacramental virtue of constitutional government." For, he continues: "No parchment yet manufactured, and no constitution drafted by the sons of men, can do away with the foundations of national character. Flashy phrases and elegant declamations may persuade people that they have been transmuted; but they alter no facts, and in Persia's case the facts point to utter incapacity for self-government." Referring to the Persian revolution, Doctor Dillon continues: "At bottom, only names of persons and things have been altered; men may come and men may go, but anarchy goes on for ever.... Financial support of the new government is impossible. For foreign capitalists will not give money to be squandered by filibusters and irresponsible agitators who, like bubbles in boiling water, appear on the surface and disappear at once."[120]

A high French colonial official thus characterizes the Algerians and other Moslem populations of French North Africa: "Our natives need to be governed. They are big children, incapable of going alone. We should guide them firmly, stand no nonsense from them, and crush intriguers and agents of sedition. At the same time, we should protect them, direct them paternally, and especially obtain influence over them by the constant example of our moral superiority. Above all: no vain humanitarian illusions, both in the interest of France and of the natives themselves."[121]

Many observers, particularly colonial officials, have been disappointed with the way Orientals have used experimental first steps in self-government like Advisory Councils granted by the European rulers; have used them, that is, to play politics and grasp for more power, instead of devoting themselves to the duties assigned. As Lord Kitchener said in his 1913 report on the state of Egypt: "Representative bodies can only be safely developed when it is shown that they are capable of performing adequately their present functions, and that there is good hope that they could undertake still more important and arduous responsibilities. If representative government, in its simplest form, is found to be unworkable, there is little prospect of its becoming more useful when its scope is extended. No government would be insane enough to consider that, because an Advisory Council had proved itself unable to carry out its functions in a reasonable and satisfactory manner, it should therefore be given a larger measure of power and control."[122]

These nationalist agitations arise primarily among the native upper classes and Western-educated élites, however successful they may be in inflaming the ignorant masses, who are often quite contented with the material benefits of enlightened European rule. This point is well brought out by a leading American missionary in India, with a lifetime of experience in that country, who wrote some years ago: "The common people of India are, now, on the whole, more contented with their government than they ever were before. It is the classes, rather, who reveal the real spirit of discontent.... If the common people were let alone by the agitators, there would not be a more loyal people on earth than the people of India. But the educated classes are certainly possessed of a new ambition, politically, and will no longer remain satisfied with inferior places of responsibility and lower posts of emolument.... These people have little or no sympathy with the kind of government which is gradually being extended to them. Ultimately they do not ask for representative institutions, which will give them a share in the government of their own land. What they really seek is absolute control. The Brahmin (only five per cent. of the community) believes that he has been divinely appointed to rule the country and would withhold the franchise from all others. The Sudra— the Bourgeois of India—would no more think of giving the ballot to the fifty million Pariahs of the land than he would give it to his dog. It is the British power that has introduced, and now maintains, the equality of rights and privileges for all the people of the land."[123]

The apprehension that India, if liberated from British control, might be exploited by a tyrannical Brahmin oligarchy is shared not only by Western observers but also by multitudes of low-caste Hindus, known collectively as the "Depressed Classes". These people oppose the Indian nationalist agitation for fear of losing their present protection under the British "Raj." They believe that India still needs generations of education and social reform before it is fit for "home rule," much less independence, and they have organized into a powerful association the "Namasudra," which is loyalist and anti-nationalist in character.

The Namasudra view-point is well expressed by its leader, Doctor Nair. "Democracy as a catchword," he says, "has already reached India and is widely used. But the spirit of democracy still pauses east of Suez, and will find it hard to secure a footing in a country where caste is strongly intrenched.... I do not want to lay the charge of oppressing the lower castes at the door of any particular caste. All the higher castes take a hand in the game. The Brahmin oppresses all the non-Brahmin castes. The high-caste non-Brahmin oppresses all the castes below him.... We want a real democracy and not an oligarchy, however camouflaged by many high-sounding words. Moreover, if an oligarchy is established now, it will be a perpetual oligarchy. We further say that we should prefer a delayed democracy to an immediate oligarchy, having more trust in a sympathetic British bureaucracy than in an unsympathetic oligarchy of the so-called high castes who have been oppressing us in the past and will do so again but for the British Government. Our attitude is based, not on 'faith' alone, but on the instinct of self-preservation."[124]

Many Mohammedans as well as Hindus feel that India is not ripe for self-government, and that the relaxing of British authority now, or in the immediate future, would be a grave disaster for India itself. The Moslem loyalists reprobate the nationalist agitation for the reasons expressed by one of their representative men, S. Khuda Bukhsh, who remarks: "Rightly or wrongly, I have always kept aloof from modern Indian politics, and I have always held that we should devote more attention to social problems and intellectual advancement and less to politics, which, in our present condition, is an unmixed evil. I am firmly persuaded that we would consult our interest better by leaving politics severely alone.... It is not a handful of men armed with the learning and culture of the West, but it is the masses that must feel, understand, and take an intelligent interest in their own affairs. The infinitesimal educated minority do not constitute the population of India. It is the masses, therefore, that must be trained, educated, brought to the level of unassailable uprightness and devotion to their country. This goal is yet far beyond measurable reach, but until we attain it our hopes will be a chimera, and our efforts futile and illusory. Even the educated minority have scarcely cast off the swaddling-clothes of political infancy, or have risen above the illusions of power and the ambitions of fortune. We have yet to learn austerity of principle and rectitude of conduct. Nor can we hope to raise the standard of private and public morality so long as we continue to subordinate the interest of our community and country to our own."[125]

Such pronouncements as these from considerable portions of the native population give pause even to those liberal English students of Indian affairs who are convinced of the theoretical desirability of Indian home rule. As one of these, Edwyn Bevan, says: "When Indian Nationalists ask for freedom, they mean autonomy; they want to get rid of the foreigner. Our answer as given in the reforms is:[126] 'Yes, autonomy you shall have, but on one condition—that you have democracy as well. We will give up the control as soon as there is an Indian people which can control its native rulers; we will not give up the control to an Indian oligarchy.' This is the root of the disagreement between those who say that India might have self-government immediately and those who say that India can only become capable of self-government with time. For the former, by 'self-government', mean autonomy, and it is perfectly true that India might be made autonomous immediately. If the foreign control were withdrawn to-day, some sort of indigenous government or group of governments would, no doubt, after a period of confusion, come into being in India. But it would not be democratic government; it would be the despotic rule of the stronger or more cunning."[127]

The citations just quoted portray the standpoint of those critics, both Western and Oriental, who maintain that the peoples of the Near and Middle East are incapable of self-government in our sense, at least to-day or in the immediate future. Let us now examine the views of those who hold a more optimistic attitude. Some observers stress strongly Islam's liberal tendencies as a foundation on which to erect political structures in the modern sense. Vambéry says, "Islam is still the most democratic religion in the world, a religion favouring both liberty and equality. If there ever was a constitutional government, it was that of the first Caliphs."[128] A close English student of the Near East declares: "Tribal Arabia has the only true form of democratic government, and the Arab tribesman goes armed to make sure that it continues democratic—as many a would-be despot knows to his cost."[129] Regarding the Young-Turk revolution of 1908, Professor Lybyer remarks: "Turkey was not so unprepared for parliamentary institutions as might at first sight appear. There lay hidden some precedent, much preparation, and a strong desire, for parliamentary government. Both the religious and the secular institutions of Turkey involve precedents for a parliament. Mohammed himself conferred with the wisest of his companions. The Ulema[130] have taken counsel together up to the present time. The Sacred Law (Sheriat) is fundamentally democratic and opposed in essence to absolutism. The habit of regarding it as fundamental law enables even the most ignorant of Mohammedans to grasp the idea of a Constitution." He points out that the early sultans had their "Divan," or assemblage of high officials, meeting regularly to give the sultan information and advice, while more recently there have been a Council of State and a Council of Ministers. Also, there were the parliaments of 1877 and 1878. Abortive though these were and followed by Hamidian absolutism, they were legal precedents, never forgotten. From all this Professor Lybyer concludes: "The Turkish Parliament may therefore be regarded, not as a complete innovation, but as an enlargement and improvement of familiar institutions."[131]

Regarding Persia, the American W. Morgan Shuster, whom the Persian Revolutionary Government called in to organize the country's finances, and who was ousted in less than a year by Russo-British pressure, expresses an optimistic regard for the political capacities of the Persian people.

"I believe," he says, "that there has never been in the history of the world an instance where a people changed suddenly from an absolute monarchy to a constitutional or representative form of government and at once succeeded in displaying a high standard of political wisdom and knowledge of legislative procedure. Such a thing is inconceivable and not to be expected by any reasonable person. The members of the first Medjlis[132] were compelled to fight for their very existence from the day that the Parliament was constituted.... They had no time for serious legislative work, and but little hope that any measures which they might enact would be put into effect.

"The second and last Medjlis, practically all of whose members I knew personally, was doubtless incompetent if it were to be judged by the standards of the British Parliament or the American Congress. It would be strange indeed if an absolutely new and untried government in a land filled with the decay of ages should, from the outset, be able to conduct its business as well as governments with generations and even centuries of experience behind them. We should make allowances for lack of technical knowledge; for the important question, of course, is that the Medjlis in the main represented the new and just ideals and aspirations of the Persian people. Its members were men of more than average education; some displayed remarkable talent, character, and courage.... They responded enthusiastically to any patriotic suggestion which was put before them. They themselves lacked any great knowledge of governmental finances, but they realized the situation and were both willing and anxious to put their full confidence in any foreign advisers who showed themselves capable of resisting political intrigues and bribery and working for the welfare of the Persian people.

"No Parliament can rightly be termed incompetent when it has the support of an entire people, when it recognizes its own limitations, and when its members are willing to undergo great sacrifices for their nation's dignity and sovereign rights....

"As to the Persian people themselves, it is difficult to generalize. The great mass of the population is composed of peasants and tribesmen, all densely ignorant. On the other hand, many thousands have been educated abroad, or have travelled after completing their education at home. They, or at least certain elements among them which had had the support of the masses, proved their capacity to assimilate Western civilization and ideals. They changed despotism into democracy in the face of untold obstacles. Opportunities were equalized to such a degree that any man of ability could occupy the highest official posts. As a race they showed during the past five years an unparalleled eagerness for education. Hundreds of schools were established during the Constitutional régime. A remarkable free press sprang up overnight, and fearless writers came forward to denounce injustice and tyranny whether from within their country or without. The Persians were anxious to adopt wholesale the political, ethical, and business codes of the most modern and progressive nations. They burned with that same spirit of Asiatic unrest which pervades India, which produced the 'Young-Turk' movement, and which has more recently manifested itself in the establishment of the Chinese Republic."[133]

Mr. Shuster concludes: "Kipling has intimated that you cannot hustle the East. This includes a warning and a reflection. Western men and Western ideals can hustle the East, provided the Orientals realize that they are being carried along lines reasonably beneficial to themselves. As a matter of fact, the moral appeal and the appeal of race-pride and patriotism, are as strong in the East as in the West, though it does not lie so near the surface, and naturally the Oriental displays no great desire to be hustled when it is along lines beneficial only to the Westerner."[134]

Indeed, many Western liberals believe that European rule, however benevolent and efficient, will never prepare the Eastern peoples for true self-government; and that the only way they will learn is by trying it out themselves. This view-point is admirably stated by the well-known British publicist Lionel Curtis. Speaking of India, Mr. Curtis says that education and kindred benefits conferred by British rule will not, of themselves, "avail to prepare Indians for the task of responsible government. On the contrary, education will prove a danger and positive mischief, unless accompanied by a definite instalment of political responsibility. It is in the workshops of actual experience alone that electorates will acquire the art of self-government, however highly educated they may be.

"There must, I urge, be a devolution of definite powers on electorates. The officers of Government[135] must give every possible help and advice to the new authorities, for which those authorities may ask. They must act as their foster-mothers, not as stepmothers. But if the new authorities are to learn the art of responsible government, they must be free from control from above. Not otherwise will they learn to feel themselves responsible to the electorate below. Nor will the electorates themselves learn that the remedy for their sufferings rests in their own hands. Suffering there will be, and it is only by suffering, self-inflicted and perhaps long endured, that a people will learn the faculty of self-help, and genuine electorates be brought into being....

"I am proud to think that England has conferred immeasurable good on India by creating order and showing Indians what orderly government means. But, this having been done, I do not believe the system can now be continued as it is, without positive damage to the character of the people. The burden of trusteeship must be transferred, piece by piece, from the shoulders of Englishmen to those of Indians in some sort able to bear it. Their strength and numbers must be developed. But that can be done by the exercise of actual responsibility steadily increased as they can bear it. It cannot be done by any system of school-teaching, though such teaching is an essential concomitant of the process.

"The goal now set by the recent announcement of the Secretary of State[136] will only be reached through trouble. Yet troublous as the times before us may be, we have at last reached that stage of our work in India which is truly consonant with our own traditions. The task is one worthy of this epoch in our history, if only because it calls for the effacement of ourselves."[137]

Mr. Curtis's concluding words foreshadow a process which is to-day actually going on, not only in India but in other parts of the East as well. The Great War has so strengthened Eastern nationalist aspirations and has so weakened European power and prestige that a widespread relaxing of Europe's hold over the Orient is taking place. This process may make for good or for ill, but it is apparently inevitable; and a generation (perhaps a decade) hence may see most of the Near and Middle East autonomous or even independent. Whether the liberated peoples will misuse their opportunities and fall into despotism or anarchy, or whether they succeed in establishing orderly, progressive, constitutional governments, remains to be seen. We have examined the factors, pro and con. Let us leave the problem in the only way in which to-day it can scientifically be left—on a note of interrogation.

FOOTNOTES:

[111] T. Morison, Imperial Rule in India, p. 43 (London, 1899).

[112] Quoted from Arminius Vambéry, Western Culture in Eastern Lands, pp. 305-306 (London, 1906).

[113] A.H. Lybyer, "The Turkish Parliament," Proceedings of the American Political Science Association, Vol. VII., p. 67 (1910).

[114] Vambéry, op. cit., p. 307.

[115] A good account of these liberal movements during the nineteenth century is found in Vambéry, "Freiheitliche Bestrebungen im moslimischen Asien," Deutsche Rundschau, October, 1893; a shorter summary of Vambéry's views is found in his Western Culture in Eastern Lands, especially chap. v. Also, see articles by Léon Cahun, previously noted, in Lavisse et Rambaud, Histoire Générale, Vols. XI. and XII.

[116] Vambéry, supra, p. 332.

[117] Vambéry, La Turquie d'aujourd'hui et d'avant Quarante Ans, p. 22 (Paris, 1898).

[118] W. Morgan Shuster, The Strangling of Persia, p. xxi (New York, 1912).

[119] Cromer, Political and Literary Essays, pp. 25-28.

[120] E. J. Dillon, "Persia not Ripe for Self-Government," Contemporary Review, April, 1910.

[121] E. Mercier, La Question indigène, p. 220 (Paris, 1901).

[122] "Egypt," No. 1 (1914), p. 6.

[123] Rev. J. P. Jones, "The Present Situation in India," Journal of Race Development, July, 1910.

[124] Dr. T. Madavan Nair, "Caste and Democracy," Edinburgh Review, October, 1918.

[125] Bukhsh, Essays: Indian and Islamic, pp. 213-214 (London, 1912).

[126] I. e., the increase of self-government granted India by Britain as a result of the Montagu-Chelmsford Report.

[127] E. Bevan, "The Reforms in India," The New Europe, January 29, 1920.

[128] Vambéry, La Turquie d'aujourd'hui et d'avant Quarante Ans, p. 58.

[129] G. W. Bury, Pan-Islam, pp. 202-203 (London, 1919).

[130] The assembly of religious notables.

[131] A. H. Lybyer, "The Turkish Parliament," Proceedings of the American Political Science Association, Vol. VII., pp. 66-67 (1910).

[132] The name of the Persian Parliament.

[133] Shuster, The Strangling of Persia, pp. 240-246.

[134] Ibid., p. 333.

[135] I. e., the British Government of India.

[136] I. e., the Montagu-Chelmsford reforms, previously noted.

[137] Lionel Curtis, Letters to the People of India on Responsible Government, pp. 159-160 (London, 1918).

CHAPTER V

NATIONALISM

The spirit of nationality is one of the great dynamics of modern times. In Europe, where it first attained self-conscious maturity, it radically altered the face of things during the nineteenth century, so that that century is often called the Age of Nationalities. But nationalism is not merely a European phenomenon. It has spread to the remotest corners of the earth, and is apparently still destined to effect momentous transformations.

Given a phenomenon of so vital a character, the question at once arises: What is nationalism? Curiously enough, this question has been endlessly debated. Many theories have been advanced, seeking variously to identify nationalism with language, culture, race, politics, geography, economics, or religion. Now these, and even other, matters may be factors predisposing or contributing to the formation of national consciousness. But, in the last analysis, nationalism is something over and above all its constituent elements, which it works into a new and higher synthesis. There is really nothing recondite or mysterious about nationalism, despite all the arguments that have raged concerning its exact meaning. As a matter of fact, nationalism is a state of mind. Nationalism is a belief, held by a fairly large number of individuals, that they constitute a "Nationality"; it is a sense of belonging together as a "Nation." This "Nation," as visualized in the minds of its believers, is a people or community associated together and organized under one government, and dwelling together in a distinct territory. When the nationalist ideal is realized, we have what is known as a body-politic or "State." But we must not forget that this "State" is the material manifestation of an ideal, which may have pre-existed for generations as a mere pious aspiration with no tangible attributes like state sovereignty or physical frontiers. Conversely, we must remember that a state need not be a nation. Witness the defunct Hapsburg Empire of Austria-Hungary, an assemblage of discordant nationalities which flew to pieces under the shock of war.

The late war was a liberal education regarding nationalistic phenomena, especially as applied to Europe, and most of the fallacies regarding nationality were vividly disclosed. It is enough to cite Switzerland—a country whose very existence flagrantly violates "tests" like language, culture, religion, or geography, and where nevertheless a lively sense of nationality emerged triumphant from the ordeal of Armageddon.

So familiar are these matters to the general public that only one point need here be stressed: the difference between nationality and race. Unfortunately the two terms have been used very loosely, if not interchangeably, and are still much confused in current thinking. As a matter of fact, they connote utterly different things. Nationality is a psychological concept or state of mind. Race is a physiological fact, which may be accurately determined by scientific tests such as skull-measurement, hair-formation, and colour of eyes and skin. In other words, race is what people anthropologically really are; nationality is what people politically think they are.

Right here we encounter a most curious paradox. There can be no question that, as between race and nationality, race is the more fundamental, and, in the long run, the more important. A man's innate capacity is obviously dependent upon his heredity, and no matter how stimulating may be his environment, the potential limits of his reaction to that environment are fixed at his birth. Nevertheless, the fact remains that men pay scant attention to race, while nationalism stirs them to their very souls. The main reason for this seems to be because it is only about half a century since even savants realized the true nature and importance of race. Even after an idea is scientifically established, it takes a long time for it to be genuinely accepted by the public, and only after it has been thus accepted will it form the basis of practical conduct. Meanwhile the far older idea of nationality has permeated the popular consciousness, and has thereby been able to produce tangible effects. In fine, our political life is still dominated by nationalism rather than race, and practical politics are thus conditioned, not by what men really are, but by what they think they are.

The late war is a striking case in point. That war is very generally regarded as having been one of "race." The idea certainly lent to the struggle much of its bitterness and uncompromising fury. And yet, from the genuine racial standpoint, it was nothing of the kind. Ethnologists have proved conclusively that, apart from certain palæolithic survivals and a few historically recent Asiatic intruders, Europe is inhabited by only three stocks: (1) The blond, long-headed "Nordic" race, (2) the medium-complexioned, round-headed "Alpine" race, (3) the brunet, long-headed "Mediterranean" race. These races are so dispersed and intermingled that every European nation is built of at least two of these stocks, while most are compounded of all three. Strictly speaking, therefore, the European War was not a race-war at all, but a domestic struggle between closely knit blood-relatives.

Now all this was known to most well-educated Europeans long before 1914. And yet it did not make the slightest difference. The reason is that, in spite of everything, the vast majority of Europeans still believe that they fit into an entirely different race-category. They think they belong to the "Teutonic" race, the "Latin" race, the "Slav" race, or the "Anglo-Saxon" race. The fact that these so-called "races" simply do not exist but are really historical differentiations, based on language and culture, which cut sublimely across genuine race-lines—all that is quite beside the point. Your European may apprehend this intellectually, but so long as it remains an intellectual novelty it will have no appreciable effect upon his conduct. In his heart of hearts he will still believe himself a Latin, a Teuton, an Anglo-Saxon, or a Slav.

For his blood-race he will not stir; for his thought-race he will die. For the glory of the dolichocephalic "Nordic" or the brachycephalic "Alpine" he will not prick his finger or wager a groat; for the triumph of the "Teuton" or the "Slav" he will give his last farthing and shed his heart's blood. In other words: Not what men really are, but what they think they are.

At first it may seem strange that in contemporary Europe thought-race should be all-powerful while blood-race is impotent. Yet there are very good reasons. Not only has modern Europe's great dynamic been nationalism, but also nationalism has seized upon the nascent racial concept and has perverted it to its own ends. Until quite recent times "Nationality" was a distinctly intensive concept, connoting approximate identity of culture, language, and historic past. It was the logical product of a relatively narrow European outlook. Indeed, it grew out of a still narrower outlook which had contented itself with the regional, feudal, and dialectic loyalties of the Middle Ages. But the first half of the nineteenth century saw a still further widening of the European outlook to a continental or even to a world horizon. At once the early concept of nationality ceased to satisfy. Nationalism became extensive. It tended to embrace all those of kindred speech, culture, and historic tradition, however distant such persons might be. Obviously a new terminology was required. The keyword was presently discovered—"Race." Hence we get that whole series of pseudo "race" phrases—"Pan-Germanism," "Pan-Slavism," "Pan-Angleism," "Pan-Latinism," and the rest. Of course these are not racial at all. They merely signify nationalism brought up to date. But the European peoples, with all the fervour of the nationalist faith that is in them, believe and proclaim them to be racial. Hence, so far as practical politics are concerned, they are racial and will so continue while the nationalist dynamic endures.

This new development of nationalism (the "racial" stage, as we may call it) was at first confined to the older centres of European civilization, but with the spread of Western ideas it presently appeared in the most unexpected quarters. Its advent in the Balkans, for example, quickly engendered those fanatical propagandas, "Pan-Hellenism," "Pan-Serbism," etc., which turned that unhappy region first into a bear-garden and latterly into a witches' sabbath.

Meanwhile, by the closing decades of the nineteenth century, the first phase of nationalism had patently passed into Asia. The "Young-Turk" and "Young-Egyptian" movements, and the "Nationalist" stirrings in regions so far remote from each other as Algeria, Persia, and India, were unmistakable signs that Asia was gripped by the initial throes of nationalist self-consciousness. Furthermore, with the opening years of the twentieth century, numerous symptoms proclaimed the fact that in Asia, as in the Balkans, the second or "racial" stage of nationalism had begun. These years saw the definite emergence of far-flung "Pan-" movements: "Pan-Turanism," "Pan-Arabism," and (most amazing of apparent paradoxes) "Pan-Islamic Nationalism."

I

Let us now trace the genesis and growth of nationalism in the Near and Middle East, devoting the present chapter to nationalist developments in the Moslem world with the exception of India. India requires special treatment, because there nationalist activity has been mainly the work of the non-Moslem Hindu element. Indian nationalism has followed a course differing distinctly from that of Islam, and will therefore be considered in the following chapter.

Before it received the Western impact of the nineteenth century, the Islamic world was virtually devoid of self-conscious nationalism. There were, to be sure, strong local and tribal loyalties. There was intense dynastic sentiment like the Turks' devotion to their "Padishas," the Ottoman sultans. There was also marked pride of race such as the Arabs' conviction that they were the "Chosen People." Here, obviously, were potential nationalist elements. But these elements were as yet dispersed and unco-ordinated. They were not yet fused into the new synthesis of self-conscious nationalism. The only Moslem people which could be said to possess anything like true nationalist feeling were the Persians, with their traditional devotion to their plateau-land of "Iran." The various peoples of the Moslem world had thus, at most, a rudimentary, inchoate nationalist consciousness: a dull, inert unitary spirit; capable of development, perhaps, but as yet scarcely perceptible even to outsiders and certainly unperceived by themselves.

Furthermore, Islam itself was in many respects hostile to nationalism. Islam's insistence upon the brotherhood of all True Believers, and the Islamic political ideal of the "Imâmât," or universal theocratic democracy, naturally tended to inhibit the formation of sovereign, mutually exclusive national units; just as the nascent nationalities of Renaissance Europe conflicted with the mediæval ideals of universal papacy and "Holy Roman Empire."

Given such an unfavourable environment, it is not strange to see Moslem nationalist tendencies germinating obscurely and confusedly throughout the first half of the nineteenth century. Not until the second half of the century is there any clear conception of "Nationalism" in the Western sense. There are distinct nationalist tendencies in the teachings of Djemal-ed-Din el-Afghani (who is philosophically the connecting link between Pan-Islamism and Moslem nationalism), while the Turkish reformers of the mid-nineteenth century were patently influenced by nationalism as they were by other Western ideas. It was, in fact, in Turkey that a true nationalist consciousness first appeared. Working upon the Turks' traditional devotion to their dynasty and pride in themselves as a ruling race lording it over many subject peoples both Christian and Moslem, the Turkish nationalist movement made rapid progress.

Precisely as in Europe, the nationalist movement in Turkey began with a revival of historic memories and a purification of the language. Half a century ago the Ottoman Turks knew almost nothing about their origins or their history. The martial deeds of their ancestors and the stirring annals of their empire were remembered only in a vague, legendary fashion, the study of the national history being completely neglected. Religious discussions and details of the life of Mohammed or the early days of Islam interested men more than the spread of Ottoman power in three continents. The nationalist pioneers taught their fellow-countrymen their historic glories and awakened both pride of past and confidence in the future.

Similarly with the Turkish language; the early nationalists found it virtually cleft in twain. On the one hand was "official" Turkish—a clumsy hotchpotch, overloaded with flowers of rhetoric and cryptic expressions borrowed from Arabic and Persian. This extraordinary jargon, couched in a bombastic style, was virtually unintelligible to the masses. The masses, on the other hand, spoke "popular" Turkish—a primitive, limited idiom, divided into many dialects and despised as uncouth and boorish by "educated" persons. The nationalists changed all this. Appreciating the simple, direct strength of the Turkish tongue, nationalist enthusiasts trained in European principles of grammar and philology proceeded to build up a real Turkish language in the Western sense. So well did they succeed that in less than a generation they produced a simplified, flexible Turkish which was used effectively by both journalists and men of letters, was intelligible to all classes, and became the unquestioned vehicle for thought and the canon of style.[138]

Of course the chief stimulus to Turkish nationalism was Western political pressure. The more men came to love their country and aspire to its future, the more European assaults on Turkish territorial integrity spurred them to defend their threatened independence. The nationalist ideal was "Ottomanism"—the welding of a real "nation" in which all citizens, whatever their origin or creed, should be "Ottomans," speaking the Turkish language and inspired by Ottoman patriotism. This, however, conflicted sharply with the rival (and prior) nationalisms of the Christian peoples of the empire, to say nothing of the new Arab nationalism which was taking shape at just this same time. Turkish nationalism was also frowned on by Sultan Abdul Hamid. Abdul Hamid had an instinctive aversion to all nationalist movements, both as limitations to his personal absolutism and as conflicting with that universal Pan-Islamic ideal on which he based his policy. Accordingly, even those Turkish nationalists who proclaimed complete loyalty were suspect, while those with liberal tendencies were persecuted and driven into exile.

The revolution of 1908, however, brought nationalism to power. Whatever their differences on other matters, the Young-Turks were all ardent nationalists. In fact, the very ardour of their nationalism was a prime cause of their subsequent misfortunes. With the rashness of fanatics the Young-Turks tried to "Ottomanize" the whole empire at once. This enraged all the other nationalities, alienated them from the revolution, and gave the Christian Balkan states their opportunity to attack disorganized Turkey in 1912.

The truth of the matter was that Turkish nationalism was evolving in a direction which could only mean heightened antagonism between the Turkish element on the one side and the non-Turkish elements, Christian or Moslem, on the other. Turkish nationalism had, in fact, now reached the second or "racial" stage. Passing the bounds of the limited, mainly territorial, idea connoted by the term "Ottomanism," it had embraced the far-flung and essentially racial concepts known as "Pan-Turkism" and "Pan-Turanism." These wider developments we shall consider later on in this chapter. Before so doing let us examine the beginnings of nationalism's "first stage" in other portions of the Moslem world.

Shortly after the Ottoman Turks showed signs of a nationalistic awakening, kindred symptoms began to appear among the Arabs. As in all self-conscious nationalist movements, it was largely a protest against some other group. In the case of the Arabs this protest was naturally directed against their Turkish rulers. We have already seen how Desert Arabia (the Nejd) had always maintained its freedom, and we have also seen how those Arab lands like Syria, Mesopotamia, and the Hedjaz which fell under Turkish control nevertheless continued to feel an ineradicable repugnance at seeing themselves, Islam's "Chosen People," beneath the yoke of a folk which, in Arab eyes, were mere upstart barbarians. Despite a thousand years of Turkish domination the two races never got on well together, their racial temperaments being too incompatible for really cordial relations. The profound temperamental incompatibility of Turk and Arab has been well summarized by a French writer. Says Victor Bérard: "Such are the two languages and such the two peoples: in the latitude of Rome and in the latitude of Algiers, the Turk of Adrianople, like the Turk of Adalia, remains a man of the north and of the extreme north; in all climates the Arab remains a man of the south and of the extreme south. To the Arab's suppleness, mobility, imagination, artistic feeling, democratic tendencies, and anarchic individualism, the Turk opposes his slowness, gravity, sense of discipline and regularity, innate militarism. The Turkish master has always felt disdain for the 'artistic canaille,' whose pose, gesticulations, and indiscipline, shock him profoundly. On their side, the Arabs see in the Turk only a blockhead; in his placidity and taciturnity only stupidity and ignorance; in his respect for law only slavishness; and in his love of material well-being only gross bestiality. Especially do the Arabs jeer at the Turk's artistic incapacity: after having gone to school to the Chinese, Persians, Arabs, and Greeks, the Turk remains, in Arab eyes, just a big booby of barrack and barnyard."[139]

Add to this the fact that the Arabs regard the Turks as perverters of the Islamic faith, and we need not be surprised to find that Turkey's Arab subjects have ever displayed symptoms of rebellious unrest. We have seen how the Wahabi movement was specifically directed against Turkish control of the holy cities, and despite the Wahabi defeat, Arab discontent lived on. About 1820 the German explorer Burckhardt wrote of Arabia: "When Turkish power in the Hedjaz declines, the Arabs will avenge themselves for their subjection."[140] And some twenty years later the Shereef of Mecca remarked to a French traveller: "We, the direct descendants of the Prophet, have to bow our heads before miserable Pashas, most of them former Christian slaves come to power by the most shameful courses."[141] Throughout the nineteenth century every Turkish defeat in Europe was followed by a seditious outburst in its Arab provinces.

Down to the middle of the nineteenth century these seditious stirrings remained sporadic, unco-ordinated outbursts of religious, regional, or tribal feeling, with no genuinely "Nationalistic" programme of action or ideal. But in the later sixties a real nationalist agitation appeared. Its birthplace was Syria. That was what might have been expected, since Syria was the part of Turkey's Arab dominions most open to Western influences. This first Arab nationalist movement, however, did not amount to much. Directed by a small group of noisy agitators devoid of real ability, the Turkish Government suppressed it without much difficulty.

The disastrous Russian war of 1877, however, blew the scattered embers into a fresh flame. For several years Turkey's Arab provinces were in full ferment. The nationalists spoke openly of throwing off the Turkish yoke and welding the Arab lands into a loose-knit confederation headed by a religious potentate, probably the Shereef of Mecca. This was obviously an adaptation of Western nationalism to the traditional Arab ideal of a theocratic democracy already realized in the Meccan caliphate and the Wahabi government of the Nejd.

This second stirring of Arab nationalism was likewise of short duration. Turkey was now ruled by Sultan Abdul Hamid, and Abdul Hamid's Pan-Islamic policy looked toward good relations with his Arab subjects. Accordingly, Arabs were welcomed at Constantinople, favours were heaped upon Arab chiefs and notables, while efforts were made to promote the contentment of the empire's Arab populations. At the same time the construction of strategic railways in Syria and the Hedjaz gave the Turkish Government a stronger grip over its Arab provinces than ever before, and conversely rendered successful Arab revolts a far more remote possibility. Furthermore, Abdul Hamid's Pan-Islamic propaganda was specially directed toward awakening a sense of Moslem solidarity between Arabs and Turks as against the Christian West. These efforts achieved a measure of success. Certainly, every European aggression in the Near East was an object-lesson to Turks and Arabs to forget, or at least adjourn, their domestic quarrels in face of the common foe.

Despite the partial successes of Abdul Hamid's efforts, a considerable section of his Arab subjects remained unreconciled, and toward the close of the nineteenth century a fresh stirring of Arab nationalist discontent made its appearance. Relentlessly persecuted by the Turkish authorities, the Arab nationalist agitators, mostly Syrians, went into exile. Gathering in near-by Egypt (now of course under British governance) and in western Europe, these exiles organized a revolutionary propaganda. Their formal organization dates from the year 1895, when the "Arabian National Committee" was created at Paris. For a decade their propaganda went on obscurely, but evidently with effect, for in 1905 the Arab provinces of Hedjaz and Yemen burst into armed insurrection. This insurrection, despite the best efforts of the Turkish Government, was never wholly suppressed, but dragged on year after year, draining Turkey of troops and treasure, and contributing materially to her Tripolitan and Balkan disasters in 1911-12.

The Arab revolt of 1905 focussed the world's attention upon "The Arab Question," and the nationalist exiles made the most of their opportunity by redoubling their propaganda, not only at home but in the West as well. Europe was fully informed of "Young Arabia's" wrongs and aspirations, notably by an extremely clever book by one of the nationalist leaders, entitled The Awakening of the Arab Nation,[142] which made a distinct sensation. The aims of the Arab nationalists are clearly set forth in the manifesto of the Arabian National Committee, addressed to the Great Powers and published early in 1906. Says this manifesto: "A great pacific change is on the eve of occurring in Turkey. The Arabs, whom the Turks tyrannized over only by keeping them divided on insignificant questions of ritual and religion, have become conscious of their national, historic, and racial homogeneity, and wish to detach themselves from the worm-eaten Ottoman trunk in order to form themselves into an independent state. This new Arab Empire will extend to its natural frontiers, from the valleys of the Tigris and Euphrates to the Isthmus of Suez, and from the Mediterranean to the Sea of Oman. It will be governed by the constitutional and liberal monarchy of an Arabian sultan. The present Vilayet of the Hedjaz, together with the territory of Medina, will form an independent empire whose sovereign will be at the same time the religious Khalif of all the Mohammedans. Thus, one great difficulty, the separation of the civil and the religious powers in Islam, will have been solved for the greater good of all."

To their fellow Arabs the committee issued the following proclamation: "Dear Compatriots! All of us know how vile and despicable the glorious and illustrious title of Arabian Citizen has become in the mouths of all foreigners, especially Turks. All of us see to what depths of misery and ignorance we have fallen under the tyranny of these barbarians sprung from Central Asia. Our land, the richest and finest on earth, is to-day an arid waste. When we were free, we conquered the world in a hundred years; we spread everywhere sciences, arts, and letters; for centuries we led world-civilization. But, since the spawn of Ertogrul[143] usurped the caliphate of Islam, they have brutalized us so as to exploit us to such a degree that we have become the poorest people on earth." The proclamation then goes on to declare Arabia's independence.[144]

Of course "Young Arabia" did not then attain its independence. The revolt was kept localized and Turkey maintained its hold over most of its Arab dominions. Nevertheless, there was constant unrest. During the remainder of Abdul Hamid's reign his Arab provinces were in a sort of unstable equilibrium, torn between the forces of nationalist sedition on the one hand and Pan-Islamic, anti-European feeling on the other.

The Young-Turk revolution of 1908 caused a new shift in the situation. The Arab provinces, like the other parts of the empire, rejoiced in the downfall of despotism and hoped great things for the future. In the Turkish Parliament the Arab provinces were well represented, and their deputies asked for a measure of federal autonomy. This the Young-Turks, bent upon "Ottomanization," curtly refused. The result was profound disillusionment in the Arab provinces and a revival of separatist agitation. It is interesting to note that the new independence agitation had a much more ambitious programme than that of a few years before. The Arab nationalists of Turkey were by this time definitely linking up with the nationalists of Egypt and French North Africa—Arabic-speaking lands where the populations were at least partly Arab in blood. Arab nationalism was beginning to speak aloud what it had previously whispered—the programme of a great "Pan-Arab" empire stretching right across North Africa and southern Asia from the Atlantic to the Indian Oceans. Thus, Arab nationalism, like Turkish nationalism, was evolving into the "second," or racial, stage.

Deferring discussion of this broader development, let us follow a trifle further the course of the more restricted Arab nationalism within the Turkish Empire. Despite the Pan-Islamic sentiment evoked by the European aggressions of 1911-12, nationalist feeling was continually aroused by the Ottomanizing measures of the Young-Turk government, and the independence agitation was presently in full swing once more. In 1913 an Arabian nationalist congress convened in Paris and revolutionary propaganda was inaugurated on an increased scale. When the Great War broke out next year, Turkey's Arab provinces were seething with seditious unrest.[145] The Turkish authorities took stern measures against possible trouble, imprisoning and executing all prominent nationalists upon whom they could lay their hands, while the proclamation of the "Holy War" rallied a certain portion of Arab public opinion to the Turkish side, especially since the conquest of Egypt was a possibility. But as the war dragged on the forces of discontent once more raised their heads. In 1916 the revolt of the Shereef of Mecca gave the signal for the downfall of Turkish rule. This revolt, liberally backed by England, gained the active or passive support of the Arab elements throughout the Turkish Empire. Inspired by Allied promises of national independence of a most alluring character, the Arabs fought strenuously against the Turks and were a prime factor in the débâcle of Ottoman military power in the autumn of 1918.[146]

Before discussing the momentous events which have occurred in the Arab provinces of the former Ottoman Empire since 1918, let us consider nationalist developments in the Arabized regions of North Africa lying to the westward. Of these developments the most important is that of Egypt. The mass of the Egyptian people is to-day, as in Pharaoh's time, of the old "Nilotic" stock. A slow, self-contained peasant folk, the Egyptian "fellaheen" have submitted passively to a long series of conquerors, albeit this passivity has been occasionally broken by outbursts of volcanic fury presently dying away into passivity once more. Above the Nilotic masses stands a relatively small upper class descended chiefly from Egypt's more recent Asiatic conquerors—Arabs, Kurds, Circassians, Albanians, and Turks. In addition to this upper class, which until the English occupation monopolized all political power, there are large European "colonies" with "extraterritorial" rights, while a further complication is added by the persistence of a considerable native Christian element, the "Copts," who refused to turn Mohammedan at the Arab conquest and who to-day number fully one-tenth of the total population.

With such a medley of races, creeds, and cultures, and with so prolonged a tradition of foreign domination, Egypt might seem a most unlikely milieu for the growth of nationalism. On the other hand, Egypt has been more exposed to Western influences than any other part of the Near East. Bonaparte's invasion at the close of the eighteenth century profoundly affected Egyptian life, and though the French were soon expelled, European influences continued to permeate the valley of the Nile. Mehemet Ali, the able Albanian adventurer who made himself master of Egypt after the downfall of French rule, realized the superiority of European methods and fostered a process of Europeanization which, however superficial, resulted in a wide dissemination of Western ideas. Mehemet Ali's policy was continued by his successors. That magnificent spendthrift Khedive Ismail, whose reckless contraction of European loans was the primary cause of European intervention, prided himself on his "Europeanism" and surrounded himself with Europeans.

Indeed, the first stirrings of Egyptian nationalism took the form of a protest against the noxious, parasitical "Europeanism" of Khedive Ismail and his courtiers. Sober-minded Egyptians became increasingly alarmed at the way Ismail was mortgaging Egypt's independence by huge European loans and sucking its life-blood by merciless taxation. Inspired consciously or unconsciously by the Western concepts of "nation" and "patriotism," these men desired to stay Ismail's destructive course and to safeguard Egypt's future. In fact, their efforts were directed not merely against the motley crew of European adventurers and concessionaires who were luring the Khedive into fresh extravagances, but also against the complaisant Turkish and Circassian pashas, and the Armenian and Syrian usurers, who were the instruments of Ismail's will. The nascent movement was thus basically a "patriotic" protest against all those, both foreigners and native-born, who were endangering the country. This showed clearly in the motto adopted by the agitators—the hitherto unheard-of slogan: "Egypt for the Egyptians!"

Into this incipient ferment there was presently injected the dynamic personality of Djemal-ed-Din. Nowhere else did this extraordinary man exert so profound and lasting an influence as in Egypt. It is not too much to say that he is the father of every shade of Egyptian nationalism. He influenced not merely violent agitators like Arabi Pasha but also conservative reformers like Sheikh Mohammed Abdou, who realized Egypt's weakness and were content to labour patiently by evolutionary methods for distant goals.

For the moment the apostles of violent action had the stage. In 1882 a revolutionary agitation broke out headed by Arabi Pasha, an army officer, who, significantly enough, was of fellah origin, the first man of Nilotic stock to sway Egypt's destinies in modern times. Raising their slogan, "Egypt for the Egyptians," the revolutionists sought to drive all "foreigners," both Europeans and Asiatics, from the country. Their attempt was of course foredoomed to failure. A massacre of Europeans in the port-city of Alexandria at once precipitated European intervention. An English army crushed the revolutionists at the battle of Tel-el-Kebir, and after this one battle, disorganized, bankrupt Egypt submitted to British rule, personified by Evelyn Baring, Lord Cromer. The khedivial dynasty was, to be sure, retained, and the native forms of government respected, but all real power centred in the hands of the British "Financial Adviser," the representative of Britain's imperial will.

For twenty-five years Lord Cromer ruled Egypt, and the record of this able proconsul will place him for ever in the front rank of the world's great administrators. His strong hand drew Egypt from hopeless bankruptcy into abounding prosperity. Material well-being, however, did not kill Egyptian nationalism. Scattered to the winds before the British bayonet charges, the seeds of unrest slowly germinated beneath the fertile Nilotic soil. Almost imperceptible at first under the numbing shock of Tel-el-Kebir, nationalist sentiment grew steadily as the years wore on, and by the closing decade of the nineteenth century it had become distinctly perceptible to keen-sighted European observers. Passing through Egypt in 1895, the well-known African explorer Schweinfurth was struck with the psychological change which had occurred since his earlier visits to the valley of the Nile. "A true national self-consciousness is slowly beginning to awaken," he wrote. "The Egyptians are still very far from being a true Nationality, but the beginning has been made."[147]

With the opening years of the twentieth century what had previously been visible only to discerning eyes burst into sudden and startling bloom. This resurgent Egyptian nationalism had, to be sure, its moderate wing, represented by conservative-minded men like Mohammed Abdou, Rector of El Azhar University and respected friend of Lord Cromer, who sought to teach his fellow-countrymen that the surest road to freedom was along the path of enlightenment and progress. In the main, however, the movement was an impatient and violent protest against British rule and an intransigeant demand for immediate independence. Perhaps the most significant point was that virtually all Egyptians were nationalists at heart, conservatives as well as radicals declining to consider Egypt as a permanent part of the British Empire. The nationalists had a sound legal basis for this attitude, owing to the fact that British rule rested upon insecure diplomatic foundations. England had intervened in Egypt as a self-constituted "Mandatory" of European financial interests. Its action had roused much opposition in Europe, particularly in France, and to allay this opposition the British Government had repeatedly announced that its occupation of Egypt was of a temporary nature. In fact, Egyptian discontent was deliberately fanned by France right down to the conclusion of the Entente Cordiale in 1904. This French sympathy for Egyptian aspirations was of capital importance in the development of the nationalist movement. In Egypt, France's cultural prestige was predominant. In Egyptian eyes a European education was synonymous with a French education, so the rising generation inevitably sat under French teachers, either in Egypt or in France, and these French preceptors, being usually Anglophobes, rarely lost an opportunity for instilling dislike of England and aversion to British rule.

The radical nationalists were headed by a young man named Mustapha Kamel. He was a very prince of agitators; ardent, magnetic, enthusiastic, and possessed of a fiery eloquence which fairly swept away both his hearers and his readers. An indefatigable propagandist, he edited a whole chain of newspapers and periodicals, and as fast as one organ was suppressed by the British authorities he started another. His uncompromising nationalism may be gauged from the following examples from his writings. Taking for his motto the phrase "The Egyptians for Egypt; Egypt for the Egyptians," he wrote as early as 1896: "Egyptian civilization cannot endure in the future unless it is founded by the people itself; unless the fellah, the merchant, the teacher, the pupil, in fine, every single Egyptian, knows that man has sacred, intangible rights; that he is not created to be a tool, but to lead an intelligent and worthy life; that love of country is the most beautiful sentiment which can ennoble a soul; and that a nation without independence is a nation without existence! It is by patriotism that backward peoples come quickly to civilization, to greatness, and to power. It is patriotism that forms the blood which courses in the veins of virile nations, and it is patriotism that gives life to every living being."

The English, of course, were bitterly denounced. Here is a typical editorial from his organ El Lewa: "We are the despoiled. The English are the despoilers. We demand a sacred right. The English are the usurpers of that right. This is why we are sure of success sooner or later. When one is in the right, it is only a question of time."

Despite his ardent aspirations, Mustapha Kamel had a sense of realities, and recognized that, for the moment at least, British power could not be forcibly overthrown. He did not, therefore, attempt any open violence which he knew would merely ruin himself and his followers. Early in 1908 he died, only thirty-four years of age. His mantle fell upon his leading disciple, Mohammed Farid Bey. This man, who was not of equal calibre, tried to make up for his deficiency in true eloquence by the violence of his invective. The difference between the two leaders can be gauged by the editorial columns of El Lewa. Here is an editorial of September, 1909: "This land was polluted by the English, putrefied with their atrocities as they suppressed our beloved dustour [constitution], tied our tongues, burned our people alive and hanged our innocent relatives, and perpetrated other horrors at which the heavens are about to tremble, the earth to split, and the mountains to fall down. Let us take a new step. Let our lives be cheap while we seek our independence. Death is far better than life for you if you remain in your present condition."

Mohammed Farid's fanatical impatience of all opposition led him into tactical blunders like alienating the native Christian Copts, whom Mustapha Kamel had been careful to conciliate. The following diatribe (which, by the way, reveals a grotesque jumble of Western and Eastern ideas) is an answer to Coptic protests at the increasing violence of his propaganda: "The Copts should be kicked to death. They still have faces and bodies similar to those of demons and monkeys, which is a proof that they hide poisonous spirits within their souls. The fact that they exist in the world confirms Darwin's theory that human beings are generated from monkeys. You sons of adulterous women! You descendants of the bearers of trays! You tails of camels with your monkey faces! You bones of bodies!"

In this more violent attitude the nationalists were encouraged by several reasons. For one thing, Lord Cromer had laid down his proconsulate in 1907 and had been succeeded by Sir Eldon Gorst. The new ruler represented the ideas of British Liberalism, now in power, which wished to appease Egyptian unrest by conciliation instead of by Lord Cromer's autocratic indifference. In the second place, the Young-Turk revolution of 1908 gave an enormous impetus to the Egyptian cry for constitutional self-government. Lastly, France's growing intimacy with England dashed the nationalist's cherished hope that Britain would be forced by outside pressure to redeem her diplomatic pledges and evacuate the Nile valley, thus driving the nationalists to rely more on their own exertions.

Given this nationalist temper, conciliatory attempt was foredoomed to failure. For, however conciliatory Sir Eldon Gorst might be in details, he could not promise the one thing which the nationalists supremely desired—independence. This demand England refused even to consider. Practically all Englishmen had become convinced that Egypt with the Suez Canal was a vital link between the eastern and western halves of the British Empire, and that permanent control of Egypt was thus an absolute necessity. There was thus a fundamental deadlock between British imperial and Egyptian national convictions. Accordingly, the British Liberal policy of conciliation proved a fiasco. Even Sir Eldon Gorst admitted in his official reports that concessions were simply regarded as signs of weakness.

Before long seditious agitation and attendant violence grew to such proportions that the British Government became convinced that only strong measures would save the situation. Therefore, in 1911, Sir Eldon Gorst was replaced by Lord Kitchener—a patent warning to the nationalists that sedition would be given short shrift by the iron hand which had crushed the Khalifa and his Dervish hordes at Omdurman. Kitchener arrived in Egypt with the express mandate to restore order, and this he did with thoroughness and exactitude. The Egyptians were told plainly that England neither intended to evacuate the Nile valley nor considered its inhabitants fit for self-government within any discernible future. They were admonished to turn their thoughts from politics, at which they were so bad, to agriculture, at which they were so good. As for seditious propaganda, new legislation enabled Lord Kitchener to deal with it in summary fashion. Practically all the nationalist papers were suppressed, while the nationalist leaders were imprisoned, interned, or exiled. In fact, the British Government did its best to distract attention everywhere from Egypt, the British press co-operating loyally by labelling the subject taboo. The upshot was that Egypt became quieter than it had been for a generation.

However, it was only a surface calm. Driven underground, Egyptian unrest even attained new virulence which alarmed close observers. In 1913 the well-known English publicist Sidney Low, after a careful investigation of the Egyptian situation, wrote: "We are not popular in Egypt. Feared we may be by some; respected I doubt not by many others; but really liked, I am sure, by very few."[148] Still more outspoken was an article significantly entitled "The Darkness over Egypt," which appeared on the eve of the Great War.[149] Its publication in a semi-scientific periodical for specialists in Oriental problems rendered it worthy of serious attention. "The long-continued absence of practically all discussion or even mention of Egyptian internal affairs from the British press," asserted this article, "is not indicative of a healthy condition. In Egypt the superficial quiet is that of suppressed discontent—of a sullen, hopeless mistrust toward the Government of the Occupation. Certain recent happenings have strengthened in Egyptian minds the conviction that the Government is making preparations for the complete annexation of the country.... We are not concerned to question how far the motives attributed to the Government are true. The essential fact is that the Government of the Occupation has not yet succeeded in endearing, or even recommending, itself to the Egyptian people, but is, on the contrary, an object of suspicion, an occasion of enmity." The article expresses grave doubt whether Lord Kitchener's repressive measures have done more than drive discontent underground, and shows "how strong is the Nationalist feeling in Egypt to-day in spite of the determined attempts to stamp out all freedom of political opinion. As might be expected, this wholesale muzzling of the press has not only reduced the Mohammedan majority to a condition of internal ferment, but has seriously alienated the hitherto loyal Copts. It may be that the Government can discover no better means of recommending itself to the confidence and good-will of the Egyptian people; it may be that only by the instant repression of every outward sign of discontent can it feel secure in its occupation; but if such be the case, it is an admission of extreme weakness, or recognized insecurity of tenure." The article concludes with the following warning as to the problem's wider implications: "Egypt, though a subject of profound indifference to the English voter, is being feverishly watched by the Indian Mohammedans, and by the whole of our West and Central African subjects—themselves strongly Moslem in sympathy, and at the present time jealously suspicious of the political activities of Christian Imperialism."

Such being the state of Egyptian feeling in 1914, the outbreak of the Great War was bound to produce intensified unrest. England's position in Egypt was, in truth, very difficult. Although in fact England exercised complete control, in law Egypt was still a dependency of the Ottoman Empire, Britain merely exercising a temporary occupation. Now it soon became evident that Turkey was going to join England's enemies, the Teutonic empires, while it was equally evident that the Egyptians sympathized with the Turks, even the Khedive Abbas Hilmi making no secret of his pro-Turkish views. During the first months of the European War, while Turkey was still nominally neutral, the Egyptian native press, despite the British censorship, was full of veiled seditious statements, while the unruly attitude of the Egyptian populace and the stirrings among the Egyptian native regiments left no doubt as to how the wind was blowing. England was seriously alarmed. Accordingly, when Turkey entered the war in November, 1914, England took the decisive plunge, deposed Abbas Hilmi, nominated his cousin Hussein Kamel "Sultan," and declared Egypt a protectorate of the British Empire.

This stung the nationalists to fury. Anything like formal rebellion was rendered impossible by the heavy masses of British and colonial troops which had been poured into the country. Nevertheless, there was a good deal of sporadic violence, suppressed only by a stern application of the "State of Siege." A French observer thus vividly describes these critical days: "The Jehadd is rousing the anti-Christian fanaticism which always stirs in the soul of every good Moslem. Since the end of October one could read in the eyes of the low-class Mohammedan natives their hope—the massacre of the Christians. In the streets of Cairo they stared insolently at the European passers-by. Some even danced for joy on learning that the Sultan had declared the Holy War. Denounced to the police for this, they were incontinently bastinadoed at the nearest police-station. The same state of mind reigned at El Azhar, and I am told that Europeans who visit the celebrated Mohammedan University have their ears filled with the strongest epithets of the Arab repertory—that best-furnished language in the world."[150]

The nationalist exiles vehemently expressed abroad what their fellows could not say at home. Their leader, Mohammed Farid Bey, issued from Geneva an official protest against "the new illegal régime proclaimed by England the 18th of last December. England, which pretends to make war on Germany to defend Belgium, ought not to trample underfoot the rights of Egypt, nor consider the treaties relative thereto as 'scraps of paper.'"[151] These exiles threw themselves vehemently into the arms of Germany, as may be gauged from the following remarks of Abd-el-Malek Hamsa, secretary of the nationalist party, in a German periodical: "There is hardly an Egyptian who does not pray that England may be beaten and her Empire fall in ruins. During the early days of the war, while I was still in Egypt, I was a witness of this popular feeling. In cities and villages, from sage to simple peasant, all are convinced in the Kaiser's love for Islam and friendship for its caliph, and they are hoping and praying for Germany's victory."[152]

Of course, in face of the overwhelming British garrison in Egypt, such pronouncements were as idle as the wind. The hoped-for Turkish attacks were beaten back from the Suez Canal, the "State of Siege" functioned with stern efficiency, and Egypt, flooded with British troops, lapsed into sullen silence, not to be broken until the end of the war.

Turning back at this point to consider nationalist developments in the rest of North Africa, we do not, as in Egypt, find a well-marked territorial patriotism. Anti-European hatred there is in plenty, but such "patriotic" sentiments as exist belong rather to those more diffused types of nationalist feeling known as "Pan-Arabism" and "Pan-Islamic Nationalism," which we shall presently discuss.

The basic reason for this North African lack of national feeling, in its restricted sense, is that nowhere outside of Egypt is there a land which ever has been, or which shows distinct signs of becoming, a true "nation." The mass of the populations inhabiting the vast band of territory between the Mediterranean Sea and the Sahara desert are "Berbers"—an ancient stock, racially European rather than Asiatic or negroid, and closely akin to the "Latin" peoples across the Mediterranean. The Berbers remind one of the Balkan Albanians: they are extremely tenacious of their language and customs, and they have an instinctive racial feeling; but they are inveterate particularists, having always been split up into many tribes, sometimes combining into partial confederations but never developing true national patriotism.[153]

Alongside the Berbers we find everywhere a varying proportion of Arabs. The Arabs have colonized North Africa ever since the Moslem conquest twelve centuries ago. They converted the Berbers to Islam and Arab culture, but they never made North Africa part of the Arab world as they did Syria and Mesopotamia, and in somewhat lesser degree Egypt. The two races have never really fused. Despite more than a thousand years of Arab tutelage, the Berbers' manner of life remains distinct. They have largely kept their language, and there has been comparatively little intermarriage. Pure-blooded Arabs abound, often in large tribal groups, but they are still, in a way, foreigners.[154]

With such elements of discord, North Africa's political life has always been troubled. The most stable region has been Morocco, though even there the sultan's authority has never really extended to the mountain tribes. As for the so-called "Barbary States" (Algiers, Tunis, and Tripoli), they were little more than port-cities along the coast, the hinterland enjoying practically complete tribal independence. Over this confused turmoil spread the tide of French conquest, beginning with Algiers in 1830 and ending with Morocco to-day.[155] France brought peace, order, and material prosperity, but here, as in other Eastern lands, these very benefits of European tutelage created a new sort of unity among the natives in their common dislike of the European conqueror and their common aspiration toward independence. Accordingly, the past generation has witnessed the appearance of "Young Algerian" and "Young Tunisian" political groups, led by French-educated men who have imbibed Western ideas of "self-government" and "liberty."[156] However, as we have already remarked, their goal is not so much the erection of distinct Algerian and Tunisian "Nations" as it is creation of a larger North African, perhaps Pan-Islamic, unity. It must not be forgotten that they are in close touch with the Sennussi and kindred influences which we have already examined in the chapter on Pan-Islamism.

So much for "first-stage" nationalist developments in the Arab or Arabized lands. There is, however, one more important centre of nationalist sentiment in the Moslem world to be considered—Persia. Persia is, in fact, the land where a genuine nationalist movement would have been most logically expected, because the Persians have for ages possessed a stronger feeling of "country" than any other Near Eastern people.

In the nineteenth century Persia had sunk into such deep decrepitude that its patent weakness excited the imperialistic appetites of Czarist Russia and, in somewhat lesser degree, of England. Persia's decadence and external perils were, however, appreciated by thinking Persians, and a series of reformist agitations took place, beginning with the religious movement of the Bab early in the nineteenth century and culminating with the revolution of 1908.[157] That revolution was largely precipitated by the Anglo-Russian Agreement of 1907 by which England and Russia virtually partitioned Persia; the country being divided into a Russian "sphere of influence" in the north and a British "sphere of influence" in the south, with a "neutral zone" between. The revolution was thus in great part a desperate attempt of the Persian patriots to set their house in order and avert, at the eleventh hour, the shadow of European domination which was creeping over the land. But the revolution was not merely a protest against European aggression. It was also aimed at the alien Khadjar dynasty which had so long misruled Persia. These Khadjar sovereigns were of Turkoman origin. They had never become really Persianized, as shown by the fact that the intimate court language was Turki, not Persian. They occupied a position somewhat analogous to that of the Manchus before the Chinese revolution. The Persian revolution was thus basically an Iranian patriotic outburst against all alien influences, whether from East or West.

We have already seen how this patriotic movement was crushed by the forcible intervention of European imperialism.[158] By 1912 Russia and England were in full control of the situation, the patriots were proscribed and persecuted, and Persia sank into despairing silence. As a British writer then remarked: "For such broken spirit and shattered hopes, as for the 'anarchy' now existing in Persia, Russia and Great Britain are directly responsible, and if there be a Reckoning, will one day be held to account. It is idle to talk of any improvement in the situation, when the only Government in Persia consists of a Cabinet which does not command the confidence of the people, terrorized by Russia, financially starved by both Russia and England, allowed only miserable doles of money on usurious terms, and forbidden to employ honest and efficient foreign experts like Mr. Shuster; when the King is a boy, the Regent an absentee, the Parliament permanently suspended, and the best, bravest, and most honest patriots either killed or driven into exile, while the wolf-pack of financiers, concession-hunters and land-grabbers presses ever harder on the exhausted victim, whose struggles grow fainter and fainter. Little less than a miracle can now save Persia."[159]

So ends our survey of the main "first-stage" nationalist movements in the Moslem world. We should of course remember that a nationalist movement was developing concurrently in India, albeit following an eccentric orbit of its own. We should also remember that, in addition to the main movements just discussed, there were minor nationalist stirrings among other Moslem peoples such as the Russian Tartars, the Chinese Mohammedans, and even the Javanese of the Dutch Indies. Lastly, we should remember that these nationalist movements were more or less interwoven with the non-national movement of Pan-Islamism, and with those "second-stage," "racial" nationalist movements which we shall now consider.

II

Earlier in this chapter we have already remarked that the opening years of the twentieth century witnessed the appearance in Asia of nationalism's second or racial stage, especially among the Turkish and Arab peoples. This wider stage of nationalism has attained its highest development among the Turks; where, indeed, it has gone through two distinct phases, describable respectively by the terms "Pan-Turkism" and "Pan-Turanism." We have described the primary phase of Turkish nationalism in its restricted "Ottoman" sense down to the close of the Balkan wars of 1912-13. It is at that time that the secondary or "racial" aspects of Turkish nationalism first come prominently to the fore.

By this time the Ottoman Turks had begun to realize that they did not stand alone in the world; that they were, in fact, the westernmost branch of a vast band of peoples extending right across eastern Europe and Asia, from the Baltic to the Pacific and from the Mediterranean to the Arctic Ocean, to whom ethnologists have assigned the name of "Uralo-Altaic race," but who are more generally termed "Turanians." This group embraces the most widely scattered folk—the Ottoman Turks of Constantinople and Anatolia, the Turkomans of Persia and Central Asia, the Tartars of South Russia and Transcaucasia, the Magyars of Hungary, the Finns of Finland and the Baltic provinces, the aboriginal tribes of Siberia, and even the distant Mongols and Manchus. Diverse though they are in culture, tradition, and even personal appearance, these people nevertheless possess certain well-marked traits in common. Their languages are all similar, while their physical and mental make-up displays undoubted affinities. They are all noted for great physical vitality combined with unusual toughness of nerve-fibre. Though somewhat deficient in imagination and creative artistic sense, they are richly endowed with patience, tenacity, and dogged energy. Above all, they have usually displayed extraordinary military capacity, together with a no less remarkable aptitude for the masterful handling of subject peoples. The Turanians have certainly been the greatest conquerors that the world has ever seen. Attila and his Huns, Arpad and his Magyars, Isperich and his Bulgars, Alp Arslan and his Seljuks, Ertogrul and his Ottomans, Jenghiz Khan and Tamerlane with their "inflexible" Mongol hordes, Baber in India, even Kubilai Khan and Nurhachu in far-off Cathay: the type is ever the same. The hoof-print of the Turanian "man on horseback" is stamped deep all over the palimpsest of history.

Glorious or sinister according to the point of view, Turan's is certainly a stirring past. Of course one may query whether these diverse peoples actually do form one genuine race. But, as we have already seen, so far as practical politics go, that makes no difference. Possessed of kindred tongues and temperaments, and dowered with such a wealth of soul-stirring tradition, it would suffice for them to think themselves racially one to form a nationalist dynamic of truly appalling potency.

Until about a generation ago, to be sure, no signs of such a movement were visible. Not only were distant stocks like Finns and Manchus quite unaware of any common Turanian bond, but even obvious kindred like Ottoman Turks and Central Asian Turkomans regarded one another with indifference or contempt. Certainly the Ottoman Turks were almost as devoid of racial as they were of national feeling. Arminius Vambéry tells how, when he first visited Constantinople in 1856, "the word Turkluk (i. e., 'Turk') was considered an opprobrious synonym of grossness and savagery, and when I used to call people's attention to the racial importance of the Turkish stock (stretching from Adrianople to the Pacific) they answered: 'But you are surely not classing us with Kirghiz and with the gross nomads of Tartary.' ... With a few exceptions, I found no one in Constantinople who was seriously interested in the questions of Turkish nationality or language."[160]

It was, in fact, the labours of Western ethnologists like the Hungarian Vambéry and the Frenchman Léon Cahun that first cleared away the mists which enshrouded Turan. These labours disclosed the unexpected vastness of the Turanian world. And this presently acquired a most unacademic significance. The writings of Vambéry and his colleagues spread far and wide through Turan and were there devoured by receptive minds already stirring to the obscure promptings of a new time. The normality of the Turanian movement is shown by its simultaneous appearance at such widely sundered points as Turkish Constantinople and the Tartar centres along the Russian Volga. Indeed, if anything, the leaven began its working on the Volga sooner than on the Bosphorus. This Tartar revival, though little known, is one of the most extraordinary phenomena in all nationalist history. The Tartars, once masters of Russia, though long since fallen from their high estate, have never vanished in the Slav ocean. Although many of them have been for four centuries under Russian rule, they have stubbornly maintained their religious, racial, and cultural identity. Clustered thickly along the Volga, especially at Kazan and Astrakhan, retaining much of the Crimea, and forming a considerable minority in Transcaucasia, the Tartars remained distinct "enclaves" in the Slav Empire, widely scattered but indomitable.

The first stirrings of nationalist self-consciousness among the Russian Tartars appeared as far back as 1895, and from then on the movement grew with astonishing rapidity. The removal of governmental restrictions at the time of the Russian revolution of 1904 was followed by a regular literary florescence. Streams of books and pamphlets, numerous newspapers, and a solid periodical press, all attested the vigour and fecundity of the Tartar revival. The high economic level of the Russian Tartars assured the material sinews of war. The Tartar oil millionaires of Baku here played a conspicuous rôle, freely opening their capacious purses for the good of the cause. The Russian Tartars also showed distinct political ability and soon gained the confidence of their Turkoman cousins of Russian Central Asia, who were also stirring to the breath of nationalism. The first Russian Duma contained a large Mohammedan group so enterprising in spirit and so skilfully led that Russian public opinion became genuinely uneasy and encouraged the government to diminish Tartar influence in Russian parliamentary life by summary curtailments of Mohammedan representation.[161]

Of course the Russian Mohammedans were careful to proclaim their political loyalty to the Russian Empire. Nevertheless, many earnest spirits revealed their secret aspirations by seeking a freer and more fruitful field of labour in Turkish Stambul, where the Russian Tartars played a prominent part in the Pan-Turk and Pan-Turanian movements within the Ottoman Empire. In fact, it was a Volga Tartar, Yusuf Bey Akchura Oglu, who was the real founder of the first Pan-Turanian society at Constantinople, and his well-known book, Three Political Systems, became the text on which most subsequent Pan-Turanian writings have been based.[162]

Down to the Young-Turk revolution of 1908, Pan-Turanism was somewhat under a cloud at Stambul. Sultan Abdul Hamid, as already remarked, was a Pan-Islamist and had a rooted aversion to all nationalist movements. Accordingly, the Pan-Turanians, while not actually persecuted, were never in the Sultan's favour. With the advent of Young-Turk nationalism to power, however, all was changed. The "Ottomanizing" leaders of the new government listened eagerly to Pan-Turanian preaching, and most of them became affiliated with the movement. It is interesting to note that Russian Tartars continued to play a prominent part. The chief Pan-Turanian propagandist was the able publicist Ahmed Bey Agayeff, a Volga Tartar. His well-edited organ, Turk Yurdu (Turkish Home), penetrated to every corner of the Turko-Tartar world and exercised great influence on the development of its public opinion.

Although leaders like Ahmed Bey Agayeff clearly visualized the entire Turanian world from Finland to Manchuria as a potential whole, and were thus full-fledged "Pan-Turanians," their practical efforts were at first confined to the closely related Turko-Tartar segment; that is, to the Ottomans of Turkey, the Tartars of Russia, and the Turkomans of central Asia and Persia. Since all these peoples were also Mohammedans, it follows that this propaganda had a religious as well as a racial complexion, trending in many respects toward Pan-Islamism. Indeed, even disregarding the religious factor, we may say that, though Pan-Turanian in theory, the movement was at that time in practice little more than "Pan-Turkism."

It was the Balkan wars of 1912-13 which really precipitated full-fledged Pan-Turanism. Those wars not merely expelled the Turks from the Balkans and turned their eyes increasingly toward Asia, but also roused such hatred of the victorious Serbs in the breasts of Hungarians and Bulgarians that both these peoples proclaimed their "Turanian" origins and toyed with ideas of "Pan-Turanian" solidarity against the menace of Serbo-Russian "Pan-Slavism."[163] The Pan-Turanian thinkers were assuredly evolving a body of doctrine grandiose enough to satisfy the most ambitious hopes. Emphasizing the great virility and nerve-force everywhere patent in the Turanian stocks, these thinkers saw in Turan the dominant race of the morrow. Zealous students of Western evolutionism and ethnology, they were evolving their own special theory of race grandeur and decadence. According to Pan-Turanian teaching, the historic peoples of southern Asia—Arabs, Persians, and Hindus—are hopelessly degenerate. As for the Europeans, they have recently passed their apogee, and, exhausted by the consuming fires of modern industrialism, are already entering upon their decline. It is the Turanians, with their inherent virility and steady nerves unspoiled by the wear and tear of Western civilization, who must be the great dynamic of the future. Indeed, some Pan-Turanian thinkers go so far as to proclaim that it is the sacred mission of their race to revitalize a whole senescent, worn-out world by the saving infusion of regenerative Turanian blood.[164]

Of course the Pan-Turanians recognized that anything like a realization of their ambitious dreams was dependent upon the virtual destruction of the Russian Empire. In fact, Russia, with its Tartars, Turkomans, Kirghiz, Finns, and numerous kindred tribes, was in Pan-Turanian eyes merely a Slav alluvium laid with varying thickness over a Turanian subsoil. This turning of Russia into a vast "Turania irredenta" was certainly an ambitious order. Nevertheless, the Pan-Turanians counted on powerful Western backing. They realized that Germany and Austria-Hungary were fast drifting toward war with Russia, and they felt that such a cataclysm, however perilous, would also offer most glorious possibilities.

These Pan-Turanian aspirations undoubtedly had a great deal to do with driving Turkey into the Great War on the side of the Central Empires. Certainly, Enver Pasha and most of the other leaders of the governing group had long been more or less affiliated with the Pan-Turanian movement. Of course the Turkish Government had more than one string to its bow. It tried to drive Pan-Turanism and Pan-Islamism in double harness, using the "Holy War" agitation for pious Moslems everywhere, while it redoubled Pan-Turanian propaganda among the Turko-Tartar peoples. A good statement of Pan-Turanian ambitions in the early years of the war is that of the publicist Tekin Alp in his book, The Turkish and Pan-Turkish Ideal, published in 1915. Says Tekin Alp: "With the crushing of Russian despotism by the brave German, Austrian, and Turkish armies, 30,000,000 to 40,000,000 Turanians will receive their independence. With the 10,000,000 Ottoman Turks, this will form a nation of 50,000,000, advancing toward a great civilization which may perhaps be compared with that of Germany, in that it will have the strength and energy to rise even higher. In some ways it will be superior to the degenerate French and English civilizations."

With the collapse of Russia after the Bolshevik revolution at the end of 1917, Pan-Turanian hopes knew no bounds. So certain were they of triumph that they began to flout even their German allies, thus revealing that hatred of all Europeans which had always lurked at the back of their minds. A German staff-officer thus describes the table-talk of Halil Pasha, the Turkish commander of the Mesopotamian front and uncle of Enver: "First of all, every tribe with a Turkish mother-tongue must be forged into a single nation. The national principle was supreme; so it was the design to conquer Turkestan, the cradle of Turkish power and glory. That was the first task. From that base connections must be established with the Yakutes of Siberia, who were considered, on account of their linguistic kinship, the remotest outposts of the Turkish blood to the eastward. The closely related Tartar tribes of the Caucasus must naturally join this union. Armenians and Georgians, who form minority nationalities in that territory, must either submit voluntarily or be subjugated.... Such a great compact Turkish Empire, exercising hegemony over all the Islamic world, would exert a powerful attraction upon Afghanistan and Persia.... In December, 1917, when the Turkish front in Mesopotamia threatened to yield, Halil Pasha said to me, half vexed, half jokingly: 'Supposing we let the English have this cursed desert hole and go to Turkestan, where I will erect a new empire for my little boy.' He had named his youngest son after the great conqueror and destroyer, Jenghiz Khan."[165]

As a matter of fact, the summer of 1918 saw Transcaucasia and northern Persia overrun by Turkish armies headed for Central Asia. Then came the German collapse in the West and the end of the war, apparently dooming Turkey to destruction. For the moment the Pan-Turanians were stunned. Nevertheless, their hopes were soon destined to revive, as we shall presently see.

Before describing the course of events in the Near East since 1918, which need to be treated as a unit, let us go back to consider the earlier developments of the other "second-stage" nationalist movements in the Moslem world. We have already seen how, concurrently with Turkish nationalism, Arab nationalism was likewise evolving into the "racial" stage, the ideal being a great "Pan-Arab" empire, embracing not merely the ethnically Arab peninsula-homeland, Syria, and Mesopotamia, but also the Arabized regions of Egypt, Tripoli, French North Africa, and the Sudan.

Pan-Arabism has not been as intellectually developed as Pan-Turanism, though its general trend is so similar that its doctrines need not be discussed in detail. One important difference between the two movements is that Pan-Arabism is much more religious and Pan-Islamic in character, the Arabs regarding themselves as "The Chosen People" divinely predestined to dominate the whole Islamic world. Pan-Arabism also lacks Pan-Turanism's unity of direction. There have been two distinct intellectual centres—Syria and Egypt. In fact, it is in Egypt that Pan-Arab schemes have been most concretely elaborated, the Egyptian programme looking toward a reunion of the Arab-speaking lands under the Khedive—perhaps at first subject to British tutelage, though ultimately throwing off British control by concerted Pan-Arab action. The late Khedive Abbas Hilmi, deposed by the British in 1914, is supposed to have encouraged this movement.[166]

The Great War undoubtedly stimulated Pan-Arabism, especially by its creation of an independent Arab kingdom in the Hedjaz with claims on Syria and Mesopotamia. However, the various Arab peoples are so engrossed with local independence agitations looking toward the elimination of British, French, and Italian control from specific regions like Egypt, Syria, Mesopotamia, and Tripoli, that the larger concept of Pan-Arabism, while undoubtedly an underlying factor, is not to-day in the foreground of Arab nationalist programmes.

85

Furthermore, as I have already said, Pan-Arabism is interwoven with the non-racial concepts of Pan-Islamism and "Pan-Islamic Nationalism." This latter concept may seem a rather grotesque contradiction of terms. So it may be to us Westerners. But it is not necessarily so to Eastern minds. However eagerly the East may have seized upon our ideas of nationality and patriotism, those ideas have entered minds already full of concepts like Islamic solidarity and the brotherhood of all True Believers. The result has been a subtle coloration of the new by the old, so that even when Moslems use our exact words, "nationality," "race," etc., their conception of what those words mean is distinctly different from ours. These differences in fact extend to all political concepts. Take the word "State," for example. The typical Mohammedan state is not, like the typical Western state, a sharply defined unit, with fixed boundaries and full sovereignty exercised everywhere within its frontiers. It is more or less an amorphous mass, with a central nucleus, the seat of an authority which shades off into ill-defined, anarchic independence. Of course, in the past half-century, most Mohammedan states have tried to remodel themselves on Western lines, but the traditional tendency is typified by Afghanistan, where the tribes of the Indian north-west frontier, though nominally Afghan, enjoy practical independence and have frequently conducted private wars of their own against the British which the Ameer has disavowed and for which the British have not held him responsible.

Similarly with the term "Nationality." In Moslem eyes, a man need not be born or formally naturalized to be a member of a certain Moslem "Nationality." Every Moslem is more or less at home in every part of Islam, so a man may just happen into a particular country and thereby become at once, if he wishes, a national in good standing. For example: "Egypt for the Egyptians" does not mean precisely what we think. Let a Mohammedan of Algiers or Damascus settle in Cairo. Nothing prevents him from acting, and being considered as, an "Egyptian Nationalist" in the full sense of the term. This is because Islam has always had a distinct idea of territorial as well as spiritual unity. All predominantly Mohammedan lands are believed by Moslems to constitute "Dar-ul-Islam,"[167] which is in a sense the joint possession of all Moslems and which all Moslems are jointly obligated to defend. That is the reason why alien encroachments on any Moslem land are instantly resented by Moslems at the opposite end of the Moslem world, who could have no possible material interest in the matter.

We are now better able to understand how many Moslem thinkers, combining the Western concept of nationality with the traditional idea of Dar-ul-Islam, have evolved a new synthesis of the two, expressed by the term "Pan-Islamic Nationalism." This trend of thought is well set forth by an Indian Moslem, who writes: "In the West, the whole science of government rests on the axiom that the essential divisions of humanity are determined by considerations of race and geography; but for Orientals these ideas are very far from being axioms. For them, humanity divides according to religious beliefs. The unity is no longer the nation or the State, but the 'Millah.'[168] Europeans see in this a counterpart to their Middle Ages—a stage which Islam should pass through on its way to modernity in the Western sense. How badly they understand how religion looks to a Mohammedan! They forget that Islam is not only a religion, but also a social organization, a form of culture, and a nationality.... The principle of Islamic fraternity—of Pan-Islamism, if you prefer the word—is analogous to patriotism, but with this difference: this Islamic fraternity, though resulting in identity of laws and customs, has not (like Western Nationality) been brought about by community of race, country, or history, but has been received, as we believe, directly from God."[169]

Pan-Islamic nationalism is a relatively recent phenomenon and has not been doctrinally worked out. Nevertheless it is visible throughout the Moslem world and is gaining in strength, particularly in regions like North Africa and India, where strong territorial patriotism has, for one reason or another, not developed. As a French writer remarks: "Mohammedan Nationalism is not an isolated or sporadic agitation. It is a broad tide, which is flowing over the whole Islamic world of Asia, India, and Africa. Nationalism is a new form of the Mohammedan faith, which, far from being undermined by contact with European civilization, seems to have discovered a surplus of religious fervour, and which, in its desire for expansion and proselytism, tends to realize its unity by rousing the fanaticism of the masses, by directing the political tendencies of the élites, and by sowing everywhere the seeds of a dangerous agitation."[170] Pan-Islamic nationalism may thus, in the future, become a major factor which will have to be seriously reckoned with.[171]

III

So ends our survey of nationalist movements in the Moslem world. Given such a tangled complex of aspirations, enormously stimulated by Armageddon, it was only natural that the close of the Great War should have left the Orient a veritable welter of unrest. Obviously, anything like a constructive settlement could have been effected only by the exercise of true statesmanship of the highest order. Unfortunately, the Versailles peace conference was devoid of true statesmanship, and the resulting "settlement" not only failed to give peace to Europe but disclosed an attitude toward the East inspired by the pre-war spirit of predatory imperialism and cynical Realpolitik. Apparently oblivious of the mighty psychological changes which the war had wrought, and of the consequent changes of attitude and policy required, the victorious Allies proceeded to treat the Orient as though Armageddon were a skirmish and Asia the sleeping giant of a century ago.

In fact, disregarding both the general pronouncements of liberal principles and the specific promises of self-determination for Near Eastern peoples which they had made during the war, the Allies now paraded a series of secret treaties (negotiated between themselves during those same war-years when they had been so unctuously orating), and these secret treaties clearly divided up the Ottoman Empire among the victors, in absolute disregard of the wishes of the inhabitants. The purposes of the Allies were further revealed by the way in which the Versailles conference refused to receive the representatives of Persia (theoretically still independent), but kept them cooling their heels in Paris while British pressure at Teheran forced the Shah's government to enter into an "agreement" that made Persia a virtual protectorate of the British Empire. As for the Egyptians, who had always protested against the protectorate proclaimed by England solely on its own initiative in 1914, the conference refused to pay any attention to their delegates, and they were given to understand that the conference regarded the British protectorate over Egypt as a fait accompli. The upshot was that, as a result of the war, European domination over the Near and Middle East was riveted rather than relaxed.

But the strangest feature of this strange business remains to be told. One might imagine that the Allied leaders would have realized that they were playing a dangerous game, which could succeed only by close team-work and quick action. As a matter of fact, the very reverse was the case. After showing their hand, and thereby filling the East with disillusionment, despair, and fury, the Allies proceeded to quarrel over the spoils. Nearly two years passed before England, France, and Italy were able to come to an even superficial agreement as to the partition of the Ottoman Empire, and meanwhile they had been bickering and intriguing against each other all over the Near East. This was sheer madness. The destined victims were thereby informed that European domination rested not only on disregard of the moral "imponderables" but on diplomatic bankruptcy as well. The obvious reflection was that a domination resting on such rotten foundations might well be overthrown.

That, at any rate, is the way multitudes of Orientals read the situation, and their rebellious feelings were stimulated not merely by consciousness of their own strength and Western disunion, but also by the active encouragement of a new ally—Bolshevik Russia. Russian Bolshevism had thrown down the gauntlet to Western civilization, and in the desperate struggle which was now on, the Bolshevik leaders saw with terrible glee the golden opportunities vouchsafed them in the East. The details of Bolshevik activity in the Orient will be considered in the chapter on Social Unrest. Suffice it to remember here that Bolshevik propaganda is an important element in that profound ferment which extends over the whole Near and Middle East; a ferment which has reduced some regions to the verge of chaos and which threatens to increase rather than diminish in the immediate future.

To relate all the details of contemporary Eastern unrest would fill a book in itself. Let us here content ourselves with considering the chief centres of this unrest, remembering always that it exists throughout the Moslem world from French North Africa to Central Asia and the Dutch Indies. The centres to be here surveyed will be Egypt, Persia, and the Turkish and Arab regions of the former Ottoman Empire. A fifth main centre of unrest—India—will be discussed in the next chapter.

The gathering storm first broke in Egypt. During the war Egypt, flooded with British troops and subjected to the most stringent martial law, had remained quiet, but it was the quiet of repression, not of passivity. We have seen how, with the opening years of the twentieth century, virtually all educated Egyptians had become more or less impregnated with nationalist ideas, albeit a large proportion of them believed in evolutionary rather than revolutionary methods. The chief hope of the moderates had been the provisional character of English rule. So long as England declared herself merely in "temporary occupation" of Egypt, anything was possible. But the proclamation of the protectorate in 1914, which declared Egypt part of the British Empire, entirely changed the situation. Even the most moderate nationalists felt that the future was definitely prejudged against them and that the door had been irrevocably closed upon their ultimate aspirations. The result was that the moderates were driven over to the extremists and were ready to join the latter in violent action as soon as opportunity might offer.

The extreme nationalists had of course protested bitterly against the protectorate from the first, and the close of the war saw a delegation composed of both nationalist wings proceed to Paris to lay their claims before the Versailles conference. Rebuffed by the conference, which recognized the British protectorate over Egypt as part of the peace settlement, the Egyptian delegation issued a formal protest warning of trouble. This protest read:

"We have knocked at door after door, but have received no answer. In spite of the definite pledges given by the statesmen at the head of the nations which won the war, to the effect that their victory would mean the triumph of Right over Might and the establishment of the principle of self-determination for small nations, the British protectorate over Egypt was written into the treaties of Versailles and Saint Germain without the people of Egypt being consulted as to their political status.

"This crime against our nation, a breach of good faith on the part of the Powers who have declared that they are forming in the same Treaty a Society of Nations, will not be consummated without a solemn warning that the people of Egypt consider the decision taken at Paris null and void.... If our voice is not heard, it will be only because the blood already shed has not been enough to overthrow the old world-order and give birth to a new world-order."[172]

Before these lines had appeared in type, trouble in Egypt had begun. Simultaneously with the arrival of the Egyptian delegation at Paris, the nationalists in Egypt laid their demands before the British authorities. The nationalist programme demanded complete self-government for Egypt, leaving England only a right of supervision over the public debt and the Suez Canal. The nationalists' strength was shown by the fact that these proposals were indorsed by the Egyptian cabinet recently appointed by the Khedive at British suggestion. In fact, the Egyptian Premier, Roushdi Pasha, asked to be allowed to go to London with some of his colleagues for a hearing. This placed the British authorities in Egypt in a distinctly trying position. However, they determined to stand firm, and accordingly answered that England could not abandon its responsibility for the continuance of order and good government in Egypt, now a British protectorate and an integral part of the empire, and that no useful purpose would be served by allowing the Egyptian leaders to go to London and there advance immoderate demands which could not possibly be entertained.

The English attitude was firm. The Egyptian attitude was no less firm. The cabinet at once resigned, no new cabinet could be formed, and the British High Commissioner, General Allenby, was forced to assume unveiled control. Meanwhile the nationalists announced that they were going to hold a plebiscite to determine the attitude of the Egyptian people. Forbidden by the British authorities, the plebiscite was nevertheless illegally held, and resulted, according to the nationalists, in an overwhelming popular indorsement of their demands. This defiant attitude determined the British on strong action. Accordingly, in the spring of 1919, most of the nationalist leaders were seized and deported to Malta.

Egypt's answer was an explosion. From one end of the country to the other, Egypt flamed into rebellion. Everywhere it was the same story. Railways and telegraph lines were systematically cut. Trains were stalled and looted. Isolated British officers and soldiers were murdered. In Cairo alone, thousands of houses were sacked by the mob. Soon the danger was rendered more acute by the irruption out of the desert of swarms of Bedouin Arabs bent on plunder. For a few days Egypt trembled on the verge of anarchy, and the British Government admitted in Parliament that all Egypt was in a state of insurrection.

The British authorities met the crisis with vigour and determination. The number of British troops in Egypt was large, trusty black regiments were hurried up from the Sudan, and the well-disciplined Egyptian native police generally obeyed orders. After several weeks of sharp fighting and heavy loss of life, Egypt was again gotten under control.

Order was restored, but the outlook was ominous in the extreme. Only the presence of massed British and Sudanese troops enabled order to be maintained. Even the application of stern martial law could not prevent continuous nationalist demonstrations, sometimes ending in riots, fighting, and heavy loss of life. The most serious aspect of the situation was that not only were the upper classes solidly nationalist, but they had behind them the hitherto passive fellah millions. The war-years had borne hard on the fellaheen. Military exigencies had compelled Britain to conscript fully a million of them for forced labour in the Near East and even in Europe, while there had also been wholesale requisitions of grain, fodder, and other supplies. These things had caused profound discontent and had roused among the fellaheen not merely passive dislike but active hatred of British rule. Authoritative English experts on Egypt were seriously alarmed. Shortly after the riots Sir William Willcocks, the noted engineer, said in a public statement: "The keystone of the British occupation of Egypt was the fact that the fellaheen were for it. The Sheikhs, Omdehs, governing classes, and high religious heads might or might not be hostile, but nothing counted for much while the millions of fellaheen were solid for the occupation. The British have undoubtedly to-day lost the friendship and confidence of the fellaheen." And Sir Valentine Chirol stated in the

London Times: "We are now admittedly face to face with the ominous fact that for the first time since the British occupation large numbers of the Egyptian fellaheen, who owe far more to us than does any other class of Egyptians, have been worked up into a fever of bitter discontent and hatred. Very few people at home, even in responsible quarters, have, I think, the slightest conception of the very dangerous degree of tension which has now been reached out here."

All foreign observers were impressed by the nationalist feeling which united all creeds and classes. Regarding the monster demonstrations held during the summer of 1919, an Italian publicist wrote: "For the first time in history, the banners flown showed the Crescent interwoven with the Cross. Until a short time ago the two elements were as distinct from each other as each of them was from the Jews. To-day, precisely as has happened in India among the Mussulmans and the Hindus, every trace of religious division has departed. All Egyptians are enrolled under a single banner. Every one behind his mask of silence is burning with the same faith, and confident that his cause will ultimately triumph."[173] And a Frenchwoman, a lifelong resident of Egypt, wrote: "We have seen surprising things in this country, so often divided by party and religious struggles: Coptic priests preaching in mosques, ulemas preaching in Christian churches; Syrian, Maronite, or Mohammedan students; women, whether of Turkish or Egyptian blood, united in the same fervour, the same ardent desire to see break over their ancient land the radiant dawn of independence. For those who, like myself, have known the Egypt of Tewfik, the attitude of the women these last few years is the most surprising transformation that has happened in the valley of the Nile. One should have seen the nonchalant life, the almost complete indifference to anything savouring of politics, to appreciate the enormous steps taken in the last few months. For example: last summer a procession of women demonstrators was surrounded by British soldiers with fixed bayonets. One of the women, threatened by a soldier, turned on him, baring her breast, and cried: 'Kill me, then, so that there may be another Miss Cavell.'"[174]

Faced by this unprecedented nationalist fervour, Englishmen on the spot were of two opinions. Some, like Sir William Willcocks and Sir Valentine Chirol, stated that extensive concessions must be made.[175] Other qualified observers asserted that concessions would be weakness and would spell disaster. Said Sir M. McIlwraith: "Five years of a Nationalist régime would lead to hopeless chaos and disorder.... If Egypt is not to fall back into the morass of bankruptcy and anarchy from which we rescued her in 1882, with the still greater horrors of Bolshevism, of which there are already sinister indications, superadded, Britain must not loosen her control."[176] In England the Egyptian situation caused grave disquietude, and in the summer of 1919 the British Government announced the appointment of a commission of inquiry headed by Lord Milner to investigate fully into Egyptian affairs.

The appointment was a wise one. Lord Milner was one of the ablest figures in British political life, a man of long experience with imperial problems, including that of Egypt, and possessed of a temperament equally remote from the doctrinaire liberal or the hidebound conservative. In short, Lord Milner was a realist, in the true sense of the word, as his action soon proved. Arriving in Egypt at the beginning of 1920, Lord Milner and his colleagues found themselves confronted with a most difficult situation. In Egypt the word had gone forth to boycott the commission, and not merely nationalist politicians but also religious leaders like the Grand Mufti refused even to discuss matters unless the commissioners would first agree to Egyptian independence. This looked like a deadlock. Nevertheless, by infinite tact and patience, Lord Milner finally got into free and frank discussion with Zagloul Pasha and the other responsible nationalist leaders.

His efforts were undoubtedly helped by certain developments within Egypt itself. In Egypt, as elsewhere in the East, there were appearing symptoms not merely of political but also of social unrest. New types of agitators were springing up, preaching to the populace the most extreme revolutionary doctrines. These youthful agitators disquieted the regular nationalist leaders, who felt themselves threatened both as party chiefs and as men of social standing and property. The upshot was that, by the autumn of 1920, Lord Milner and Zagloul Pasha had agreed upon the basis of what looked like a genuine compromise. According to the intimations then given out to the press, and later confirmed by the nature of Lord Milner's official report, the lines of the tentative agreement ran as follows: England was to withdraw her protectorate and was to declare Egypt independent. This independence was qualified to about the same extent that Cuba's is toward the United States. Egypt was to have complete self-government, both the British garrison and British civilian officials being withdrawn. Egypt was, however, to make a perpetual treaty of alliance with Great Britain, was to agree not to make treaties with other Powers save with Britain's consent, and was to grant Britain a military and naval station for the protection of the Suez Canal and of Egypt itself in case of sudden attack by foreign enemies. The vexed question of the Sudan was left temporarily open.

These proposals bore the earmarks of genuinely constructive compromise. Unfortunately, they were not at once acted upon.[177] Both in England and in Egypt they roused strong opposition. In England adverse official influences held up the commission's report till February, 1921. In Egypt the extreme nationalists denounced Zagloul Pasha as a traitor, though moderate opinion seemed substantially satisfied. The commission's report, as finally published, declared that the grant of self-government to Egypt could not be safely postponed; that the nationalist spirit could not be extinguished; that an attempt to govern Egypt in the teeth of a hostile people would be "a difficult and disgraceful task"; and that it would be a great misfortune if the present opportunity for a settlement were lost. However, the report was not indorsed by the British Government in its entirety, and Lord Milner forthwith resigned. As for Zagloul Pasha, he still maintains his position as nationalist leader, but his authority has been gravely shaken. Such is the situation of Egypt at this present writing: a situation frankly not so encouraging as it was last year.

Meanwhile the storm which had begun in Egypt had long since spread to other parts of the Near East. In fact, by the opening months of 1920, the storm-centre had shifted to the Ottoman Empire. For this the Allies themselves were largely to blame. Of course a constructive settlement of these troubled regions would have been very difficult. Still, it might not have proved impossible if Allied policy had been fair and above-board. The close of the war found the various peoples of the Ottoman Empire hopeful that the liberal war-aims professed by the Allied spokesmen would be redeemed. The Arab elements were notably hopeful, because they had been given a whole series of Allied promises (shortly to be repudiated, as we shall presently see), while even the beaten Turks were not entirely bereft of hope in the future. Besides the general pronouncements of liberal treatment as formulated in the "Fourteen Points" programme of President Wilson and indorsed by the Allies, the Turks had pledges of a more specific character, notably by Premier Lloyd George, who, on January 5, 1918, had said: "Nor are we fighting to deprive Turkey of its capital or of the rich and renowned lands of Asia Minor and Thrace, which are predominantly Turkish in race." In other words, the Turks were given unequivocally to understand that, while their rule over non-Turkish regions like the Arab provinces must cease, the Turkish regions of the empire were not to pass under alien rule, but were to form a Turkish national state. The Turks did not know about a series of secret treaties between the Allies, begun in 1915, which partitioned practically the whole of Asia Minor between the Allied Powers. These were to come out a little later. For the moment the Turks might hope.

In the case of the Arabs there were far brighter grounds for nationalist hopes—and far darker depths of Allied duplicity. We have already mentioned the Arab revolt of 1916, which, beginning in the Hedjaz under the leadership of the Shereef of Mecca, presently spread through all the Arab provinces of the Ottoman Empire and contributed so largely to the collapse of Turkish resistance. This revolt was, however, not a sudden, unpremeditated thing. It had been carefully planned, and was due largely to Allied backing—and Allied promises. From the very beginning of the war Arab nationalist malcontents had been in touch with the British authorities in Egypt. They were warmly welcomed and encouraged in their separatist schemes, because an Arab rebellion would obviously be of invaluable assistance to the British in safeguarding Egypt and the Suez Canal, to say nothing of an advance into Turkish territory.

The Arabs, however, asked not merely material aid but also definite promises that their rebellion should be rewarded by the formation of an Arab state embracing the Arab provinces of the Ottoman Empire. Unfortunately for Arab nationalist aspirations, the British and French Governments had their own ideas as to the future of Turkey's Arab provinces. Both England and France had long possessed "spheres of influence" in those regions. The English sphere was in southern Mesopotamia at the head of the Persian Gulf. The French sphere was the Lebanon, a mountainous district in northern Syria just inland from the Mediterranean coast, where the population, known as Maronites, were Roman Catholics, over whom France had long extended her diplomatic protection. Of course both these districts were legally Turkish territory. Also, both were small in area. But "spheres of influence" are elastic things. Under favourable circumstances they are capable of sudden expansion to an extraordinary degree. Such a circumstance was the Great War. Accordingly the British and French Foreign Offices put their heads together and on March 5, 1915, the two governments signed a secret treaty by the terms of which France was given a "predominant position" in Syria and Britain a predominant position in Mesopotamia. No definite boundaries were then assigned, but the intent was to stake out claims which would partition Turkey's Arab provinces between England and France.

Naturally the existence of this secret treaty was an embarrassment to the British officials in Egypt in their negotiations with the Arabs. However, an Arab rebellion was too valuable an asset to be lost, and the British negotiators finally evolved a formula which satisfied the Arab leaders. On October 25, 1915, the Shereef of Mecca's representative at Cairo was given a document by the Governor-General of Egypt, Sir Henry McMahon, in which Great Britain undertook, conditional upon an Arab revolt, to recognize the independence of the Arabs of the Ottoman Empire except in southern Mesopotamia, where British interests required special measures of administrative control, and also except areas where Great Britain was "not free to act without detriment to the interests of France." This last clause was of course a "joker." However, it achieved its purpose. The Arabs, knowing nothing about the secret treaty, supposed it referred merely to the restricted district of the Lebanon. They went home jubilant, to prepare the revolt which broke out next year.

The revolt began in November, 1916. It might not have begun at all had the Arabs known what had happened the preceding May. In that month England and France signed another secret treaty, the celebrated Sykes-Picot Agreement. This agreement definitely partitioned Turkey's Arab provinces along the lines suggested in the initial secret treaty of the year before. By the Sykes-Picot Agreement most of Mesopotamia was to be definitely British, while the Syrian coast from Tyre to Alexandretta was to be definitely French, together with extensive Armenian and Asia Minor regions to the northward. Palestine was to be "international," albeit its chief seaport, Haifa, was to be British, and the implication was that Palestine fell within the English sphere. As to the great hinterland lying between Mesopotamia and the Syrian coast, it was to be "independent Arab under two spheres of influence," British and French;

the French sphere embracing all the rest of Syria from Aleppo to Damascus, the English sphere embracing all the rest of Mesopotamia—the region about Mosul. In other words, the independence promised the Arabs by Sir Henry McMahon had vanished into thin air.

This little shift behind the scenes was of course not communicated to the Arabs. On the contrary, the British did everything possible to stimulate Arab nationalist hopes—this being the best way to extract their fighting zeal against the Turks. The British Government sent the Arabs a number of picked intelligence officers, notably a certain Colonel Lawrence, an extraordinary young man who soon gained unbounded influence over the Arab chiefs and became known as "The Soul of the Arabian Revolution."[178] These men, chosen for their knowledge of, and sympathy for, the Arabs, were not informed about the secret treaties, so that their encouragement of Arab zeal might not be marred by any lack of sincerity. Similarly, the British generals were prodigal of promises in their proclamations.[179] The climax of this blessed comedy occurred at the very close of the war, when the British and French Governments issued the following joint declaration which was posted throughout the Arab provinces: "The aim which France and Great Britain have in view in waging in the East the war let loose upon the world by German ambition, is to insure the complete and final emancipation of all those peoples, so long oppressed by Turks, and to establish national governments and administrations which shall derive their authority from the initiative and free will of the people themselves."

This climax was, however, followed by a swift dénouement. The war was over, the enemy was beaten, the comedy was ended, the curtain was rung down, and on that curtain the Arabs read—the inner truth of things. French troops appeared to occupy the Syrian coast, the secret treaties came out, and the Arabs learned how they had been tricked. Black and bitter was their wrath. Probably they would have exploded at once had it not been for their cool-headed chiefs, especially Prince Feisal, the son of the Shereef of Mecca, who had proved himself a real leader of men during the war and who had now attained a position of unquestioned authority. Feisal knew the Allies' military strength and realized how hazardous war would be, especially at that time. Feeling the moral strength of the Arab position, he besought his countrymen to let him plead Arabia's cause before the impending peace conference, and he had his way. During the year 1919 the Arab lands were quiet, though it was the quiet of suspense.

Prince Feisal pleaded his case before the peace conference with eloquence and dignity. But Feisal failed. The covenant of the League of Nations might contain the benevolent statement that "certain communities formerly belonging to the Turkish Empire have reached a stage of development where their existence as independent nations can be provisionally recognized subject to the rendering of administrative advice and assistance by a mandatory until such time as they are able to stand alone."[180] The Arabs knew what "mandatories" meant. Lloyd George might utter felicitous phrases such as "Arab forces have redeemed the pledges given to Great Britain, and we should redeem our pledges."[181] The Arabs had read the secret treaties. "In vain is the net spread in the sight of any bird." The game no longer worked. The Arabs knew that they must rely on their own efforts, either in diplomacy or war.

Feisal still counselled peace. He was probably influenced to this not merely by the risks of armed resistance but also by the fact that the Allies were now quarrelling among themselves. These quarrels of course extended all over the Near East, but there was none more bitter than the quarrel which had broken out between England and France over the division of the Arab spoils. This dispute originated in French dissatisfaction with the secret treaties. No sooner had the Sykes-Picot Agreement been published than large and influential sections of French opinion began shouting that they had been duped. For generations French imperialists had had their eye on Syria,[182] and since the beginning of the war the imperialist press had been conducting an ardent propaganda for wholesale annexations in the Near East. "La Syrie intégrale!" "All Syria!" was the cry. And this "all" included not merely the coast-strip assigned France by the Sykes-Picot Agreement, but also Palestine and the vast Aleppo-Damascus hinterland right across to the rich oil-fields of Mosul. To this entire region, often termed in French expansionist circles "La France du Levant," the imperialists asserted that France had "imprescriptible historic rights running back to the Crusades and even to Charlemagne." Syria was a "second Alsace," which held out its arms to France and would not be denied. It was also the indispensable fulcrum of French world-policy. These imperialist aspirations had powerful backing in French Government circles. For example, early in 1915, M. Leygues had said in the Chamber of Deputies: "The axis of French policy is in the Mediterranean. One of its poles is in the West, at Algiers, Tunis, and Morocco. The other must lie in the East, with Syria, Lebanon, Palestine."[183]

After such high hopes, the effect of the Sykes-Picot Agreement on French imperialists can be imagined. Their anger turned naturally upon the English, who were roundly denounced and blamed for everything that was happening in the East, Arab nationalist aspirations being stigmatized as nothing but British propaganda. Cried one French writer: "Some psychiatrist ought to write a study of these British colonial officials, implacable imperialists, megalomaniacs, who, night and day, work for their country without even asking counsel from London, and whose constant care is to annihilate in Syria, as they once annihilated in Egypt, the supremacy of France."[184] In answer to such fulminations, English writers scored French "greed" and "folly" which was compromising England's prestige and threatening to set the whole East on fire.[185] In fine, there was a very pretty row on between people who, less than a year before, had been pledging their "sacred union" for all eternity. The Arabs were certainly much edified, and the other Eastern peoples as well.

Largely owing to these bickerings, Allied action in the Near East was delayed through 1919. But by the spring of 1920 the Allies came to a measure of agreement. The meeting of the Allied Premiers at San Remo elaborated the terms of the treaty to be imposed on Turkey, dividing Asia Minor into spheres of influence and exploitation, while the Arab provinces were assigned England and France according to the terms of the Sykes-Picot Agreement—properly camouflaged, of course, as "mandates" of the League of Nations. England, France, and their satellite, Greece, prepared for action. British reinforcements were sent to Mesopotamia and Palestine; French reinforcements were sent to Syria; an Anglo-Franco-Greek force prepared to occupy Constantinople, and Premier Venizelos promised a Greek army for Asia Minor contingencies. The one rift in the lute was Italy. Italy saw big trouble brewing and determined not to be directly involved. Said Premier Nitti to an English journalist after the San Remo conference: "You will have war in Asia Minor, and Italy will not send a single soldier nor pay a single lira. You have taken from the Turks their sacred city of Adrianople; you have placed their capital city under foreign control; you have taken from them every port and the larger part of their territory; and the five Turkish delegates whom you will select will sign a treaty which will not have the sanction of the Turkish people or the Turkish Parliament."

Premier Nitti was a true prophet. For months past the Turkish nationalists, knowing what was in store for them, had been building up a centre of resistance in the interior of Asia Minor. Of course the former nationalist leaders such as Enver Pasha had long since fled to distant havens like Transcaucasia or Bolshevik Russia, but new leaders appeared, notably a young officer of marked military talent, Mustapha Kemal Pasha. With great energy Mustapha Kemal built up a really creditable army, and from his "capital," the city of Angora in the heart of Asia Minor, he now defied the Allies, emphasizing his defiance by attacking the French garrisons in Cilicia (a coast district in Asia Minor just north of Syria), inflicting heavy losses.

The Arabs also were preparing for action. In March a "Pan-Syrian Congress" met at Damascus, unanimously declared the independence of Syria, and elected Feisal king. This announcement electrified all the Arab provinces. In the French-occupied coastal zone riots broke out against the French; in Palestine there were "pogroms" against the Jews, whom the Arabs, both Moslem and Christian, hated for their "Zionist" plans; while in Mesopotamia there were sporadic uprisings of tribesmen.

Faced by this ominous situation, the "mandatories" took military counter-measures. The French took especially vigorous action. France now had nearly 100,000 men in Syria and Cilicia, headed by General Gouraud, a veteran of many colonial wars and a believer in "strong-arm" methods. On July 15 Gouraud sent Feisal an ultimatum requiring complete submission. Feisal, diplomatic to the last, actually accepted the ultimatum, but Gouraud ignored this acceptance on a technicality and struck for Damascus with 60,000 men. Feisal attempted no real resistance, fighting only a rearguard action and withdrawing into the desert. On July 25 the French entered Damascus, the Arab capital, deposed Feisal, and set up thoroughgoing French rule. Opposition was punished with the greatest severity. Damascus was mulcted of a war-contribution of 10,000,000 francs, after the German fashion in Belgium, many nationalist leaders were imprisoned or shot, while Gouraud announced that the death of "one French subject or one Christian" would be followed by wholesale "most terrible reprisals" by bombing aeroplanes.[186]

Before this Napoleonic "thunder-stroke" Syria bent for the moment, apparently terrorized. In Mesopotamia, however, the British were not so fortunate. For some months trouble had patently been brewing, and in March the British commander had expressed himself as "much struck with the volcanic possibilities of the country." In July all Mesopotamia flamed into insurrection, and though Britain had fully 100,000 troops in the province, they were hard put to it to stem the rebellion.

Meanwhile, the Allies had occupied Constantinople, to force acceptance of the draft treaty of peace. Naturally, there was no resistance, Constantinople being entirely at the mercy of the Allied fleet. But the silence of the vast throngs gathered to watch the incoming troops filled some Allied observers with disquietude. A French journalist wrote: "The silence of the multitude was more impressive than boisterous protests. Their eyes glowed with sullen hatred. Scattered through this throng of mute, prostrated, hopeless people circulated watchful and sinuous emissaries, who were to carry word of this misfortune to the remotest confines of Islam. In a few hours they would be in Anatolia. A couple of days later the news would have spread to Konia, Angora, and Sivas. In a brief space of time it would be heralded throughout the regions of Bolshevist influence, extending to the Caucasus and beyond. In a few weeks all these centres of agitation will be preparing their counter-attack. Asia and Africa will again cement their union of faith. Intelligent agents will record in the retentive minds of people who do not read, the history of our blunders. These missionaries of insurrection and fanaticism come from every race and class of society. Educated and refined men disguise themselves as beggars and outcasts, in order to spread the news apace and to prepare for bitter vengeance."[187]

Events in Turkey now proceeded precisely as the Italian Premier Nitti had foretold. The Allied masters of Constantinople compelled the Sultan to appoint a "friendly" cabinet which solemnly denounced Mustapha Kemal and his "rebels," and sent a hand-picked delegation to Sèvres, France, where they dutifully "signed on the dotted line" the treaty that the Allies had prepared. The Allies had thus "imposed their will"—on paper. For every sensible man knew that the whole business was a roaring farce; knew that the "friendly" government, from Sultan to meanest clerk, was as nationalist as Mustapha Kemal himself; knew that the real Turkish capital was not Constantinople but Angora, and that the Allies' power was measured by the range of their guns. As for Mustapha Kemal, his comment on the Sèvres Treaty was: "I will fight to the end of the world."

The Allies were thus in a decidedly embarrassing situation, especially since "The Allies" now meant only England and France. Italy was out of the game. As Nitti had warned at San Remo, she would "not send a single soldier nor pay a single lira." With 200,000 soldiers holding down the Arabs, and plenty of trouble elsewhere, neither France nor Britain had the troops to crush Mustapha Kemal—a job which the French staff estimated would take 300,000 men. One weapon, however, they still possessed—Greece. In return for large territorial concessions, Premier Venizelos offered to bring the Turks to reason. His offer was accepted, and 100,000 Greek troops landed at Smyrna. But the Greek campaign was not a success. Even 100,000 men soon wore thin when spread out over the vast Asia Minor plateau. Mustapha Kemal avoided decisive battle, harassing the Greeks by guerilla warfare just as he was harassing the French in Cilicia at the other end of the line. The Greeks "dug in," and a deadlock ensued which threatened to continue indefinitely. This soon caused a new complication. Venizelos might be willing to "carry on" as the Allies' submandatory, but the Greek people were not. Kept virtually on a war-footing since 1912, the Greeks kicked over the traces. In the November elections they repudiated Venizelos by a vote of 990,000 to 10,000, and recalled King Constantine, who had been deposed by the Allies three years before. This meant that Greece, like Italy, was out of the game. To be sure, King Constantine presently started hostilities with the Turks on his own account. This was, however, something very different from Greece's attitude under the Venizelist régime. The Allies' weapon had thus broken in their hands.

Meanwhile Mustapha Kemal was not merely consolidating his authority in Asia Minor but was gaining allies of his own. In the first place, he was establishing close relations with the Arabs. It may appear strange to find such bitter foes become friends; nevertheless, Franco-British policy had achieved even this seeming miracle. The reason was clearly explained by no less a person than Lawrence ("The Soul of the Arab Revolution"), who had returned to civil life and was thus free to speak his mind on the Eastern situation, which he did in no uncertain fashion. In one of several statements given to the British press, Lawrence said: "The Arabs rebelled against the Turks during the war, not because the Turkish Government was notably bad, but because they wanted independence. They did not risk their lives in battle to change masters, to become British subjects or French citizens, but to win a State of their own." The matter was put even more pointedly by an Arab nationalist leader in the columns of a French radical paper opposed to the Syrian adventure. Said this leader: "Both the French and the English should know once for all that the Arabs are joined by a common religion with the Turks, and have been politically identified with them for centuries, and therefore do not wish to separate themselves from their fellow believers and brothers-in-arms merely to submit to the domination of a European nation, no matter what form the latter's suzerainty may assume.... It is no use for M. Millerand to say: 'We have never thought of trespassing in any respect upon the independence of these people.' No one is deceived by such statements as that. The armistice was signed in accordance with the conditions proclaimed by Mr. Wilson, but as soon as Germany and its allies were helpless, the promises of the armistice were trodden underfoot, as well as the Fourteen Points. Such a violation of the promises of complete independence, so prodigally made to the Arabs on so many occasions, has resulted in re-uniting closer than ever the Arabs and the Turks. It has taken but a few months to restore that intimacy.... It is probable that France, by maintaining an army of 150,000 men in

Syria, and by spending billions of francs, will be able to subdue the Syrian Arabs. But that will not finish the task. The interior of that country borders upon other lands inhabited by Arabs, Kurds, and Turks, and by the immense desert. In starting a conflict with 4,000,000 Syrians, France will be making enemies of 15,000,000 Arabs in the Levant, most of whom are armed tribes, without including the other Mohammedan peoples, who are speedily acquiring solidarity and organization under the blows that are being dealt them by the Entente. If you believe I am exaggerating, all you have to do is to investigate the facts yourself. But what good will it do to confirm the truth too late, and after floods of blood have flowed?"[188]

In fact, signs of Turco-Arab co-operation became everywhere apparent. To be sure, this co-operation was not openly avowed either by Mustapha Kemal or by the deposed King Feisal who, fleeing to Italy, continued his diplomatic manœuvres. But Arabs fought beside Turks against the French in Cilicia; Turks and Kurds joined the Syrian Arabs in their continual local risings; while Kemal's hand was clearly apparent in the rebellion against the British in Mesopotamia.

This Arab entente was not the whole of Mustapha Kemal's foreign policy. He was also reaching out north-eastward to the Tartars of Transcaucasia and the Turkomans of Persian Azerbaidjan. The Caucasus was by this time the scene of a highly complicated struggle between Moslem Tartars and Turkomans, Christian Armenians and Georgians, and various Russian factions, which was fast reducing that unhappy region to chaos. Among the Tartar-Turkomans, long leavened by Pan-Turanian propaganda, Mustapha Kemal found enthusiastic adherents; and his efforts were supported by a third ally—Bolshevik Russia. Bolshevik policy, which, as we have already stated, was seeking to stir up trouble against the Western Powers throughout the East, had watched Kemal's rise with great satisfaction. At first the Bolsheviki could do very little for the Turkish nationalists because they were not in direct touch, but the collapse of Wrangel's "White" army in November, 1920, and the consequent overrunning of all south Russia by the Red armies, opened a direct line from Moscow to Angora via the Caucasus, and henceforth Mustapha Kemal was supplied with money, arms, and a few men.

Furthermore, Kemal and the Bolsheviki were starting trouble in Persia. That country was in a most deplorable condition. During the war Persia, despite her technical neutrality, had been a battle-ground between the Anglo-Russians on the one hand and the Turco-Germans on the other. Russia's collapse in 1917 had led to her military withdrawal from Persia, and England, profiting by the situation, had made herself supreme, legalizing her position by the famous "Agreement" "negotiated" with the Shah's government in August, 1919.[189] This treaty, though signed and sealed in due form, was bitterly resented by the Persian people. Here was obviously another ripe field for Bolshevik propaganda. Accordingly, the Bolshevik government renounced all rights in Persia acquired by the Czarist régime and proclaimed themselves the friends of the Persian people against Western imperialism. Naturally the game worked, and Persia soon became honeycombed with militant unrest. In the early summer of 1920 a Bolshevist force actually crossed the Caspian Sea and landed on the Persian shore. They did not penetrate far into the country. They did not need to, for the country simply effervesced in a way which made the British position increasingly untenable. For many months a confused situation ensued. In fact, at this writing the situation is still obscure. But there can be no doubt that Britain's hold on Persia is gravely shaken, and she may soon be compelled to evacuate the country, with the possible exception of the extreme south.

Turning back to the autumn of 1920: the position of England and France in the Near East had become far from bright. Deserted by Italy and Greece, defied by the Turks, harried by the Arabs, worried by the Egyptians and Persians, and everywhere menaced by the subtle workings of Bolshevism, the situation was not a happy one. The burden of empire was proving heavy. In Mesopotamia alone the bill was already 100,000,000 sterling, with no relief in sight.

Under these circumstances, it is not surprising that in both England and France Near Eastern policies were subjected to a growing flood of criticism. In England especially the tide ran very strong. The Mesopotamian imbroglio was denounced as both a crime and a blunder. For example, Colonel Lawrence stated: "We are to-day not far from disaster. Our government is worse than the old Turkish system. They kept 14,000 local conscripts in the ranks and killed yearly an average of 200 Arabs in maintaining peace. We keep 90,000 men, with aeroplanes, armoured cars, gunboats, and armoured trains. We have killed about 10,000 Arabs in the rising this summer."[190] Influenced by such criticisms and by the general trend of events, the British Government modified its attitude, sending out Sir Percy Cox to negotiate with the Arabs. Sir Percy Cox was a man of the Milner type, with a firm grip on realities and an intimate experience with Eastern affairs. Authorized to discuss large concessions, he met the nationalist leaders frankly and made a good impression upon them. At this writing matters have not been definitely settled, but it looks as though England was planning to limit her direct control to the extreme south of Mesopotamia at the head of the Persian Gulf—practically her old sphere of influence before 1914.

Meanwhile, in Syria, France has thus far succeeded in maintaining relative order by strong-arm methods. But the situation is highly unstable. All classes of the population have been alienated. Even the Catholic Maronites, traditionally pro-French, have begun agitating. General Gouraud promptly squelched the agitation by deporting the leaders to Corsica; nevertheless, the fact remains that France's only real friends in Syria are dissatisfied. Up to the present these things have not changed France's attitude. A short time ago ex-Premier Leygues remarked of Syria, "France will occupy all of it, and always"; while still more recently General Gouraud stated: "France must remain in Syria, both for political and economic reasons. The political consequences of our abandonment of the country would be disastrous. Our prestige and influence in the Levant and the Mediterranean would be doomed. The economic interests of France also compel us to remain there. When fully developed, Syria and Cilicia will have an economic value fully equal to that of Egypt."

However, despite the French Government's firmness, there is an increasing public criticism of the "Syrian adventure," not merely from radical anti-imperialist quarters, but from unimpeachably conservative circles as well. The editor of one of the most conservative French political periodicals has stated: "Jealous of its autonomy, the Arab people, liberated from the Ottoman yoke, do not desire a new foreign domination. To say that Syria demands our protection is a lie. Syria wishes to be entirely independent."[191] And recently Senator Victor Bérard, one of France's recognized authorities on Eastern affairs made a speech in the French Senate strongly criticising the Government's Syrian policy from the very start and declaring that a "free Syria" was "a question of both interest and honour."

Certainly, the French Government, still so unyielding toward the Arabs, has reversed its attitude toward the Turks. Side-stepping the Sèvres Treaty, it has lately agreed on provisional peace terms with the Turkish nationalists, actually agreeing to evacuate Cilicia. In fact, both France and England know that the Sèvres Treaty is unworkable, and that Turkish possession of virtually the whole of Asia Minor will have to be recognized.

In negotiating with Mustapha Kemal, France undoubtedly hopes to get him to throw over the Arabs. But this is scarcely thinkable. The whole trend of events betokens an increasing solidarity of the Near Eastern peoples against Western political control. A most remarkable portent in this direction is the Pan-Islamic conference held at Sivas early in 1921. This conference, called to draw up a definite scheme for effective Moslem co-operation the world over, was attended not merely by the high orthodox Moslem dignitaries and political leaders, but also by heterodox chiefs like the Shiah Emir of Kerbela, the Imam Yahya, and the Zaidite Emir of Yemen—leaders of heretical sects between whom and the orthodox Sunnis co-operation had previously been impossible. Most notable of all, the press reports state that the conference was presided over by no less a personage than El Sennussi. This may well be so, for we have already seen how the Sennussi have always worked for a close union of all Islam against Western domination.

Such is the situation in the Near East—a situation very grave and full of trouble. The most hopeful portent is the apparent awakening of the British Government to the growing perils of the hour, and its consequent modifications of attitude. The labours of men like Lord Milner and Sir Percy Cox, however hampered by purblind influences, can scarcely be wholly barren of results. Such men are the diplomatic descendants of Chatham and of Durham; the upholders of that great political tradition which has steered the British Empire safely through crises that appeared hopeless.

On the other hand, the darkest portent in the Near East is the continued intransigeance of France. Steeped in its old traditions, French policy apparently refuses to face realities. If an explosion comes, as come it must unless France modifies her attitude; if, some dark day, thirty or forty French battalions are caught in a simoom of Arab fury blowing out of the desert and are annihilated in a new Adowa; the regretful verdict of many versed in Eastern affairs can only be: "French policy has deserved it."

Leaving the Near Eastern problem at this critical juncture to the inscrutable solution of the future, let us now turn to the great political problem of the Middle East—the nationalist movement in India.

FOOTNOTES:

[138] For these early stages of the Turkish nationalist movement, see Vambéry, La Turquie d'aujourd'hui et d'avant Quarante Ans; and his Western Culture in Eastern Lands. Also the articles by Léon Cahun in Lavisse et Rambaud, previously cited; and L. Rousseau, L'Effort Ottoman (Paris, 1907).

[139] Bérard, Le Sultan, l'Islam et les Puissances, p. 16 (Paris, 1907).

[140] Cited by Bérard, p. 19.

[141] Cited by Bérard, p. 20.

[142] Le Revéil de la Nation arabe, by Negib Azoury (Paris, 1905).

[143] The semi-legendary founder of the Ottoman Empire.

[144] The texts of both the above documents can be most conveniently found in E. Jung, Les Puissances devant la Révolte arabe: La Crise mondiale de Demain, pp. 23-25 (Paris, 1906).

[145] A good analysis of Arab affairs on the eve of the Great War is that of the Moslem publicist "X," "Les Courants politiques dans le Monde arabe," Revue du Monde musulman, December, 1913. Also see G. W. Bury, Arabia Infelix, or the Turks in Yemen (London, 1915).

[146] For Arab affairs during the Great War, see E. Jung, "L'Indépendance arabe et la Révolte actuelle," La Revue, 1 August, 1916; I. D. Levine, "Arabs versus Turks," American Review of Reviews, November, 1916; A. Musil, Zur Zeitgeschichte von Arabien (Leipzig, 1918); G. W. Bury, Pan-Islam (London, 1919); S. Mylrea, "The Politico-Religious Situation in Arabia," The Moslem World, July, 1919; L. Thomas, "Lawrence: The Soul of the Arabian Revolution," Asia, April, May, June, 1920.

[147] Georg Schweinfurth, Die Wiedergeburt Ägyptens im Lichte eines aufgeklärten Islam (Berlin, 1895).

[148] Low, Egypt in Transition, p. 260 (London, 1914).

[149] The Asiatic Review, April, 1914.

[150] "L'Égypte et les Débuts du Protectorat," Revue des Sciences Politiques, 15 June, 1915.

[151] Mohammed Farid Bey, "L'Égypte et la Guerre," Revue Politique Internationale, May, 1915.

[152] Abd-el-Malek Hamsa, "Die ägyptische Frage," Asien, November, 1916.

[153] A good summary of Berber history is H. Weisgerber, Les Blancs d'Afrique (Paris, 1910).

[154] For analyses of differences between Arabs and Berbers, see Caix de Saint-Aymour, Arabes et Kabyles (Paris, 1891); A. Bel, Coup d'Œil sur l'Islam en Berbérie (Paris, 1917).

[155] For short historical summary, see A. C. Coolidge, "The European Reconquest of North Africa," American Historical Review, July, 1912.

[156] For these nationalist movements in French North Africa, see A. Servier, Le Nationalisme musulman (Constantine, Algeria, 1913); P. Lapie, Les Civilisations tunisiennes (Paris, 1898); P. Millet, "Les Jeunes-Algériens," Revue de Paris, 1 November, 1913.

[157] A good analysis of the pre-revolutionary reformist movements is found in "X," "La Situation politique de la Perse," Revue du Monde musulman, June, 1914. See also Vambéry, Western Culture in Eastern Lands; General Sir T. E. Gordon, "The Reform Movement in Persia," Proceedings of the Central Asian Society, 13 March, 1907.

[158] See W. Morgan Shuster, The Strangling of Persia (New York, 1912). Also, for earlier phase of the revolution, see E. G. Browne, The Revolution in Persia (London, 1910).

[159] E. G. Browne, "The Present Situation in Persia," Contemporary Review, November, 1912.

[160] Vambéry, La Turquie d'aujourd'hui et d'avant Quarante Ans, pp. 11-12.

[161] For the Tartar revival, see S. Brobovnikov, "Moslems in Russia," The Moslem World, January, 1911; Févret, "Les Tatars de Crimée," Revue du Monde musulman, August, 1907; A. Le Chatelier, "Les Musulmans russes," Revue du Monde musulman, December, 1906; Fr. von Mackay, "Die Erweckung Russlands asiatischen Völkerschaften," Deutsche Rundschau, March, 1918; Arminius Vambéry, Western Culture in Eastern Lands; H. Williams, "The

Russian Mohammedans," Russian Review, February, 1914; "X," "Le Pan-Islamisme et le Pan-Turquisme," Revue du Monde musulman, March, 1913.

[162] For these activities, see article by "X," quoted above; also Ahmed Emin, The Development of Modern Turkey as Measured by its Press (New York, 1914).

[163] For these Pan-Turanian tendencies in Hungary and Bulgaria, see my article "Pan-Turanism," American Political Science Review, February, 1917.

[164] See article by "X," quoted above; also his article "Les Courants politiques dans la Turquie contemporaine," Revue du Monde musulman, December, 1912.

[165] Ex-Chief of General Staff (Ottoman) Ernst Paraquin, in the Berliner Tageblatt, January 24, 1920. For Turkish nationalist activities and attitudes during the war, see further I. D. 1199—A Manual on the Turanians and Pan-Turanianism. Compiled by the Geographical Section of the Naval Intelligence Division, Naval Staff, Admiralty (London, 1919); E. F. Benson, Crescent and Iron Cross (London, 1918); M. A. Czaplicka, The Turks of Central Asia: An Inquiry into the Pan-Turanian Problem (Oxford, 1918); H. Morgenthau, Ambassador Morgenthau's Story (New York, 1918); Dr. Harry Stürmer, Two War-Years in Constantinople (New York, 1917); A. Mandelstam, "The Turkish Spirit," New Europe, April 22, 1920.

[166] For Pan-Arab developments, see A. Musil, Zur Zeitgeschichte von Arabien (Leipzig, 1918); M. Pickthall, "Turkey, England, and the Present Crisis," Asiatic Review, October 1, 1914; A. Servier, Le Nationalisme musulman; Sheick Abd-el-Aziz Schauisch, "Das Machtgebiet der arabischen Sprache," Preussische Jahrbücher, September, 1916.

[167] Literally "House of Islam." All non-Moslem lands are collectively known as "Dar-ul-Harb" or "House of War."

[168] I. e., the organized group of followers of a particular religion.

[169] Mohammed Ali, "Le Mouvement musulman dans l'Inde," Revue Politique Internationale, January, 1914. He headed the so-called "Khilafat Delegation" sent by the Indian Moslems to England in 1919 to protest against the partition of the Ottoman Empire by the peace treaties.

[170] A. Servier, Le Nationalisme musulman, p. 181.

[171] For Pan-Islamic nationalism, besides Servier and Mohammed Ali, quoted above, see A. Le Chatelier, L'Islam au dix-neuvième Siècle (Paris, 1888); same author, "Politique musulmane," Revue du Monde Musulman, September, 1910; Sir T. Morison, "England and Islam," Nineteenth Century and After, July, 1919; G. Démorgny, La Question Persane, pp. 23-31 (Paris, 1916); W. E. D. Allen, "Transcaucasia, Past and Present," Quarterly Review, October, 1920.

[172] Egyptian White Book: Collection of Official Correspondence of the Egyptian Delegation to the Peace Conference (Paris, 1919).

[173] G. Civimini, in the Corriere della Sera, December 30, 1919.

[174] Madame Jehan d'Ivray, "En Égypte," Revue de Paris, September 15, 1920. Madame d'Ivray cites other picturesque incidents of a like character. See also Annexes to Egyptian White Book, previously quoted. These Annexes contain numerous depositions, often accompanied by photographs, alleging severities and atrocities by the British troops.

[175] Contained in the press statements previously mentioned.

[176] Sir M. McIlwraith, "Egyptian Nationalism," Edinburgh Review, July, 1919. See also Hon. W. Ormsby-Gore, "The Future in Egypt," New Europe, November 6, 1919.

[177] For unfortunate aspects of this delay, see Sir Valentine Chirol, "Conflicting Policies in the East," New Europe, July 1, 1920.

[178] For a good account of Lawrence and his work, see series of articles by L. Thomas, "Lawrence: The Soul of the Arabian Revolution," Asia, April, May, June, July, 1920.

[179] A notable example is General Maude's proclamation to the Mesopotamian Arabs in March, 1917.

[180] Article xxii.

[181] From a speech delivered September 19, 1919.

[182] For examples of this pre-war imperialist propaganda, see G. Poignant, "Les Intérêts français en Syrie," Questions diplomatiques et coloniales, March 1-16, 1913. Among other interesting facts, the author cites Premier Poincaré's declaration before the Chamber of Deputies, December 21, 1912: "I need not remark that in the Lebanon and Syria particularly we have traditional interests and that we intend to make them respected." See also J. Atalla, "Les Trois Solutions de la Question syrienne," Questions diplomatiques et coloniales, October 16, 1913; L. Le Fur, Le Protectorat de la France sur les Catholiques d'Orient (Paris, 1914).

[183] Quoted by Senator E. Flandrin in his article "Nos Droits en Syrie et en Palestine,"[1] Revue Hebdomadaire, June 5, 1915. For other examples of French imperialist propaganda, see, besides above article, C. G. Bassim, La Question du Liban (Paris, 1915); H. Baudouin, "La Syrie: Champ de Bataille politique," La Revue Mondiale, February 1-15, 1920; Comte Cressaty, La Syrie française (Paris, 1916); F. Laudet, "La France du Levant," Revue Hebdomadaire, March 1, 1919.

[184] Baudouin, supra. For other violent anti-British comment, see Laudet, supra.

[185] For sharp British criticisms of the French attitude in Syria, see Beckles Wilson, "Our Amazing Syrian Adventure," National Review, September, 1920; W. Urinowski, "The Arab Cause," Balkan Review, September, 1920. Both of these writers were officers in the British forces in the Arab area. See also strong articles by "Taira" in the Balkan Review, August and October, 1920.

[186] For accounts of French severities, see articles just quoted.

[187] B. G. Gaulis in L'Opinion, April 24, 1920.

[188] Le Populaire, February 16, 1920.

[189] For the details of these events, see my article on Persia in The Century, January, 1920.

[190] Statement given to the press in August, 1920.

[191] Henri de Chambon, editor of La Revue Parlementaire. Quoted by Beckles Wilson, "Our Amazing Syrian Adventure," National Review, September, 1920.

CHAPTER VI

NATIONALISM IN INDIA

India is a land of paradox. Possessing a fundamental geographical unity, India has never known real political union save that recently imposed externally by the British "Raj." Full of warlike stocks, India has never been able to repel invaders. Occupied by many races, these races have never really fused, but have remained distinct and mutually hostile, sundered by barriers of blood, speech, culture, and creed. Thus India, large and populous as Europe or China, has neither, like China, evolved a generalized national unity; nor, like Europe, has developed a specialized national diversity; but has remained an amorphous, unstable indeterminate, with tendencies in both directions which were never carried to their logical conclusion.

India's history has been influenced mainly by three great invasions: the Aryan invasion, commencing about 1500 b.c.; the Mohammedan invasion, extending roughly from a.d. 1000 to 1700, and the English invasion, beginning about a.d. 1750 and culminating a century later in a complete conquest which has lasted to the present day.

The Aryans were a fair-skinned people, unquestionably of the same general stock as ourselves. Pressing down from Central Asia through those north-western passes where alone land-access is possible to India, elsewhere impregnably guarded by the mountain wall of the Himalayas, the Aryans subdued the dark-skinned Dravidian aborigines, and settled down as masters. This conquest was, however, superficial and partial. The bulk of the Aryans remained in the north-west, the more adventurous spirits scattering thinly over the rest of the vast peninsula. Even in the north large areas of hill-country and jungle remained in the exclusive possession of the aborigines, while very few Aryans ever penetrated the south. Over most of India, therefore, the Aryans were merely a small ruling class superimposed upon a much more numerous subject population. Fearing to be swallowed up in the Dravidian ocean, the Aryans attempted to preserve their political ascendancy and racial purity by the institution of "caste," which has ever since remained the basis of Indian social life. Caste was originally a "colour line." But it was enforced not so much by civil law as by religion. Society was divided into three castes: Brahmins, or priests; Kshatriyas, or warriors; and Sudras, or workers. The Aryans monopolized the two upper castes, the Sudras being the Dravidian subject population. These castes were kept apart by a rigorous series of religious taboos. Intermarriage, partaking of food and drink, even physical propinquity, entailed ceremonial defilement sometimes inexpiable. Disobedience to these taboos was punished with the terrible penalty of "outcasting," whereby the offender did not merely fall to a lower rank in the caste hierarchy but sank even below the Sudra and became a "Pariah," or man of no-caste, condemned to the most menial and revolting occupations, and with no rights which even the Sudra was bound to respect. Thus Indian society was governed, not by civil, but by ceremonially religious law; while, conversely, the nascent Indian religion ("Brahminism") became not ethical but social in character.

These things produced the most momentous consequences. As a "colour line," caste worked very imperfectly. Despite its prohibitions, even the Brahmins became more or less impregnated with Dravidian blood.[192] But as a social system caste continued to function in ways peculiar to itself. The three original castes gradually subdivided into hundreds and even thousands of sub-castes. These sub-castes had little or nothing of the original racial significance. But they were all just as exclusive as the primal trio, and the outcome was a shattering of Indian society into a chaos of rigid social atoms, between which co-operation or even understanding was impossible. The results upon Indian history are obvious. Says a British authority: "The effect of this permanent maintenance of human types is that the population is heterogeneous to the last degree. It is no question of rich and poor, of town and country, of employer and employed: the differences lie far deeper. The population of a district or a town is a collection of different nationalities—almost different species—of mankind that will not eat or drink or intermarry with one another, and that are governed in the more important affairs of life by committees of their own. It is hardly too much to say that by the caste system the inhabitants of India are differentiated into over two thousand species, which, in the intimate physical relations of life, have as little in common as the inmates of a zoological garden."[193]

Obviously, a land socially atomized and politically split into many principalities was destined to fall before the first strong invader. This invader was Islam. The Mohammedans attacked India soon after their conquest of Persia, but these early attacks were mere border raids without lasting significance. The first real Mohammedan invasion was that of Mahmud of Ghazni, an Afghan prince, in a.d. 1001. Following the road taken by the Aryans ages before, Mahmud conquered north-western India, the region known as the Punjab. Islam had thus obtained a firm foothold in India, and subsequent Moslem leaders spread gradually eastward until most of northern India was under Moslem rule. The invaders had two notable advantages: they were fanatically united against the despised "Idolaters," and they drew many converts from the native population. The very antithesis of Brahminism, Islam, with its doctrine that all Believers are brothers, could not fail to attract multitudes of low-castes and out-castes, who by conversion might rise to the status of the conquerors. This is the main reason why the Mohammedans in India to-day number more than 70,000,000—over one-fifth of the total population. These Indian Moslems are descended, not merely from Afghan, Turkish, Arab, and Persian invaders, but even more from the millions of Hindu converts who embraced Islam.

For many generations the Moslem hold on India was confined to the north. Then, early in the sixteenth century, the great Turko-Mongol leader Baber entered India and founded the "Mogul" Empire. Baber and his successors overran even the south, and united India politically as it had never been united before. But even this conquest was superficial. The Brahmins, threatened with destruction, preached a Hindu revival; the Mogul dynasty petered out; and at the beginning of the eighteenth century the Mogul Empire collapsed, leaving India a welter of warring principalities, Mohammedan and Hindu, fighting each other for religion, for politics, or for sheer lust of plunder.

Out of this anarchy the British rose to power. The British were at first merely one of several other European elements—Portuguese, Dutch, and French—who established small settlements along the Indian coasts. The Europeans never dreamed of conquering India while the Mogul power endured. In fact, the British connection with India began as a purely trading venture—the East India Company. But when India collapsed into anarchy the Europeans were first obliged to acquire local authority to protect their "factories," and later were lured into more ambitious schemes by the impotence of petty rulers. Gradually the British ousted their European rivals and established a solid political foothold in India. The one stable element in a seething chaos, the British inevitably extended their authority. At first they did so reluctantly. The East India Company long remained primarily a trading venture, aiming at dividends rather than dominion. However, it later evolved into a real government with an ambitious policy of annexation. This in turn awakened the fears of many Indians and brought on the "Mutiny" of 1857. The mutiny was quelled, the East India Company abolished, and India came directly under the British Crown, Queen Victoria being later proclaimed Empress of India. These events in turn resulted not only in a strengthening of British political authority but also in an increased penetration of Western influences of every description. Roads, railways, and canals opened up and unified India as never before; the piercing of the Isthmus of Suez facilitated communication with Europe; while education on European lines spread Western ideas.

Over this rapidly changing India stood the British "Raj"—a system of government unique in the world's history. It was the government of a few hundred highly skilled administrative experts backed by a small professional army, ruling a vast agglomeration of subject peoples. It was frankly an absolute paternalism, governing as it saw fit, with no more responsibility to the governed than the native despots whom it had displaced. But it governed well. In efficiency, honesty, and sense of duty, the government of India is probably the best example of benevolent absolutism that the world has ever seen. It gave India profound peace. It played no favourites, holding the scales even between rival races, creeds, and castes. Lastly, it made India a real political entity—something which India had never been before. For the first time in its history, India was firmly united under one rule—the rule of the Pax Britannica.

Yet the very virtues of British rule sowed the seeds of future trouble. Generations grew up, peacefully united in unprecedented acquaintanceship, forgetful of past ills, seeing only European shortcomings, and, above all, familiar with Western ideas of self-government, liberty, and nationality. In India, as elsewhere in the East, there was bound to arise a growing movement of discontent against Western rule—a discontent varying from moderate demands for increasing autonomy to radical demands for immediate independence.

Down to the last quarter of the nineteenth century, organized political agitation against the British "Raj" was virtually unknown. Here and there isolated individuals uttered half-audible protests, but these voices found no popular echo. The Indian masses, pre-occupied with the ever-present problem of getting a living, accepted passively a government no more absolute, and infinitely more efficient, than its predecessors. Of anything like self-conscious Indian "Nationalism" there was virtually no trace.

The first symptom of organized discontent was the formation of the "Indian National Congress" in the year 1885. The very name showed that the British Raj, covering all India, was itself evoking among India's diverse elements a certain common point of view and aspiration. However, the early congresses were very far from representing Indian public opinion, in the general sense of the term. On the contrary, these congresses represented merely a small class of professional men, journalists, and politicians, all of them trained in Western ideas. The European methods of education which the British had introduced had turned out an Indian intelligentsia, conversant with the English language and saturated with Westernism.

This new intelligentsia, convinced as it was of the value of Western ideals and achievements, could not fail to be dissatisfied with many aspects of Indian life. In fact, its first efforts were directed, not so much to politics, as to social and economic reforms like the suppression of child-marriage, the remarriage of widows, and wider education. But, as time passed, matters of political reform came steadily to the fore. Saturated with English history and political philosophy as they were, the Indian intellectuals felt more and more keenly their total lack of self-government, and aspired to endow India with those blessings of liberty so highly prized by their English rulers. Soon a vigorous native press developed, preaching the new gospel, welding the intellectuals into a self-conscious unity, and moulding a genuine public opinion. By the close of the nineteenth century the Indian intelligentsia was frankly agitating for sweeping political innovations like representative councils, increasing control over taxation and the executive, and the opening of the public services to Indians all the way up the scale.

Down to the closing years of the nineteenth century Indian discontent was, as already said, confined to a small class of more or less Europeanized intellectuals who, despite their assumption of the title, could hardly be termed "Nationalists" in the ordinary sense of the word. With a few exceptions, their goal was neither independence nor the elimination of effective British oversight, but rather the reforming of Indian life along Western lines, including a growing degree of self-government under British paramount authority.

But by the close of the nineteenth century there came a change in the situation. India, like the rest of the Orient, was stirring to a new spirit of political and racial self-consciousness. True nationalist symptoms began to appear. Indian scholars delved into their musty chronicles and sacred texts, and proclaimed the glories of India's historic past. Reformed Hindu sects like the Arya Somaj lent religious sanctions. The little band of Europeanized intellectuals was joined by other elements, thinking, not in terms of piecemeal reforms on Western models, but of a new India, rejuvenated from its own vital forces, and free to work out its own destiny in its own way. From the nationalist ranks now arose the challenging slogan: "Bandemataram!" ("Hail, Motherland!")[194]

The outstanding feature about this early Indian nationalism was that it was a distinctively Hindu movement. The Mohammedans regarded it with suspicion or hostility. And for this they had good reasons. The ideal of the new nationalists was Aryan India, the India of the "Golden Age." "Back to the Vedas!" was a nationalist watchword, and this implied a veneration for the past, including a revival of aggressive Brahminism. An extraordinary change came over the intelligentsia. Men who, a few years before, had proclaimed the superiority of Western ideas and had openly flouted "superstitions" like idol-worship, now denounced everything Western and reverently sacrificed to the Hindu gods. The "sacred soil" of India must be purged of the foreigner.[195] But the "foreigner," as these nationalists conceived him, was not merely the Englishman; he was the Mohammedan as well. This was stirring up the past with a vengeance. For centuries the great Hindu-Mohammedan division had run like a chasm athwart India. It had never been closed, but it had been somewhat veiled by the neutral overlordship of the British Raj. Now the veil was torn aside, and the Mohammedans saw themselves menaced by a recrudescence of militant Hinduism like that which had shattered the Mogul Empire after the death of the Emperor Aurangzeb two hundred years before. The Mohammedans were not merely alarmed; they were infuriated as well. Remembering the glories of the Mogul Empire just as the Hindus did the glories of Aryan India, they considered themselves the rightful lords of the land, and had no mind to fall under the sway of despised "Idolaters." The Mohammedans had no love for the British, but they hated the Hindus, and they saw in the British Raj a bulwark against the potential menace of hereditary enemies who outnumbered them nearly five to one. Thus the Mohammedans denounced Hindu nationalism and proclaimed their loyalty to the Raj. To be sure, the Indian Moslems were also affected by the general spirit of unrest which was sweeping over the East. They too felt a quickened sense of self-consciousness. But, being a minority in India, their feelings took the form, not of territorial "patriotism," but of those more diffused sentiments, Pan-Islamism and Pan-Islamic nationalism, which we have already discussed.[196]

Early Indian nationalism was not merely Hindu in character; it was distinctly "Brahminical" as well. More and more the Brahmins became the driving-power of the movement, seeking to perpetuate their supremacy in the India of the morrow as they had enjoyed it in the India of the past. But this aroused apprehension in certain sections of Hindu society. Many low-castes and Pariahs began to fear that an independent or even autonomous India might be ruled by a tyrannical Brahmin oligarchy which would deny them the benefits they now enjoyed under British rule.[197] Also, many of the Hindu princes disliked the thought of a theocratic régime which might reduce them to shadows.[198] Thus the nationalist movement stood out as an alliance between the Brahmins and the Western-educated intelligentsia, who had pooled their ambitions in a programme for jointly ruling India.

Quickened by this ambition and fired by religious zeal, the nationalist movement rapidly acquired a fanatical temper characterized by a mystical abhorrence of everything Western and a ferocious hatred of all Europeans. The Russo-Japanese War greatly inflamed this spirit, and the very next year (1905) an act of the Indian Government precipitated the gathering storm. This act was the famous Partition of Bengal. The partition was a mere administrative measure, with no political intent. But the nationalists made it a "vital issue," and about this grievance they started an intense propaganda that soon filled India with seditious unrest. The leading spirit in this agitation was Bal Gangadhar Tilak, who has been called "the father of Indian unrest." Tilak typified the nationalist movement. A Brahmin with an excellent Western education, he was the sworn foe of English rule and Western civilization. An able propagandist, his speeches roused his hearers to frenzy, while his newspaper, the Yugantar, of Calcutta, preached a campaign of hate, assassination, and rebellion. Tilak's incitements soon produced tangible results, numerous riots, "dacoities," and murders of Englishmen taking place. And of course the Yugantar was merely one of a large number of nationalist organs, some printed in the vernacular and others in English, which vied with one another in seditious invective.

The violence of the nationalist press may be judged by a few quotations. "Revolution," asserted the Yugantar, "is the only way in which a slavish society can save itself. If you cannot prove yourself a man in life, play the man in death. Foreigners have come and decided how you are to live. But how you are to die depends entirely upon yourself." "Let preparations be made for a general revolution in every household! The handful of police and soldiers will never be able to withstand this ocean of revolutionists. Revolutionists may be made prisoners and may die, but thousands of others will spring into their places. Do not be afraid! With the blood of heroes the soil of Hindustan is ever fertile. Do not be downhearted. There is no dearth of heroes. There is no dearth of money; glory awaits you! A single frown (a few bombs) from your eyes has struck terror into the heart of the foe! The uproar of panic has filled the sky. Swim with renewed energy in the ocean of bloodshed!" The assassination note was vehemently stressed. Said S. Krishnavarma in The Indian Sociologist: "Political assassination is not murder, and the rightful employment of physical force connotes 'force used defensively against force used aggressively.'" "The only subscription required," stated the Yugantar, "is that every reader shall bring the head of a European." Not even women and children were spared. Commenting on the murder of an English lady and her daughter, the Yugantar exclaimed exultantly: "Many a female demon must be killed in course of time, in order to extirpate the race of Asuras from the breast of the earth." The fanaticism of the men (usually very young men) who committed these assassinations may be judged by the statement of the murderer of a high English official, Sir Curzon-Wyllie, made shortly before his execution: "I believe that a nation held down by foreign bayonets is in a perpetual state of war. Since open battle is rendered impossible to a disarmed race, I attacked by surprise; since guns were denied to me, I drew my pistol and fired. As a Hindu I feel that wrong to my country is an insult to the gods. Her cause is the cause of Shri Ram; her service is the service of Shri Krishna. Poor in wealth and intellect, a son like myself has nothing else to offer the Mother but his own blood, and so I have sacrificed the same on Her altar. The only lesson required in India at present is to learn how to die, and the only way to teach it is to die ourselves; therefore I die and glory in my martyrdom. This war will continue between England and India so long as the Hindee and English races last, if the present unnatural relation does not cease."[199]

The government's answer to this campaign of sedition and assassination was of course stern repression. The native press was muzzled, the agitators imprisoned or executed, and the hands of the authorities were strengthened by punitive legislation. In fact, so infuriated was the European community by the murders and outrages committed by the nationalists that many Englishmen urged the withdrawal of such political privileges as did exist, the limiting of Western education, and the establishment of extreme autocratic rule. These angry counsels were at once caught up by the nationalists, resulted in fresh outrages, and were answered by more punishment and fresh menaces. Thus the extremists on both sides lashed each other to hotter fury and worsened the situation. For several years India seethed with an unrest which jailings, hangings, and deportations did little to allay.

Presently, however, things took at least a temporary turn for the better. The extremists were, after all, a small minority, and cool heads, both British and Indian, were seeking a way out of the impasse. Conservative Indian leaders like Mr. Gokhale condemned terrorism, and besought their countrymen to seek the realization of their aspirations by peaceful means. On the other hand, liberal-minded Englishmen, while refusing to be stampeded, sought a programme of conciliation. Indian affairs were then in the hands of the eminent Liberal statesman John Morley, and the fruit of his labours was the Indian Councils Act of 1909. The act was a distinct departure from the hitherto almost unlimited absolutism of British rule in India. It gave the Indian opposition greatly increased opportunities for advice, criticism, and debate, and it initiated a restricted scheme of elections to the legislative bodies which it established. The salutary effect of these concessions was soon apparent. The moderate nationalist elements, while not wholly satisfied, accepted the act as an earnest of subsequent concessions and as a proof of British good-will. The terrorism and seditious plottings of the extremists, while not stamped out, were held in check and driven underground. King George's visit to India in 1911 evoked a wave of loyal enthusiasm which swept the peninsula and augured well for the future.

The year 1911 was the high-water mark of this era of appeasement following the storms of 1905-9. The years after 1911 witnessed a gradual recrudescence of discontent as the first effect of the Councils Act wore off and the sense of unfulfilled aspiration sharpened the appetite for more. In fact, during these years, Indian nationalism was steadily broadening its base. In one sense this made for stability, for the nationalist movement ceased to be a small minority of extremists and came more under the influence of moderate leaders like Mr. Gokhale, who were content to work for distant goals by evolutionary methods. It did, however, mean an increasing pressure on the government for fresh devolutions of authority. The most noteworthy symptom of nationalist growth was the rallying of a certain section of Mohammedan opinion to the nationalist cause. The Mohammedans had by this time formed their own organization, the "All-India Moslem League." The league was the reverse of nationalist in complexion, having been formed primarily to protect Moslem interests against possible Hindu ascendancy. Nevertheless, as time passed, some Mohammedans, reassured by the friendly attitude and promises of the Hindu moderates, abandoned the league's anti-

Hindu attitude and joined the moderate nationalists, though refraining from seditious agitation. Indeed, the nationalists presently split into two distinct groups, moderates and extremists. The extremists, condemned by their fellows, kept up a desultory campaign of violence, largely directed by exiled leaders who from the shelter of foreign countries incited their followers at home to seditious agitation and violent action.

Such was the situation in India on the outbreak of the Great War; a situation by no means free from difficulty, yet far less troubled than it had been a few years before. Of course, the war produced an increase of unrest and a certain amount of terrorism. Yet India, as a whole, remained quiet. Throughout the war India contributed men and money unstintedly to the imperial cause, and Indian troops figured notably on European, Asiatic, and African battlefields.

However, though the war-years passed without any serious outbreak of revolutionary violence, it must not be thought that the far more widespread movement for increasing self-government had been either quenched or stilled. On the contrary, the war gave this movement fresh impetus. Louder and louder swelled the cry for not merely good government but government acceptable to Indian patriots because responsible to them. The very fact that India had proved her loyalty to the Empire and had given generously of her blood and treasure were so many fresh arguments adduced for the grant of a larger measure of self-direction. Numerous were the memoranda presented to the British authorities by various sections of Indian public opinion. These memoranda were an accurate reflection of the different shades of Indian nationalism. The ultimate goal of all was emancipation from British tutelage, but they differed widely among themselves as to how and when this emancipation was to be attained. The most conservative contented themselves with asking for modified self-government under British guidance, while the more ambitious asked for the full status of a dominion of the British Empire like Australia and Canada. The revolutionary element naturally held aloof, recognizing that only violence could serve their aim—immediate and unqualified independence.

Of course even the more moderate nationalist demands implied great changes in the existing governmental system and a diminution of British control such as the Government of India was not prepared at present to concede. Nevertheless, the government met these demands by a conciliatory attitude foreshadowing fresh concessions in the near future. In 1916 the Viceroy, Lord Harding, said: "I do not for a moment wish to discountenance self-government for India as a national ideal. It is a perfectly legitimate aspiration and has the sympathy of all moderate men, but in the present position of India it is not idealism that is needed but practical politics. We should do our utmost to grapple with realities, and lightly to raise extravagant hopes and encourage unrealizable demands can only tend to delay and will not accelerate political progress. I know this is the sentiment of wise and thoughtful Indians. Nobody is more anxious than I am to see the early realization of the legitimate aspirations of India, but I am equally desirous of avoiding all danger of reaction from the birth of institutions which experience might prove to be premature."

As a matter of fact, toward the close of 1917, Mr. Montagu, Secretary of State for India, came out from England with the object of thoroughly canvassing Indian public opinion on the question of constitutional reform. For months the problem was carefully weighed, conferences being held with the representatives of all races, classes, and creeds. The result of these researches was a monumental report signed by Mr. Montagu and by the Viceroy, Lord Chelmsford, and published in July, 1918.

The report recommended concessions far beyond any which Great Britain had hitherto made. It frankly envisaged the gift of home rule for India "as soon as possible," and went on to state that the gift was to be conferred not because of Indian agitation, but because of "the faith that is in us." There followed these memorable words: "We believe profoundly that the time has come when the sheltered existence which we have given India cannot be prolonged without damage to her national life; that we have a richer gift for her people than any that we have yet bestowed on them; that nationhood within the Empire represents something better than anything India has hitherto attained; that the placid, pathetic contentment of the masses is not the soil on which such Indian nationhood will grow, and that in deliberately disturbing it we are working for her highest good."

The essence of the report was its recommendation of the principle of "diarchy," or division of governmental responsibility between councillors nominated by the British executive and ministers chosen from elective legislative bodies. This diarchy was to hold for both the central and provincial governments. The legislatures were to be elected by a much more extensive franchise than had previously prevailed and were to have greatly enlarged powers. Previously they had been little more than advisory bodies; now they were to become "legislatures" in the Western sense, though their powers were still limited, many powers, particularly that of the purse, being still "reserved" to the executive. The British executive thus retained ultimate control and had the last word; thus no true "balance of power" was to exist, the scales being frankly weighted in favour of the British Raj. But the report went on to state that this scheme of government was not intended to be permanent; that it was frankly a transitional measure, a school in which the Indian people was to serve its apprenticeship, and that when these first lessons in self-government had been learned, India would be given a thoroughly representative government which would not only initiate and legislate, but which would also control the executive officials.

The Montagu-Chelmsford Report was exhaustively discussed both in India and in England, and from these frank discussions an excellent idea of the Indian problem in all its challenging complexity can be obtained. The nationalists split sharply on the issue, the moderates welcoming the report and agreeing to give the proposed scheme of government their loyal co-operation, the extremists condemning the proposals as a snare and a sham. The moderate attitude was stated in a manifesto signed by their leaders, headed by the eminent Indian economist Sir Dinshaw Wacha, which stated: "The proposed scheme forms a complicated structure capable of improvement in some particulars, especially at the top, but is nevertheless a progressive measure. The reforms are calculated to make the provinces of India reach the goal of complete responsible government. On the whole, the proposals are evolved with great foresight and conceived in a spirit of genuine sympathy with Indian political aspirations, for which the distinguished authors are entitled to the country's gratitude." The condemnation of the radicals was voiced by leaders like Mr. Tilak, who urged "standing fast by the Indian National Congress ideal," and Mr. Bepin Chander Pal, who asserted: "It is my deliberate opinion that if the scheme is accepted, the Government will be more powerful and more autocratic than it is to-day."

Extremely interesting was the protest of the anti-nationalist groups, particularly the Mohammedans and the low-caste Hindus. For it is a fact significant of the complexity of the Indian problem that many millions of Indians fear the nationalist movement and look upon the autocracy of the British Raj as a shield against nationalist oppression and discrimination. The Mohammedans of India are, on the question of self-government for India, sharply divided among themselves. The majority still dislike and fear the nationalist movement, owing to its "Hindu" character. A minority, however, as already stated, have rallied to the nationalist cause. This minority grew greatly in numbers during the war-years, their increased friendliness

110

being due not merely to desire for self-government but also to anger at the Allies' policy of dismemberment of the Ottoman Empire and kindred policies in the Near and Middle East.[200] The Hindu nationalists were quick to sympathize with the Mohammedans on these external matters, and the result was a cordiality between the two elements never known before.

The predominance of high-caste Brahmins in the nationalist movement explains the opposition of many low-caste Hindus to Indian home rule. So great is the low-caste fear of losing their present protection under the British Raj and of being subjected to the domination of a high-caste Brahmin oligarchy that in recent years they have formed an association known as the "Namasudra," led by well-known persons like Doctor Nair.[201] The Namasudra points out what might happen by citing the Brahminic pressure which occurs even in such political activity as already exists. For example: in many elections the Brahmins have terrorized low-caste voters by threatening to "out-caste" all who should not vote the Brahmin ticket, thus making them "Pariahs"—untouchables, with no rights in Hindu society.

Such protests against home rule from large sections of the Indian population gave pause even to many English students of the problem who had become convinced of home rule's theoretical desirability. And of course they greatly strengthened the arguments of those numerous Englishmen, particularly Anglo-Indians, who asserted that India was as yet unfit for self-government. Said one of these objectors in The Round Table: "The masses care not one whit for politics; Home Rule they do not understand. They prefer the English District Magistrate. They only ask to remain in eternal and bovine quiescence. They feel confidence in the Englishman because he has always shown himself the 'Protector of the Poor,' and because he is neither Hindu nor Mussulman, and has a reputation for honesty." And Lord Sydenham, in a detailed criticism of the Montagu-Chelmsford proposals, stated: "There are many defects in our system of government in India. Reforms are needed; but they must be based solely upon considerations of the welfare of the masses of India as a whole. If the policy of 'deliberately' disturbing their 'contentment' which the Viceroy and the Secretary of State have announced is carried out; if, through the 'whispering galleries of the East,' the word is passed that the only authority that can maintain law and order and secure the gradual building-up of an Indian nation is weakening; if, as is proposed, the great public services are emasculated; then the fierce old animosities will break out afresh, and, assisted by a recrudescence of the reactionary forces of Brahminism, they will within a few years bring to nought the noblest work which the British race has ever accomplished."[202]

Yet other English authorities on Indian affairs asserted that the Montagu-Chelmsford proposals were sound and must be enacted into law if the gravest perils were to be averted. Such were the opinions of men like Lionel Curtis[203] and Sir Valentine Chirol, who stated: "It is of the utmost importance that there should be no unnecessary delay. We have had object-lessons enough as to the danger of procrastination, and in India as elsewhere time is on the side of the troublemakers.... We cannot hope to reconcile Indian Extremism. What we can hope to do is to free from its insidious influence all that is best in Indian public life by opening up a larger field of useful activity."[204]

As a matter of fact, the Montagu-Chelmsford Report was accepted as the basis of discussion by the British Parliament, and at the close of the year 1919 its recommendations were formally embodied in law. Unfortunately, during the eighteen months which elapsed between the publication of the report and its legal enactment, the situation in India had darkened. Militant unrest had again raised its head, and India was more disturbed than it had been since 1909.

For this there were several reasons. In the first place, all those nationalist elements who were dissatisfied with the report began coquetting with the revolutionary irreconcilables and encouraging them to fresh terrorism, perhaps in the hope of stampeding the British Parliament into wider concessions than the report had contemplated. But there were other causes of a more general nature. The year 1918 was a black one for India. The world-wide influenza epidemic hit India particularly hard, millions of persons being carried off by the grim plague. Furthermore, India was cursed with drought, the crops failed, and the spectre of famine stalked through the land. The year 1919 saw an even worse drought, involving an almost record famine. By the late summer it was estimated that millions of persons had died of hunger, with millions more on the verge of starvation. And on top of all came an Afghan war, throwing the north-west border into tumult and further unsettling the already restless Mohammedan element.

The upshot was a wave of unrest revealing itself in an epidemic of riots, terrorism, and seditious activity which gave the British authorities serious concern. So critical appeared the situation that a special commission was appointed to investigate conditions, and the report handed in by its chairman, Justice Rowlatt, painted a depressing picture of the strength of revolutionary unrest. The report stated that not only had a considerable number of young men of the educated upper classes become involved in the promotion of anarchical movements, but that the ranks were filled with men belonging to other social orders, including the military, and that there was clear evidence of successful tampering with the loyalty of the native troops. To combat this growing disaffection, the Rowlatt committee recommended fresh repressive legislation.

Impressed with the gravity of the committee's report, the Government of India formulated a project of law officially known as the Anarchical and Revolutionary Crimes Act, though generally known as the Rowlatt Bill. By its provisions the authorities were endowed with greatly increased powers, such as the right to search premises and arrest persons on mere suspicion of seditious activity, without definite evidence of the same.

The Rowlatt Bill at once aroused bitter nationalist opposition. Not merely extremists, but many moderates, condemned it as a backward step and as a provoker of fresh trouble. When the bill came up for debate in the Indian legislative body, the Imperial Legislative Council, all the native members save one opposed it, and the bill was finally passed on strictly racial lines by the votes of the appointed English majority. However, the government considered the bill an absolute pre-requisite to the successful maintenance of order, and it was passed into law in the spring of 1919.

This brought matters to a head. The nationalists, stigmatizing the Rowlatt law as the "Black Cobra Act," were unmeasured in their condemnation. The extremists engineered a campaign of militant protest and decreed the date of the bill's enactment, April 6, 1919, as a national "Humiliation Day." On that day monster mass-meetings were held, at which nationalist orators made seditious speeches and inflamed the passions of the multitude. "Humiliation Day" was in fact the beginning of the worst wave of unrest since the mutiny. For the next three months a veritable epidemic of rioting and terrorism swept India, particularly the northern provinces. Officials were assassinated, English civilians were murdered, and there was wholesale destruction of property. At some moments it looked as though India were on the verge of revolution and anarchy.

However, the government stood firm. Violence was countered with stern repression. Riotous mobs were mowed down wholesale by rifle and machine-gun fire or were scattered by bombs dropped from low-flying aeroplanes. The most noted of these occurrences was the so-called

"Amritsar Massacre," where British troops fired into a seditious mass-meeting, killing 500 and wounding 1500 persons. In the end the government mastered the situation. Order was restored, the seditious leaders were swept into custody, and the revolutionary agitation was once more driven underground. The enactment of the Montagu-Chelmsford reform bill by the British Parliament toward the close of the year did much to relax the tension and assuage discontent, though the situation of India was still far from normal. The deplorable events of the earlier part of 1919 had roused animosities which were by no means allayed. The revolutionary elements, though driven underground, were more bitter and uncompromising than ever, while opponents of home rule were confirmed in their conviction that India could not be trusted and that any relaxation of autocracy must spell anarchy.

This was obviously not the best mental atmosphere in which to apply the compromises of the Montagu-Chelmsford reforms. In fact, the extremists were determined that they should not be given a fair trial, regarding the reforms as a snare which must be avoided at all costs. Recognizing that armed rebellion was still impossible, at least for the present, the extremists evolved the idea known as "non-co-operation." This was, in fact, a gigantic boycott of everything British. Not merely were the new voters urged to stay away from the polls and thus elect no members to the proposed legislative bodies, but lawyers and litigants were to avoid the courts, taxpayers refuse to pay imposts, workmen to go on strike, shopkeepers to refuse to buy or sell British-made goods, and even pupils to leave the schools and colleges. This wholesale "out-casting" of everything British would make the English in India a new sort of Pariah—"untouchables"; the British Government and the British community in India would be left in absolute isolation, and the Raj, rendered unworkable, would have to capitulate to the extremist demands for complete self-government.

Such was the non-co-operation idea. And the idea soon found an able exponent: a certain M. K. Gandhi, who had long possessed a reputation for personal sanctity and thus inspired the Hindu masses with that peculiar religious fervour which certain types of Indian ascetics have always known how to arouse. Gandhi's propaganda can be judged by the following extract from one of his speeches: "It is as amazing as it is humiliating that less than 100,000 white men should be able to rule 315,000,000 Indians. They do so somewhat, undoubtedly, by force, but more by securing our co-operation in a thousand ways and making us more and more helpless and dependent on them, as time goes forward. Let us not mistake reformed councils (legislatures), more law-courts, and even governorships for real freedom or power. They are but subtler methods of emasculation. The British cannot rule us by mere force. And so they resort to all means, honourable and dishonourable, in order to retain their hold on India. They want India's billions and they want India's man-power for their imperialistic greed. If we refuse to supply them with men and money, we achieve our goal: namely, Swaraj,[205] equality, manliness."

The extreme hopes of the non-co-operation movement have not been realized. The Montagu-Chelmsford reforms have been put in operation, and the first elections under them were held at the beginning of 1921. But the outlook is far from bright. The very light vote cast at the elections revealed the effect of the non-co-operation movement, which showed itself in countless other ways, from strikes in factories to strikes of school-children. India to-day is in a turmoil of unrest. And this unrest is not merely political; it is social as well. The vast economic changes which have been going on in India for the past half-century have profoundly disorganized Indian society. These changes will be discussed in later chapters. The point to be here noted is that the extremist leaders are capitalizing social discontent and are unquestionably in touch with Bolshevik Russia. Meanwhile the older factors of disturbance are by no means eliminated. The recent atrocious massacre of dissident Sikh pilgrims by orthodox Sikh fanatics, and the three-cornered riots between Hindus,

Mohammedans, and native Christians which broke out about the same time in southern India, reveal the hidden fires of religious and racial fanaticism that smoulder beneath the surface of Indian life.

The truth of the matter is that India is to-day a battle-ground between the forces of evolutionary and revolutionary change. It is an anxious and a troubled time. The old order is obviously passing, and the new order is not yet fairly in sight. The hour is big with possibilities of both good and evil, and no one can confidently predict the outcome.

FOOTNOTES:

[192] According to some historians, this race-mixture occurred almost at once. The theory is that the Aryan conquerors, who outside the north-western region had very few of their own women with them, took Dravidian women as wives or concubines, and legitimatized their half-breed children, the offspring of the conquerors, both pure-bloods and mixed-bloods, coalescing into a closed caste. Further infiltration of Dravidian blood was thus prevented, but Aryan race-purity had been destroyed.

[193] Sir Bampfylde Fuller, Studies of Indian Life and Sentiment, p. 40 (London, 1910). For other discussions of caste and its effects, see W. Archer, India and the Future (London, 1918); Sir V. Chirol, Indian Unrest (London, 1910); Rev. J. Morrison, New Ideas in India: A Study of Social, Political and Religious Developments (Edinburgh, 1906); Sir H. Risley, The People of India (London, 1908); also writings of the "Namasudra" leader, Dr. Nair, previously quoted, and S. Nihal Singh, "India's Untouchables," Contemporary Review, March, 1913.

[194] For the nationalist movement, see Archer, Chirol, and Morrison, supra. Also Sir H. J. S. Cotton, India in Transition (London, 1904); J. N. Farquhar, Modern Religious Movements in India (New York, 1915); Sir W. W. Hunter, The India of the Queen and Other Essays (London, 1903); W. S. Lilly, India and Its Problems (London, 1902); Sir V. Lovett, A History of the Indian Nationalist Movement (London, 1920); J. Ramsay Macdonald, The Government of India (London, 1920); Sir T. Morison, Imperial Rule in India (London, 1899); J. D. Rees, The Real India (London, 1908); Sir J. Strachey, India: Its Administration and Progress (Fourth Edition—London, 1911); K. Vyasa Rao, The Future Government of India (London, 1918).

[195] I have already discussed this "Golden Age" tendency in Chapter III. For more or less Extremist Indian view-points, see A. Coomaraswamy, The Dance of Siva (New York, 1918); H. Maitra, Hinduism: The World-Ideal (London, 1916); Bipin Chandra Pal, "The Forces Behind the Unrest in India," Contemporary Review, February, 1910; also various writings of Lajpat Rai, especially The Arya Samaj (London, 1915) and Young India (New York, 1916).

[196] For Indian Mohammedan points of view, mostly anti-Hindu, see H. H. The Aga Khan, India in Transition (London, 1918); S. Khuda Bukhsh, Essays: Indian and Islamic (London, 1912); Sir Syed Ahmed, The Present State of Indian Politics (Allahabad, 1888); Syed Sirdar Ali Khan, The Unrest in India (Bombay, 1907); also his India of To-day (Bombay, 1908).

[197] This attitude of the "Depressed Classes," especially as revealed in the "Namasudra Association," has already been discussed in Chapter III, and will be further touched upon later in this present chapter.

[198] Regarding the Indian native princes, see Archer and Chirol, supra. Also J. Pollen, "Native States and Indian Home Rule," Asiatic Review, January 1, 1917; The Maharajah of

114

Bobbili, Advice to the Indian Aristocracy (Madras, 1905); articles by Sir D. Barr and Sir F. Younghusband in The Empire and the Century (London, 1905).

[199] A good symposium of extremist comment is contained in Chirol, supra. Also see J. D. Rees, The Real India (London, 1908); series of extremist articles in The Open Court, March, 1917. A good sample of extremist literature is the fairly well-known pamphlet India's "Loyalty" to England (1915).

[200] Discussed in the preceding chapter.

[201] Quoted in Chapter IV.

[202] Lord Sydenham, "India," Contemporary Review, November, 1918. For similar criticisms of the Montagu-Chelmsford proposals, see G. M. Chesney, India under Experiment (London, 1918); "The First Stage towards Indian Anarchy," Spectator, December 20, 1919.

[203] Lionel Curtis, Letters to the People of India on Responsible Government, already quoted at the end of Chapter IV.

[204] Sir V. Chirol, "India in Travail," Edinburgh Review, July, 1918.

[205] I. e., self-government, in the extremist sense—practically independence.


CHAPTER VII

ECONOMIC CHANGE

One of the most interesting phenomena of modern world-history is the twofold conquest of the East by the West. The word "conquest" is usually employed in a political sense, and calls up visions of embattled armies subduing foreign lands and lording it over distant peoples. Such political conquests in the Orient did of course occur, and we have already seen how, during the past century, the decrepit states of the Near and Middle East fell an easy prey to the armed might of the European Powers.

But what is not so generally realized is the fact that this political conquest was paralleled by an economic conquest perhaps even more complete and probably destined to produce changes of an even more profound and enduring character.

The root-cause of this economic conquest was the Industrial Revolution. Just as the voyages of Columbus and Da Gama gave Europe the strategic mastery of the ocean and thereby the political mastery of the world, so the technical inventions of the later eighteenth century which inaugurated the Industrial Revolution gave Europe the economic mastery of the world. These inventions in fact heralded a new Age of Discovery, this time into the realms of science. The results were, if possible, more momentous even than those of the age of geographical discovery three centuries before. They gave our race such increased mastery over the resources of nature that the ensuing transformation of economic life swiftly and utterly transformed the face of things.

This transformation was, indeed, unprecedented in the world's history. Hitherto man's material progress had been a gradual evolution. With the exception of gunpowder, he had tapped no new sources of material energy since very ancient times. The horse-drawn mail-coach of our great-grandfathers was merely a logical elaboration of the horse-drawn Egyptian chariot; the wind-driven clipper-ship traced its line unbroken to Ulysses's lateen bark before Troy; while industry still relied on the brawn of man and beast or upon the simple action of wind and waterfall. Suddenly all was changed. Steam, electricity, petrol, the Hertzian wave, harnessed nature's hidden powers, conquered distance, and shrunk the terrestrial globe to the measure of human hands. Man entered a new material world, differing not merely in degree but in kind from that of previous generations.

When I say "Man," I mean, so far as the nineteenth century was concerned, the white man of Europe and its racial settlements overseas. It was the white man's brain which had conceived all this, and it was the white man alone who at first reaped the benefits. The two outstanding features of the new order were the rise of machine-industry with its incalculable acceleration of mass-production, and the correlative development of cheap and rapid transportation. Both these factors favoured a prodigious increase in economic power and wealth in Europe, since Europe became the workshop of the world. In fact, during the nineteenth century, Europe was transformed from a semi-rural continent into a swarming hive of industry, gorged with goods, capital, and men, pouring forth its wares to the remotest corners of the earth, and drawing thence fresh stores of raw material for new fabrication and exchange.

Such was the industrially revolutionized West which confronted an East as backward and stagnant in economics as it was in politics and the art of war. In fact, the East was virtually devoid of either industry or business, as we understand these terms to-day. Economically, the East was on an agricultural basis, the economic unit being the self-supporting, semi-isolated village. Oriental "industries" were handicrafts, carried on by relatively small numbers of artisans, usually working by and for themselves. Their products, while often exquisite in quality, were largely luxuries, and were always produced by such slow, antiquated methods that their quantity was limited and their market price relatively high. Despite very low wages, therefore, Asiatic products not only could not compete in the world-market with European and American machine-made, mass-produced articles, but were hard hit in their home-markets as well.

This Oriental inability to compete with Western industry arose not merely from methods of production but also from other factors such as the mentality of the workers and the scarcity of capital. Throughout the Near and Middle East economic life rested on the principle of status. The Western economic principles of contract and competition were virtually unknown. Agriculturalists and artisans followed blindly in the footsteps of their fathers. There was no competition, no stimulus for improvement, no change in customary wages, no desire for a better and more comfortable living. The industries were stereotyped; the apprentice merely imitated his master, and rarely thought of introducing new implements or new methods of manufacture. Instead of working for profit and advancement, men followed an hereditary "calling," usually hallowed by religious sanctions, handed down from father to son through many generations, each calling possessing its own unchanging ideals, its zealously guarded craft-secrets.

The few bolder, more enterprising spirits who might have ventured to break the iron bands of custom and tradition were estopped by lack of capital. Fluid "investment" capital, easily mobilized and ready to pour into an enterprise of demonstrable utility and profit, simply did not exist. To the Oriental, whether prince or peasant, money was regarded, not as a source of profit or a medium of exchange, but as a store of value, to be hoarded intact against a "rainy day." The East has been known for ages as a "sink of the precious metals." In India alone, the value of the gold, silver, and jewels hidden in strong-boxes, buried in the earth, or hanging about the necks of women must run into billions. Says a recent writer on India: "I had the privilege of being taken through the treasure-vaults of one of the wealthiest Maharajahs. I could have plunged my arm to the shoulder in great silver caskets filled with diamonds, pearls, emeralds, rubies. The walls were studded with hooks and on each pair of hooks rested gold bars three to four feet long and two inches across. I stood by a great cask of diamonds, and picking up a handful let them drop slowly from between my fingers, sparkling and glistening like drops of water in sunlight. There are some seven hundred native states, and the rulers of every one has his treasure-vaults on a more or less elaborate scale. Besides these, every zamindar and every Indian of high or low degree who can save anything, wants to have it by him in actual metal; he distrusts this new-fangled paper currency that they try to pass off on him. Sometimes he beats his coins into bangles for his wives, and sometimes he hides money behind a loose brick or under a flat stone in the bottom of the oven, or he goes out and digs a little hole and buries it."[206]

Remember that this description is of present-day India, after more than a century of British rule and notwithstanding a permeation of Western ideas which, as we shall presently see, has produced momentous modifications in the native point of view. Remember also that this hoarding propensity is not peculiar to India but is shared by the entire Orient. We can then realize the utter lack of capital for investment purposes in the East of a hundred years ago, especially when we remember that political insecurity and religious prohibitions of the lending of money at interest stood in the way of such far-sighted individuals as might have been inclined to employ their hoarded wealth for productive purposes. There was, indeed, one outlet for financial activity—usury, and therein virtually all the scant fluid capital of the old Orient was employed. But such capital, lent not for productive enterprise, but for luxury, profligacy, or incompetence, was a destructive rather than a creative force and merely intensified the prejudice against capital of any kind.

Such was the economic life of the Orient a hundred years ago. It is obvious that this archaic order was utterly unable to face the tremendous competition of the industrialized West. Everywhere the flood of cheap Western machine-made, mass-produced goods began invading Eastern lands, driving the native wares before them. The way in which an ancient Oriental handicraft like the Indian textiles was literally annihilated by the destructive competition of Lancashire cottons is only one of many similar instances. To be sure, some Oriental writers contend that this triumph of Western manufactures was due to political rather than economic reasons, and Indian nationalists cite British governmental activity in favour of the Lancashire cottons above mentioned as the sole cause for the destruction of the Indian textile handicrafts. But such arguments appear to be fallacious. British official action may have hastened the triumph of British industry in India, but that triumph was inevitable in the long run. The best proof is the way in which the textile crafts of independent Oriental countries like Turkey and Persia were similarly ruined by Western competition.

A further proof is the undoubted fact that Oriental peoples, taken as a whole, have bought Western-manufactured products in preference to their own hand-made wares. To many Westerners this has been a mystery. Such persons cannot understand how the Orientals could buy the cheap, shoddy products of the West, manufactured especially for the Eastern market, in preference to their native wares of better quality and vastly greater beauty. The answer, however, is that the average Oriental is not an art connoisseur but a poor man living perilously close to the margin of starvation. He not only wants but must buy things cheap, and the wide price-margin is the deciding factor. Of course there is also the element of novelty. Besides goods which merely replace articles he has always used, the West has introduced many new articles whose utility or charm are irresistible. I have already mentioned the way in which the sewing-machine and the kerosene-lamp have swept the Orient from end to end, and there are many other instances of a similar nature. The permeation of Western industry has, in fact, profoundly modified every phase of Oriental economic life. New economic wants have been created; standards of living have been raised; canons of taste have been altered. Says a lifelong American student of the Orient: "The knowledge of modern inventions and of other foods and articles has created new wants. The Chinese peasant is no longer content to burn bean-oil; he wants kerosene. The desire of the Asiatic to possess foreign lamps is equalled only by his passion for foreign clocks. The ambitious Syrian scorns the mud roof of his ancestors, and will be satisfied only with the bright red tiles imported from France. Everywhere articles of foreign manufacture are in demand.... Knowledge increases wants, and the Oriental is acquiring knowledge. He demands a hundred things to-day that his grandfather never heard of."[207]

Everywhere it is the same story. An Indian economic writer, though a bitter enemy of Western industrialism, bemoans the fact that "the artisans are losing their occupations and are turning to agriculture. The cheap kerosene-oil from Baku or New York threatens the oilman's[208] existence. Brass and copper which have been used for vessels from time immemorial are threatened by cheap enamelled ironware imported from Europe.... There is also, pari passu, a transformation of the tastes of the consumers. They abandon gur for crystal sugar. Home-woven cloths are now replaced by manufactured cloths for being too coarse. All local industries are attacked and many have been destroyed. Villages that for centuries followed customary practices are brought into contact with the world's markets all on a sudden. For steamships and railways which have established the connection have been built in so short an interval as hardly to allow breathing-time to the village which slumbered so long under the dominion of custom. Thus the sudden introduction of competition into an economic unit which had from time immemorial followed custom has wrought a mighty change."[209]

This "mighty change" was due not merely to the influx of Western goods but also to an equally momentous influx of Western capital. The opportunities for profitable investment were so numerous that Western capital soon poured in streams into Eastern lands. Virtually devoid of fluid capital of its own, the Orient was bound to have recourse to Western capital for the initiation of all economic activity in the modern sense. Railways, mines, large-scale agriculture of the "plantation" type, and many other undertakings thus came into being. Most notable of all was the founding of numerous manufacturing establishments from North Africa to China and the consequent growth of genuine "factory towns" where the whir of machinery and the smoke of tall chimneys proclaimed that the East was adopting the industrial life of the West.

The momentous social consequences of this industrialization of the Orient will be treated in subsequent chapters. In the present chapter we will confine ourselves to a consideration of its economic side. Furthermore, this book, limited as it is to the Near and Middle East, cannot deal with industrial developments in China and Japan. The reader should, however, always bear in mind Far Eastern developments, which, in the main, run parallel to those which we shall here discuss.

These industrial innovations were at first pure Western transplantings set in Eastern soil. Initiated by Western capital, they were wholly controlled and managed by Western brains. Western capital could not venture to entrust itself to Orientals, with their lack of the modern industrial spirit, their habits of "squeeze" and nepotism, their lust for quick returns, and their incapacity for sustained business team-play. As time passed, however, the success of Western undertakings so impressed Orientals that the more forward-looking among them were ready to risk their money and to acquire the technique necessary for success. At the close of Chapter II, I described the development of modern business types in the Moslem world, and the same is true of the non-Moslem populations of India. In India there were several elements such as the Parsis and the Hindu "banyas," or money-lenders, whose previous activities in commerce or usury predisposed them to financial and industrial activity in the modern sense. From their ranks have chiefly sprung the present-day native business communities of India, exemplified by the jute and textile factories of Calcutta and Bombay, and the great Tata iron-works of Bengal—undertakings financed by native capital and wholly under native control. Of course, beside these successes there have been many lamentable failures. Nevertheless, there seems to be no doubt that Western industrialism is ceasing to be an exotic and is rooting itself firmly in Eastern soil.[210]

The combined result of Western and Eastern enterprise has been, as already stated, the rise of important industrial centres at various points in the Orient. In Egypt a French writer remarks: "Both banks of the Nile are lined with factories, sugar-refineries and cotton-mills, whose belching chimneys tower above the mud huts of the fellahs."[211] And Sir Theodore Morison says of India: "In the city of Bombay the industrial revolution has already been accomplished. Bombay is a modern manufacturing city, where both the dark and the bright side of modern industrialism strike the eye. Bombay has insanitary slums where overcrowding is as great an evil as in any European city; she has a proletariat which works long hours amid the din and whir of machinery; she also has her millionaires, whose princely charities have adorned her streets with beautiful buildings. Signs of lavish wealth and, let me add, culture and taste in Bombay astonish the visitor from the inland districts. The brown villages and never-ending fields with which he has hitherto been familiar are the India which is passing away; Bombay is the presage of the future."[212]

The juxtaposition of vast natural resources and a limitless supply of cheap labour has encouraged the most ambitious hopes in Oriental minds. Some Orientals look to a combination of Western money and Eastern man-power, expressed by an Indian economic writer in the formula: "English money and Indian labour are the two cheapest things in the world."[213] Others more ambitiously dream of industrializing the East entirely by native effort, to the exclusion and even to the detriment of the West. This view was well set forth some years ago by a Hindu, who wrote in a leading Indian periodical:[214] "In one sense the Orient is really menacing the West, and so earnest and open-minded is Asia that no pretence or apology whatever is made about it. The Easterner has thrown down the industrial gauntlet, and from now on Asia is destined to witness a progressively intense trade warfare, the Occidental scrambling to retain his hold on the markets of the East, and the Oriental endeavouring to beat him in a battle in which heretofore he has been an easy victor.... In competing with the Occidental commercialists, the Oriental has awakened to a dynamic realization of the futility of pitting unimproved machinery and methods against modern methods and appliances. Casting aside his former sense of self-complacency, he is studying the sciences and arts that have given the West its material prosperity. He is putting the results of his investigations to practical use, as a rule, recasting the Occidental methods to suit his peculiar needs, and in some instances improving upon them."

This statement of the spirit of the Orient's industrial awakening is confirmed by many white observers. At the very moment when the above article was penned, an American economic writer was making a study tour of the Orient, of which he reported: "The real cause of Asia's poverty lies in just two things: the failure of Asiatic governments to educate their people, and the failure of the people to increase their productive capacity by the use of machinery. Ignorance and lack of machinery are responsible for Asia's poverty; knowledge and modern tools are responsible for America's prosperity." But, continues this writer, we must watch out. Asia now realizes these facts and is doing much to remedy the situation. Hence, "we must face in ever-increasing degree the rivalry of awakening peoples who are strong with the strength that comes from struggle with poverty and hardship, and who have set themselves to master and apply all our secrets in the coming world-struggle for industrial supremacy and for racial readjustment."[215] Another American observer of Asiatic economic conditions reports: "All Asia is being permeated with modern industry and present-day mechanical progress."[216] And Sir Theodore Morison concludes regarding India's economic future: "India's industrial transformation is near at hand; the obstacles which have hitherto prevented the adoption of modern methods of manufacture have been removed; means of transport have been spread over the face of the whole country, capital for the purchase of machinery and erection of factories may now be borrowed on easy terms; mechanics, engineers, and business managers may be hired from Europe to train the future captains of Indian industry; in English a common language has been found in which to transact business with all the provinces of India and with a great part of the Western world; security from foreign invasion and internal commotion justifies the inception of large enterprises. All the conditions are favourable for a great reorganization of industry which, when successfully accomplished, will bring about an increase hitherto undreamed of in India's annual output of wealth."[217]

The factor usually relied upon to overcome the Orient's handicaps of inexperience and inexpertness in industrialism is its cheap labour. To Western observers the low wages and long hours of Eastern industry are literally astounding. Take Egypt and India as examples of industrial conditions in the Near and Middle East. Writing of Egypt in 1908, the English economist H. N. Brailsford says: "There was then no Factory Act in Egypt. There are all over the country ginning-mills, which employ casual labour to prepare raw cotton for export during four or five months of the year. The wages were low, from 7½d. to 10d. (15 to 20 cents) a day for an adult, and 6d. (12 cents) for a child. Children and adults alike worked sometimes for twelve, usually for fifteen, and on occasion even for sixteen or eighteen hours a day. In the height of the season even the children were put on night shifts of twelve hours."[218]

In India conditions are about the same. The first thorough investigation of Indian industry was made in 1907 by a factory labour commission, and the following are some of the data published in its report: In the cotton-mills of Bombay the hours regularly worked ran from thirteen to fourteen hours. In the jute-mills of Calcutta the operatives usually worked fifteen hours. Cotton-ginning factories required their employees to work seventeen and eighteen hours a day, rice and flour mills twenty to twenty-two hours, and an extreme case was found in a printing works where the men had to work twenty-two hours a day for seven consecutive days. As to wages, an adult male operative, working from thirteen to fifteen hours a day, received from 15 to 20 rupees a month ($5 to $6.35). Child labour was very prevalent, children six and seven years old working "half-time"—in many cases eight hours a day. As a result of this report legislation was passed by the Indian Government bettering working conditions somewhat, especially for women and children. But in 1914 the French economist Albert Métin, after a careful study, reported factory conditions not greatly changed, the Factory Acts systematically evaded, hours very long, and wages extremely low. In Bombay men were earning from 10 cents to 20 cents per day, the highest wages being 30 cents. For women and children the maximum was 10 cents per day.[219]

With such extraordinarily low wages and long hours of labour it might at first sight seem as though, given adequate capital and up-to-date machinery, the Orient could not only drive Occidental products from Eastern markets but might invade Western markets as well. This, indeed, has been the fear of many Western writers. Nearly three-quarters of a century ago

Gobineau prophesied an industrial invasion of Europe from Asia,[220] and of late years economists like H. N. Brailsford have warned against an emigration of Western capital to the tempting lure of factory conditions in Eastern lands.[221] Nevertheless, so far as the Near and Middle East is concerned, nothing like this has as yet materialized. China, to be sure, may yet have unpleasant surprises in store for the West,[222] but neither the Moslem world nor India have developed factory labour with the skill, stamina, and assiduity sufficient to undercut the industrial workers of Europe and America. In India, for example, despite a swarming and poverty-stricken population, the factories are unable to recruit an adequate or dependable labour-supply. Says M. Métin: "With such long hours and low wages it might be thought that Indian industry would be a formidable competitor of the West. This is not so. The reason is the bad quality of the work. The poorly paid coolies are so badly fed and so weak that it takes at least three of them to do the work of one European. Also, the Indian workers lack not only strength but also skill, attention, and liking for their work.... An Indian of the people will do anything else in preference to becoming a factory operative. The factories thus get only the dregs of the working class. The workers come to the factories and mines as a last resort; they leave as soon as they can return to their prior occupations or find a more remunerative employment. Thus the factories can never count on a regular labour-supply. Would higher wages remedy this? Many employers say no—as soon as the workers got a little ahead they would quit, either temporarily till their money was spent, or permanently for some more congenial calling."[223] These statements are fully confirmed by an Indian economic writer, who says: "One of the greatest drawbacks to the establishment of large industries in India is the scarcity and inefficiency of labour. Cheap labour, where there is no physical stamina, mental discipline, and skill behind it, tends to be costly in the end. The Indian labourer is mostly uneducated. He is not in touch with his employers or with his work. The labouring population of the towns is a flitting, dilettante population."[224]

Thus Indian industry, despite its very considerable growth, has not come up to early expectations. As the official Year-Book very frankly states: "India, in short, is a country rich in raw materials and in industrial possibilities, but poor in manufacturing accomplishments."[225] In fact, to some observers, India's industrial future seems far from bright. As a competent English student of Indian conditions recently wrote: "Some years ago it seemed possible that India might, by a rapid assimilation of Western knowledge and technical skill, adapt for her own conditions the methods of modern industry, and so reach an approximate economic level. Some even now threaten the Western world with a vision of the vast populations of China and India rising up with skilled organization, vast resources, and comparatively cheap labour to impoverish the West. To the present writer this is a mere bogey. The peril is of a very different kind. Instead of a growing approximation, he sees a growing disparity. For every step India takes toward mechanical efficiency, the West takes two. When India is beginning to use bicycles and motor-cars (not to make them), the West is perfecting the aeroplane. That is merely symbolic. The war, as we know, has speeded up mechanical invention and produced a population of mechanics; but India has stood comparatively still. It is, up to now, overwhelmingly mediæval, a country of domestic industry and handicrafts. Mechanical power, even of the simplest, has not yet been applied to its chief industry—agriculture. Yet the period of age-long isolation is over, and India can never go back to it; nevertheless, the gap between East and West is widening. What is to be the outcome for her 300 millions? We are in danger in the East of seeing the worst evils of commercialism developed on an enormous scale, with the vast population of India the victims—of seeing the East become a world slum."[226]

Whether or not this pessimistic outlook is justified, certain it is that not merely India but the entire Orient is in a stage of profound transition; and transition periods are always painful times. We have been considering the new industrial proletariat of the towns. But the older social classes are affected in very similar fashion. The old-type handicraftsman and small merchant are obviously menaced by modern industrial and business methods, and the peasant masses are in little better shape. It is not merely a change in technique but a fundamental difference in outlook on life that is involved. The life of the old Orient, while there was much want and hardship, was an easygoing life, with virtually no thought of such matters as time, efficiency, output, and "turnover." The merchant sat cross-legged in his little booth amid his small stock of wares, passively waiting for trade, chaffering interminably with his customers, annoyed rather than pleased if brisk business came his way. The artisan usually worked by and for himself, keeping his own hours and knocking off whenever he chose. The peasant arose with the dawn, but around noon he and his animals lay down for a long nap and slept until, in the cool of afternoon, they awoke, stretched themselves, and, comfortably and casually, went to work again.

To such people the speed, system, and discipline of our economic life are painfully repugnant, and adaptation can at best be effected only very slowly and under the compulsion of the direst necessity. Meanwhile they suffer from the competition of those better equipped in the economic battle. Sir William Ramsay paints a striking picture of the way in which the Turkish population of Asia Minor, from landlords and merchants to simple peasants, have been going down-hill for the last half-century under the economic pressure not merely of Westerners but of the native Christian elements, Armenians and Greeks, who had partially assimilated Western business ideas and methods. Under the old state of things, he says, there was in Asia Minor "no economic progress and no mercantile development; things went on in the old fashion, year after year. Such simple business as was carried on was inconsistent with the highly developed Western business system and Western civilization; but it was not oppressive to the people. There were no large fortunes; there was no opportunity for making a great fortune; it was impossible for one man to force into his service the minds and the work of a large number of people, and so to create a great organization out of which he might make big profits. There was a very large number of small men doing business on a small scale."[227] Sir William Ramsay then goes on to describe the shattering of this archaic economic life by modern business methods, to the consequent impoverishment of all classes of the unadaptable Turkish population.

How the agricultural classes, peasants and landlords alike, are suffering from changing economic conditions is well exemplified by the recent history of India. Says the French writer Chailley, an authoritative student of Indian problems: "For the last half-century large fractions of the agricultural classes are being entirely despoiled of their lands or reduced to onerous tenancies. On the other hand, new classes are rising and taking their place.... Both ryots and zamindars[228] are involved. The old-type nobility has not advanced with the times. It remains idle and prodigal, while the peasant proprietors, burdened by the traditions of many centuries, are likewise improvident and ignorant. On the other hand, the economic conditions of British India are producing capitalists who seek employment for their wealth. A conflict between them and the old landholders was predestined, and the result was inevitable. Wealth goes to the cleverest, and the land must pass into the hands of new masters, to the great indignation of the agricultural classes, a portion of whom will be reduced to the position of farm-labourers."[229]

The Hindu economist Mukerjee thus depicts the disintegration and decay of the Indian village: "New economic ideas have now begun to influence the minds of the villagers. Some are compelled to leave their occupations on account of foreign competition, but more are leaving their hereditary occupations of their own accord. The Brahmins go to the cities to seek government posts or professional careers. The middle classes also leave their villages and get scattered all over the country to earn a living. The peasants also leave their ancestral acres and form a class of landless agricultural labourers. The villages, drained of their best blood, stagnate and decay. The movement from the village to the city is in fact not only working a complete revolution in the habits and ideals of our people, but its economic consequences are far more serious than are ordinarily supposed. It has made our middle classes helplessly subservient to employment and service, and has also killed the independence of our peasant proprietors. It has jeopardized our food-supply, and is fraught with the gravest peril not only to our handicrafts but also to our national industry—agriculture."[230]

Happily there are signs that, in Indian agriculture at least, the transition period is working itself out and that conditions may soon be on the mend. Both the British Government and the native princes have vied with one another in spreading Western agricultural ideas and methods, and since the Indian peasant has proved much more receptive than has the Indian artisan, a more intelligent type of farmer is developing, better able to keep step with the times. A good instance is the growth of rural co-operative credit societies. First introduced by the British Government in 1904, there were in 1915 more than 17,000 such associations, with a total of 825,000 members and a working capital of nearly $30,000,000. These agricultural societies make loans for the purchase of stock, fodder, seed, manure, sinking of wells, purchase of Western agricultural machinery, and, in emergencies, personal maintenance. In the districts where they have established themselves they have greatly diminished the plague of usury practised by the "banyas," or village money-lenders, lowering the rate of interest from its former crushing range of 20 to 75 per cent. to a range averaging from 9 to 18 per cent. Of course such phenomena are as yet merely exceptions to a very dreary rule. Nevertheless, they all point toward a brighter morrow.[231]

But this brighter agricultural morrow is obviously far off, and in industry it seems to be farther still. Meanwhile the changing Orient is full of suffering and discontent. What wonder that many Orientals ascribe their troubles, not to the process of economic transition, but to the political control of European governments and the economic exploitation of Western capital. The result is agitation for emancipation from Western economic as well as Western political control. At the end of Chapter II we examined the movement among the Mohammedan peoples known as "Economic Pan-Islamism." A similar movement has arisen among the Hindus of India—the so-called "Swadeshi" movement. The Swadeshists declare that India's economic ills are almost entirely due to the "drain" of India's wealth to England and other Western lands. They therefore advocate a boycott of English goods until Britain grants India self-government, whereupon they propose to erect protective tariffs for Indian products, curb the activities of British capital, replace high-salaried English officials by natives, and thereby keep India's wealth at home.[232]

An analysis of these Swadeshist arguments, however, reveals them as inadequate to account for India's ills, which are due far more to the general economic trend of the times than to any specific defects of the British connection. British governance and British capital do cost money, but their undoubted efficiency in producing peace, order, security, and development must be considered as offsets to the higher costs which native rule and native capital would impose. As Sir Theodore Morison well says: "The advantages which the British Navy and British credit confer on India are a liberal offset to her expenditure on pensions and gratuities to her English servants.... India derives a pecuniary advantage from her connection with the British Empire. The answer, then, which I give to the question 'What economic equivalent does India get for foreign payments?' is this: India gets the equipment of modern industry, and she gets an administration favourable to economic evolution cheaper than she could provide it herself."[233] A comparison with Japan's much more costly defence budgets, inferior credit, and higher interest charges on both public and private loans is enlightening on this point.

In fact, some Indians themselves admit the fallacy of Swadeshist arguments. As one of them remarks: "The so-called economic 'drain' is nonsense. Most of the misery of late years is due to the rising cost of living—a world-wide phenomenon." And in proof of this he cites conditions in other Oriental countries, especially Japan.[234] As warm a friend of the Indian people as the British labour leader, Ramsay Macdonald, states: "One thing is quite evident, a tariff will not re-establish the old hand-industry of India nor help to revive village handicrafts. Factory and machine production, native to India itself, will throttle them as effectively as that of Lancashire and Birmingham has done in the past."[235]

Even more trenchant are the criticisms formulated by the Hindu writer Pramatha Nath Bose.[236] The "drain," says Mr. Bose, is ruining India. But would the Home Rule programme, as envisaged by most Swadeshists, cure India's economic ills? Under Home Rule these people would do the following things: (1) Substitute Englishmen for Indians in the Administration; (2) levy protective duties on Indian products; (3) grant State encouragement to Indian industries; (4) disseminate technical education. Now, how would these matters work out? The substitution of Indian for British officials would not lessen the "drain" as much as most Home Rulers think. The high-placed Indian officials who already exist have acquired European standards of living, so the new official corps would cost almost as much as the old. Also, "the influence of the example set by the well-to-do Indian officials would permeate Indian society more largely than at present, and the demand for Western articles would rise in proportion. So commercial exploitation by foreigners would not only continue almost as if they were Europeans, but might even increase." As to a protective tariff, it would attract European capital to India which would exploit labour and skim the profits. India has shown relatively little capacity for indigenous industrial development. Of course, even at low wages, many Indians might benefit, yet such persons would form only a tithe of the millions now starving—besides the fact that this industrialization would bring in many new social evils. As to State encouragement of industries, this would bring in Western capital even more than a protective tariff, with the results already stated. As for technical education, it is a worthy project, but, says Mr. Bose, "I am afraid the movement is too late, now. Within the last thirty years the Westerners and the Japanese have gone so far ahead of us industrially that it has been yearly becoming more and more difficult to compete with them."

In fact, Mr. Bose goes on to criticize the whole system of Western education, as applied to India. Neither higher nor lower education have proven panaceas. "Higher education has led to the material prosperity of a small section of our community, comprising a few thousands of well-to-do lawyers, doctors, and State servants. But their occupations being of a more or less unproductive or parasitic character, their well-being does not solve the problem of the improvement of India as a whole. On the contrary, as their taste for imported articles develops in proportion to their prosperity, they help to swell rather than diminish the economic drain from the country which is one of the chief causes of our impoverishment." Neither has elementary education "on the whole furthered the well-being of the multitude. It has not enabled the cultivators to 'grow two blades where one grew before.' On the contrary, it has distinctly diminished their efficiency by inculcating in the literate proletariat, who constitute the cream of their class, a strong distaste for their hereditary mode of living and their hereditary callings, and an equally strong taste for shoddy superfluities and brummagem fineries, and for occupations of a more or less parasitic character. They have, directly or indirectly, accelerated rather than retarded the decadence of indigenous industries, and have thus helped to aggravate their own economic difficulties and those of the entire community. What they want is more food—and New India vies with the Government in giving them what is called 'education' that does not increase their food-earning capacity, but on the contrary fosters in them tastes and habits which make them despise indigenous products and render them fit subjects for the exploitation of scheming capitalists, mostly foreign. Political and economic causes could not have led to the extinction of indigenous industry if they had not been aided by change of taste fostered by the Western environment of which the so-called 'education' is a powerful factor."

From all this Mr. Bose concludes that none of the reforms advocated by the Home Rulers would cure India's ills. "In fact, the chances are, she would be more inextricably entangled in the toils of Western civilization, without any adequate compensating advantage, and the grip of the West would close on her to crush her more effectively." Therefore, according to Mr. Bose, the only thing for India to do is to turn her back on everything Western and plunge resolutely into the traditional past. As he expresses it: "India's salvation lies, not in the region of politics, but outside it; not in aspiring to be one of the 'great' nations of the present day, but in retiring to her humble position—a position, to my mind, of solitary grandeur and glory; not in going forward on the path of Western civilization, but in going back from it so far as practicable; not in getting more and more entangled in the silken meshes of its finely knit, widespread net, but in escaping from it as far as possible."

Such are the drastic conclusions of Mr. Bose; conclusions shared to a certain extent by other Indian idealists like Rabindranath Tagore. But surely such projects, however idealistic, are the vainest fantasies. Whole peoples cannot arbitrarily cut themselves off from the rest of the world, like isolated individuals forswearing society and setting up as anchorites in the jungle. The time for "hermit nations" has passed, especially for a vast country like India, set at the cross-roads of the East, open to the sea, and already profoundly penetrated by Western ideas.

Nevertheless, such criticisms, appealing as they do to the strong strain of asceticism latent in the Indian nature, have affected many Indians who, while unable to concur in the conclusions, still try to evolve a "middle term," retaining everything congenial in the old system and grafting on a select set of Western innovations. Accordingly, these persons have elaborated programmes for a "new order" built on a blend of Hindu mysticism, caste, Western industry, and socialism.[237]

Now these schemes are highly ingenious. But they are not convincing. Their authors should remember the old adage that you cannot eat your cake and have it too. When we realize the abysmal antithesis between the economic systems of the old East and the modern West, any attempt to combine the most congenial points of both while eschewing their defects seems an attempt to reconcile irreconcilables and about as profitable as trying to square the circle. As Lowes Dickinson wisely observes: "Civilization is a whole. Its art, its religion, its way of life, all hang together with its economic and technical development. I doubt whether a nation can pick and choose; whether, for instance, the East can say, 'We will take from the West its battleships, its factories, its medical science; we will not take its social confusion, its hurry and fatigue, its ugliness, its over-emphasis on activity.'... So I expect the East to follow us, whether it like it or no, into all these excesses, and to go right through, not round, all that we have been through on its way to a higher phase of civilization."[238]

This seems to be substantially true. Judged by the overwhelming body of evidence, the East, in its contemporary process of transformation, will follow the West—avoiding some of our more patent mistakes, perhaps, but, in the main, proceeding along similar lines. And, as already stated, this transformation is modifying every phase of Eastern life. We have already examined the process at work in the religious, political, and economic phases. To the social phase let us now turn.

FOOTNOTES:

[206] F. B. Fisher, India's Silent Revolution, p. 53 (New York, 1920).

[207] Rev. A. J. Brown, "Economic Changes in Asia," The Century, March, 1904.

[208] I. e. the purveyor of the native vegetable-oils.

[209] R. Mukerjee, The Foundations of Indian Economics, p. 5 (London, 1916).

[210] On these points, see Fisher, op. cit.; Sir T. Morison, The Economic Transition in India (London, 1911); Sir Valentine Chirol, Indian Unrest (London, 1910); D. H. Dodwell, "Economic Transition in India," Economic Journal, December, 1910; J. P. Jones, "The Present Situation in India," Journal of Race Development, July, 1910.

[211] L. Bertrand, Le Mirage oriental, pp. 20-21 (Paris, 1910).

[212] Sir T. Morison, The Economic Transition in India, p. 181.

[213] Quoted by Jones, supra.

[214] The Indian Review (Madras), 1910.

[215] Clarence Poe, "What the Orient can Teach Us," World's Work, July, 1911.

[216] C. S. Cooper, The Modernizing of the Orient, p. 5 (New York, 1914).

[217] Morison, op. cit., p. 242.

[218] H. N. Brailsford, The War of Steel and Gold, p. 114 (London, 1915).

[219] A. Métin, L'Inde d'aujourd'hui: Étude sociale, p. 336 (Paris, 1918).

[220] In his book, Trois Ans en Perse (Paris, 1858).

[221] Brailsford, op. cit., pp. 83, 114-115.

[222] Regarding conditions in China, especially the extraordinary discipline and working ability of the Chinaman, see my Rising Tide of Colour against White World-Supremacy, pp. 28-30, 243-251.

[223] Métin, op. cit., p. 337.

[224] A. Yusuf Ali, Life and Labour in India, p. 183 (London, 1907).

[225] "India in the Years 1917-1918" (official publication—Calcutta).

[226] Young and Ferrers, India in Conflict, pp. 15-17 (London, 1920).

[227] Sir W. M. Ramsay, "The Turkish Peasantry of Anatolia," Quarterly Review, January, 1918.

[228] I. e. peasants and landlords.

[229] J. Chailley Administrative Problems of British India, p. 339 (London, 1910—English translation).

[230] Mukerjee, op. cit., p. 9.

[231] On the co-operative movement in India, see Fisher, India's Silent Revolution, pp. 54-58; R. B. Ewebank, "The Co-operative Movement in India," Quarterly Review, April, 1916. India's economic problems, both agricultural and industrial, have been carefully studied by a large number of Indian economists, some of whose writings are extremely interesting. Some of the most noteworthy books, besides those of Mukerjee and Yusuf Ali, already quoted, are: Dadabhai Naoroji, Poverty and Un-British Rule in India (London, 1901); Romesh Dutt, The Economic History of India in the Victorian Age (London, 1906); H. H. Gosh, The Advancement of Industry (Calcutta, 1910); P. C. Ray, The Poverty Problem in India (Calcutta, 1895); M. G. Ranade, Essays on Indian Economics (Madras, 1920); Jadunath Sarkar, Economics of British India (Calcutta, 1911).

[232] The best compendium of Swadeshist opinion is the volume containing pronouncements from all the Swadeshi leaders, entitled, The Swadeshi Movement: A Symposium (Madras, 1910). See also writings of the economists Gosh, Mukerjee, Ray, and Sarkar, above quoted, as well as the various writings of the nationalist agitator Lajpat Rai. A good summary interpretation is found in M. Glotz, "Le Mouvement 'Swadeshi' dans l'Inde," Revue du Mois, July, 1913.

[233] Sir T. Morison, The Economic Transition in India, pp. 240-241. Also see Sir Valentine Chirol, Indian Unrest, pp. 255-279; William Archer, India and the Future, pp. 131-157.

[234] Syed Sirdar Ali Khan, India of To-day, p. 19 (Bombay, 1908).

[235] J. Ramsay Macdonald, The Government of India, p. 133 (London, 1920).

[236] In The Hindustan Review (Calcutta), 1917.

[237] Good examples are found in the writings of Mukerjee and Lajpat Rai, already quoted.

[238] G. Lowes Dickinson, An Essay on the Civilizations of India, China, and Japan, pp. 84-85 (London, 1914).


CHAPTER VIII

SOCIAL CHANGE

The momentous nature of the contemporary transformation of the Orient is nowhere better attested than by the changes effected in the lives of its peoples. That dynamic influence of the West which is modifying governmental forms, political concepts, religious beliefs, and economic processes is proving equally potent in the range of social phenomena. In the third chapter of this volume we attempted a general survey of Western influence along all the above lines. In the present chapter we shall attempt a detailed consideration of the social changes which are to-day taking place.

These social changes are very great, albeit many of them may not be so apparent as the changes in other fields. So firm is the hold of custom and tradition on individual, family, and group life in the Orient that superficial observers of the East are prone to assert that these matters are still substantially unaltered, however pronounced may have been the changes on the external, material side. Yet such is not the opinion of the closest students of the Orient, and it is most emphatically not the opinion of Orientals themselves. These generally stress the profound social changes which are going on.

And it is their judgments which seem to be the more correct. To say that the East is advancing "materially" but standing still "socially" is to ignore the elemental truth that social systems are altered quite as much by material things as by abstract ideas. Who that looks below the surface can deny the social, moral, and civilizing power of railroads, post-offices, and telegraph lines? Does it mean nothing socially as well as materially that the East is adopting from the West a myriad innovations, weighty and trivial, important and frivolous, useful and baneful? Does it mean nothing socially as well as materially that the Prophet's tomb at Medina is lit by electricity and that picture post-cards are sold outside the Holy Kaaba at Mecca? It may seem mere grotesque piquancy that the muezzin should ride to the mosque in a tram-car, or that the Moslem business man should emerge from his harem, read his morning paper, motor to an office equipped with a prayer-rug, and turn from his devotions to dictaphone and telephone. Yet why assume that his life is moulded by mosque, harem, and prayer-rug, and yet deny the things of the West a commensurate share in the shaping of his social existence? Now add to these tangible innovations intangible novelties like scientific education, Occidental amusements, and the partial emancipation of women, and we begin to get some idea of the depth and scope of the social transformation which is going on.

In those parts of the Orient most open to Western influences this social transformation has attained notable proportions for more than a generation. When the Hungarian Orientalist Vambéry returned to Constantinople in 1896 after forty years' absence, he stood amazed at the changes which had taken place, albeit Constantinople was then subjected to the worst repression of the Hamidian régime. "I had," he writes, "continually to ask myself this question: Is it possible that these are my Turks of 1856; and how can all these transformations have taken place? I was astonished at the aspect of the city; at the stone buildings which had replaced the old wooden ones; at the animation of the streets, in which carriages and tram-cars abounded, whereas forty years before only saddle-animals were used; and when the strident shriek of the locomotive mingled with the melancholy calls from the minarets, all that I saw and heard seemed to me a living protest against the old adage: 'La bidaat fil Islam'—'There is nothing to reform in Islam.' My astonishment became still greater when I entered the houses and was able to appreciate the people, not only by their exteriors but still more by their manner of thought. The effendi class[239] of Constantinople seemed to me completely transformed in its conduct, outlook, and attitude toward foreigners."[240]

Vambéry stresses the inward as well as outward evolution of the Turkish educated classes, for he says: "Not only in his outward aspect, but also in his home-life, the present-day Turk shows a strong inclination to the manners and habits of the West, in such varied matters as furniture, table-manners, sex-relations, and so forth. This is of the very greatest significance. For a people may, to be sure, assimilate foreign influences in the intellectual field, if it be persuaded of their utility and advantage; but it gives up with more difficulty customs and habits which are in the blood. One cannot over-estimate the numerous sacrifices which, despite everything, the Turks have made in this line. I find all Turkish society, even the

Mollahs,[241] penetrated with the necessity of a union with Western civilization. Opinions may differ as to the method of assimilation: some wish to impress on the foreign civilization a national character; others, on the contrary, are partisans of our intellectual culture, such as it is, and reprobate any kind of modification."[242]

Most significant of all, Vambéry found even the secluded women of the harems, "those bulwarks of obscurantism," notably changed. "Yes, I repeat, the life of women in Turkey seems to me to have been radically transformed in the last forty years, and it cannot be denied that this transformation has been produced by internal conviction as much as by external pressure." Noting the spread of female education, and the increasing share of women in reform movements, Vambéry remarks: "This is of vital importance, for when women shall begin to act in the family as a factor of modern progress, real reforms, in society as well as in the state, cannot fail to appear."[243]

In India a similar permeation of social life by Westernism is depicted by the Moslem liberal, S. Khuda Bukhsh, albeit Mr. Bukhsh, being an insider, lays greater emphasis upon the painful aspects of the inevitable transition process from old to new. He is not unduly pessimistic, for he recognizes that "the age of transition is necessarily to a certain extent an age of laxity of morals, indifference to religion, superficial culture, and gossiping levity. These are passing ills which time itself will cure." Nevertheless, he does not minimize the critical aspects of the present situation, which implies nothing less than the breakdown of the old social system. "The clearest result of this breakdown of our old system of domestic life and social customs under the assault of European ideas," he says, "is to be found in two directions—in our religious beliefs and in our social life. The old system, with all its faults, had many redeeming virtues." To-day this old system, narrow-minded but God-fearing, has been replaced by a "strange independence of thought and action. Reverence for age, respect for our elders, deference to the opinions of others, are fast disappearing.... Under the older system the head of the family was the sole guide and friend of its members. His word had the force of law. He was, so to speak, the custodian of the honour and prestige of the family. From this exalted position he is now dislodged, and the most junior member now claims equality with him."[244]

Mr. Bukhsh deplores the current wave of extravagance, due to the wholesale adoption of European customs and modes of living. "What," he asks, "has happened here in India? We have adopted European costume, European ways of living, even the European vices of drinking and gambling, but none of their virtues. This must be remedied. We must learn at the feet of Europe, but not at the sacrifice of our Eastern individuality. But this is precisely what we have not done. We have dabbled a little in English and European history, and we have commenced to despise our religion, our literature, our history, our traditions. We have unlearned the lessons of our history and our civilization, and in their place we have secured nothing solid and substantial to hold society fast in the midst of endless changes." In fine: "Destruction has done its work, but the work of construction has not yet begun."[245]

Like Vambéry, Bukhsh lays strong emphasis on the increasing emancipation of women. No longer regarded as mere "child-bearing machines," the Mohammedan women of India "are getting educated day by day, and now assert their rights. Though the purdah system[246] still prevails, it is no longer that severe, stringent, and unreasonable seclusion of women which existed fifty years ago. It is gradually relaxing, and women are getting, step by step, rights and liberties which must in course of time end in the complete emancipation of Eastern womanhood. Forty years ago women meekly submitted to neglect, indifference, and even harsh treatment from their husbands, but such is the case no longer."[247]

These two descriptions of social conditions in the Near and Middle East respectively enable one to get a fair idea of the process of change which is going on. Of course it must not be forgotten that both writers deal primarily with the educated upper classes of the large towns. Nevertheless, the leaven is working steadily downward, and with every decade is affecting wider strata of the native populations.

The spread of Western education in the East during the past few decades has been truly astonishing, because it is the exact antithesis of the Oriental educational system. The traditional "education" of the entire Orient, from Morocco to China, was a mere memorizing of sacred texts combined with exercises of religious devotion. The Mohammedan or Hindu student spent long years reciting to his master (a "holy man") interminable passages from books which, being written in classic Arabic or Sanskrit, were unintelligible to him, so that he usually did not understand a word of what he was saying. No more deadening system for the intellect could possibly have been devised. Every part of the brain except the memory atrophied, and the wonder is that any intellectual initiative or original thinking ever appeared.

Even to-day the old system persists, and millions of young Orientals are still wasting their time at this mind-petrifying nonsense. But alongside the old there has arisen a new system, running the whole educational gamut from kindergartens to universities, where Oriental youth is being educated along Western lines. These new-type educational establishments are of every kind. Besides schools and universities giving a liberal education and fitting students for government service or the professions, there are numerous technical schools turning out skilled agriculturists or engineers, while good normal schools assure a supply of teachers qualified to instruct coming student-generations. Both public and private effort furthers Western education in the East. All the European governments have favoured Western education in the lands under their control, particularly the British in India and Egypt, while various Christian missionary bodies have covered the East with a network of schools and colleges. Also many Oriental governments like Turkey and the native states of India have made sincere efforts to spread Western education among their peoples.[248]

Of course, as in any new development, the results so far obtained are far from ideal. The vicious traditions of the past handicap or partially pervert the efforts of the present. Eastern students are prone to use their memories rather than their intellects, and seek to cram their way quickly through examinations to coveted posts rather than acquire knowledge and thus really fit themselves for their careers. The result is that many fail, and these unfortunates, half-educated and spoiled for any sort of useful occupation, vegetate miserably, come to hate that Westernism which they do not understand, and give themselves up to anarchistic revolutionary agitation. Sir Alfred Lyall well describes the dark side of Western education in the East when he says of India: "Ignorance is unquestionably the root of many evils; and it was natural that in the last century certain philosophers should have assumed education to be a certain cure for human delusions; and that statesmen like Macaulay should have declared education to be the best and surest remedy for political discontent and for law-breaking. In any case, it was the clear and imperative duty of the British Government to attempt the intellectual emancipation of India as the best justification of British rule. We have since discovered by experience, that, although education is a sovereign remedy for many ills—is indeed indispensable to healthy progress—yet an indiscriminate or superficial administration of this potent medicine may engender other disorders. It acts upon the frame of an antique society as a powerful dissolvent, heating weak brains, stimulating rash ambitions, raising inordinate expectations of which the disappointment is bitterly resented."[249]

Indeed, some Western observers of the Orient, particularly colonial officials, have been so much impressed by the political and social dangers arising from the existence of this "literate

130

proletariat" of semi-educated failures that they are tempted to condemn the whole venture of Western education in the East as a mistake. Lord Cromer, for example, was decidedly sceptical of the worth of the Western-educated Egyptian,[250] while a prominent Anglo-Indian official names as the chief cause of Indian unrest, "the system of education, which we ourselves introduced—advisedly so far as the limited vision went of those responsible; blindly in view of the inevitable consequences."[251]

Yet these pessimistic judgments do not seem to make due allowance for the inescapable evils attendant on any transition stage. Other observers of the Orient have made due allowance for this factor. Vambéry, for instance, notes the high percentage of honest and capable native officials in the British Indian and French North African civil service (the bulk of these officials, of course, Western-educated men), and concludes: "Strictly conservative Orientals, and also fanatically inclined Europeans, think that with the entrance of our culture the primitive virtues of the Asiatics have been destroyed, and that the uncivilized Oriental was more faithful, more honest, and more reliable than the Asiatic educated on European principles. This is a gross error. It may be true of the half-educated, but not of the Asiatic in whose case the intellectual evolution is founded on the solid basis of a thorough, systematic education."[252]

And, whatever may be the ills attendant upon Western education in the East, is it not the only practicable course to pursue? The impact of Westernism upon the Orient is too ubiquitous to be confined to books. Granting, therefore, for the sake of argument, that colonial governments could have prevented Western education in the formal sense, would not the Oriental have learned in other ways? Surely it is better that he should learn through good texts under the supervision of qualified teachers, rather than tortuously in perverted—and more dangerous—fashion.

The importance of Western education in the East is nowhere better illustrated than in the effects it is producing in ameliorating the status of women. The depressed condition of women throughout the Orient is too well known to need elaboration. Bad enough in Mohammedan countries, it is perhaps at its worst among the Hindus of India, with child-marriage, the virtual enslavement of widows (burned alive till prohibited by English law), and a seclusion more strict even than that of the "harem" of Moslem lands. As an English writer well puts it: "'Ladies first,' we say in the West; in the East it is 'ladies last.' That sums up succinctly the difference in the domestic ideas of the two civilizations."[253]

Under these circumstances it might seem as though no breath of the West could yet have reached these jealously secluded creatures. Yet, as a matter of fact, Western influences have already profoundly affected the women of the upper classes, and female education, while far behind that of the males, has attained considerable proportions. In the more advanced parts of the Orient like Constantinople, Cairo, and the cities of India, distinctly "modern" types of women have appeared, the self-supporting, self-respecting—and respected—woman school-teacher being especially in evidence.

The social consequences of this rising status of women, not only to women themselves but also to the community at large, are very important. In the East the harem is, as Vambéry well says, the "bulwark of obscurantism."[254] Ignorant and fanatical herself, the harem woman implants her ignorance and fanaticism in her sons as well as in her daughters. What could be a worse handicap for the Eastern "intellectual" than his boyhood years spent "behind the veil"? No wonder that enlightened Oriental fathers have been in the habit of sending their boys to school at the earliest possible age in order to get them as soon as possible out of the stultifying atmosphere of harem life. Yet even this has proved merely a palliative. Childhood impressions are ever the most lasting, and so long as one-half of the Orient remained untouched by progressive influences Oriental progress had to be begun again de novo with every succeeding generation.

The increasing number of enlightened Oriental women is remedying this fatal defect. As a Western writer well says: "Give the mothers education and the whole situation is transformed. Girls who are learning other things than the unintelligible phrases of the Koran are certain to impart such knowledge, as daughters, sisters, and mothers, to their respective households. Women who learn housewifery, methods of modern cooking, sewing, and sanitation in the domestic-economy schools, are bound to cast about the home upon their return the atmosphere of a civilized community. The old-time picture of the Oriental woman spending her hours upon divans, eating sweetmeats, and indulging in petty and degrading gossip with the servants, or with women as ignorant as herself, will be changed. The new woman will be a companion rather than a slave or a toy of her husband. Marriage will advance from the stage of a paltry trade in bodies to something like a real union, involving respect towards the woman by both sons and fathers, while in a new pride of relationship the woman herself will be discovered."[255]

These men and women of the newer Orient reflect their changing ideas in their changing standards of living. Although this is most evident among the wealthier elements of the towns, it is perceptible in all classes of the population. Rich and poor, urban and rural, the Orientals are altering their living standards towards those of the West. And this involves social changes of the most far-reaching character, because few antitheses could be sharper than the living conditions prevailing respectively in the traditional East and in the modern Western world. This basic difference lies, not in wealth (the East, like the West, knows great riches as well as great poverty), but rather in comfort—using the word in its broad sense. The wealthy Oriental of the old school spends most of his money on Oriental luxuries, like fine raiment, jewels, women, horses, and a great retinue of attendants, and then hoards the rest. But of "comfort," in the Western sense, he knows virtually nothing, and it is safe to say that he lives under domestic conditions which a Western artisan would despise.[256]

To-day, however, the Oriental is discovering "comfort." And, high or low, he likes it very well. All the myriad things which make our lives easier and more agreeable—lamps, electric light, sewing-machines, clocks, whisky, umbrellas, sanitary plumbing, and a thousand others: all these things, which to us are more or less matters of course, are to the Oriental so many delightful discoveries, of irresistible appeal. He wants them, and he gets them in ever-increasing quantities. But this produces some rather serious complications. His private economy is more or less thrown out of gear. This opening of a whole vista of new wants means a portentous rise in his standard of living. And where is he going to find the money to pay for it? If he be poor, he has to skimp on his bare necessities. If he be rich, he hates to forgo his traditional luxuries. The upshot is a universal growth of extravagance. And, in this connection, it is well to bear in mind that the peoples of the Near and Middle East, taken as a whole, have never been really thrifty. Poor the masses may have been, and thus obliged to live frugally, but they have always proved themselves "good spenders" when opportunity offers. The way in which a Turkish peasant or a Hindu ryot will squander his savings and run into debt over festivals, marriages, funerals, and other social events is astounding to Western observers.[257] Now add to all this the fact that in the Orient, as in the rest of the world, the cost of the basic necessaries of life—food, clothing, fuel, and shelter, has risen greatly during the past two decades, and we can realize the gravity of the problem which higher Oriental living-standards involves.[258]

Certain it is that the struggle for existence is growing keener and that the pressure of poverty is getting more severe. With the basic necessaries rising in price, and with many things considered necessities which were considered luxuries or entirely unheard of a generation ago, the Oriental peasant or town working-man is finding it harder and harder to make both ends meet. As one writer well phrases it: "These altered economic conditions have not as yet brought the ability to meet them. The cost of living has increased faster than the resources of the people."[259]

One of the main (though not sufficiently recognized) causes of the economic-social crisis through which the Orient is to-day passing is over-population. The quick breeding tendencies of Oriental peoples have always been proverbial, and have been due not merely to strong sexual appetites but also to economic reasons like the harsh exploitation of women and children, and perhaps even more to religious doctrines enjoining early marriage and the begetting of numerous sons. As a result, Oriental populations have always pressed close upon the limits of subsistence. In the past, however, this pressure was automatically lightened by factors like war, misgovernment, pestilence, and famine, which swept off such multitudes of people that, despite high birth-rates, populations remained at substantially a fixed level. But here, as in every other phase of Eastern life, Western influences have radically altered the situation. The extension of European political control over Eastern lands has meant the putting down of internal strife, the diminution of governmental abuses, the decrease of disease, and the lessening of the blight of famine. In other words, those "natural" checks which previously kept down the population have been diminished or abolished, and in response to the life-saving activities of the West, the enormous death-rate which in the past has kept Oriental populations from excessive multiplication is falling to proportions comparable with the low death-rate of Western nations. But to lower the Orient's prodigious birth-rate is quite another matter. As a matter of fact, that birth-rate keeps up with undiminished vigour, and the consequence has been a portentous increase of population in nearly every portion of the Orient under Western political control. In fact, even those Oriental countries which have maintained their independence have more or less adopted Western life-conserving methods, and have experienced in greater or less degree an accelerated increase of population.

The phenomena of over-population are best seen in India. Most of India has been under British control for the greater part of a century. Even a century ago, India was densely populated, yet in the intervening hundred years the population has increased between two and three fold.[260] Of course, factors like improved agriculture, irrigation, railways, and the introduction of modern industry enable India to support a much larger population than it could have done at the time of the British Conquest. Nevertheless, the evidence is clear that excessive multiplication has taken place. Nearly all qualified students of the problem concur on this point. Forty years ago the Duke of Argyll stated: "Where there is no store, no accumulation, no wealth; where the people live from hand to mouth from season to season on a low diet; and where, nevertheless, they breed and multiply at such a rate; there we can at least see that this power and force of multiplication is no evidence even of safety, far less of comfort." Towards the close of the last century, Sir William Hunter termed population India's "fundamental problem," and continued: "The result of civilized rule in India has been to produce a strain on the food-producing powers of the country such as it had never before to bear. It has become a truism of Indian statistics that the removal of the old cruel checks on population in an Asiatic country is by no means an unmixed blessing to an Asiatic people."[261] Lord Cromer remarks of India's poverty: "Not only cannot it be remedied by mere philanthropy, but it is absolutely certain—cruel and paradoxical though it may appear to say so—that philanthropy enhances the evil. In the days of Akhbar or Shah Jehan, cholera, famine, and internal strife kept down the population. Only the fittest survived. Now internal strife is forbidden, and philanthropy steps in and says that no single life shall be sacrificed if science and Western energy or skill can save it. Hence the growth of a highly congested population, vast numbers of whom are living on a bare margin of subsistence. The fact that one of the greatest difficulties of governing the teeming masses of the East is caused by good and humane government should be recognized. It is too often ignored."[262]

William Archer well states the matter when, in answer to the query why improved external conditions have not brought India prosperity, he says: "The reason, in my view, is simple: namely, that the benefit of good government is, in part at any rate, nullified, when the people take advantage of it, not to save and raise their standard of living, but to breed to the very margin of subsistence. Henry George used to point out that every mouth that came into the world brought two hands along with it; but though the physiological fact is undeniable, the economic deduction suggested will not hold good except in conditions that permit of the profitable employment of the two hands.... If mouths increase in a greater ratio than food, the tendency must be towards greater poverty."[263]

It is one of the most unfortunate aspects of the situation that very few Oriental thinkers yet realize that over-population is a prime cause of Oriental poverty. Almost without exception they lay the blame to political factors, especially to Western political control. In fact, the only case that I know of where an Eastern thinker has boldly faced the problem and has courageously advocated birth-control is in the book published five years ago by P. K. Wattal, a native official of the Indian Finance Department, entitled, The Population Problem of India.[264] This pioneer volume is written with such ability and is of such apparent significance as an indication of the awakening of Orientals to a more rational attitude, that it merits special attention.

Mr. Wattal begins his book by a plea to his fellow-countrymen to look at the problem rationally and without prejudice. "This essay," he says, "should not be constituted into an attack on the spiritual civilization of our country, or even indirectly into a glorification of the materialism of the West. The object in view is that we should take a somewhat more matter-of-fact view of the main problem of life, viz., how to live in this world. We are a poor people; the fact is indisputable. Our poverty is, perhaps, due to a great many causes. But I put it to every one of us whether he has not at some of the most momentous periods of his life been handicapped by having to support a large family, and whether this encumbrance has not seriously affected the chances of advancement warranted by early promise and exceptional endowment. This question should be viewed by itself. It is a physical fact, and has nothing to do with political environment or religious obligation. If we have suffered from the consequences of that mistake, is it not a duty that we owe to ourselves and to our progeny that its evil effects shall be mitigated as far as possible? There is no greater curse than poverty—I say this with due respect to our spiritualism. It is not in a spirit of reproach that restraint in married life is urged in these pages. It is solely from a vivid realization of the hardships caused by large families and a profound sympathy with the difficulties under which large numbers of respectable persons struggle through life in this country that I have made bold to speak in plain terms what comes to every young man, but which he does not care to give utterance to in a manner that would prevent the recurrence of the evil."[265]

After this appeal to reason in his readers, Mr. Wattal develops his thesis. The first prime cause of over-population in India, he asserts, is early marriage. Contrary to Western lands, where population is kept down by prudential marriages and by birth-control, "for the Hindus marriage is a sacrament which must be performed, regardless of the fitness of the parties to bear the responsibilities of a mated existence. A Hindu male must marry and beget children—sons, if you please—to perform his funeral rites lest his spirit wander uneasily in the waste places of the earth. The very name of son, 'putra,' means one who saves his father's soul from the hell called Puta. A Hindu maiden unmarried at puberty is a source of social obloquy to her family and of damnation to her ancestors. Among the Mohammedans, who are not handicapped by such penalties, the married state is equally common, partly owing to Hindu example and partly to the general conditions of primitive society, where a wife is almost a necessity both as a domestic drudge and as a helpmate in field work."[266] The worst of the matter is that, despite the efforts of social reformers child-marriage seems to be increasing. The census of 1911 showed that during the decade 1901-10 the numbers of married females per 1000 of ages 0-5 years rose from 13 to 14; of ages 5-10 from 102 to 105; of 10-15 from 423 to 430, and of 15-20 from 770 to 800. In other words, in the year 1911, out of every 1000 Indian girls, over one-tenth were married before they were 10 years old, nearly one-half before they were 15, and four-fifths before they were 20.[267]

The result of all this is a tremendous birth-rate, but this is "no matter for congratulation. We have heard so often of our high death-rate and the means for combating it, but can it be seriously believed that with a birth-rate of 30 per 1000 it is possible to go on as we are doing with the death-rate brought down to the level of England or Scotland? Is there room enough in the country for the population to increase so fast as 20 per 1000 every year? We are paying the inevitable penalty of bringing into this world more persons than can be properly cared for, and therefore if we wish fewer deaths to occur in this country the births must be reduced to the level of the countries where the death-rate is low. It is, therefore, our high birth-rate that is the social danger; the high death-rate, however regrettable, is merely an incident of our high birth-rate."[268]

Mr. Wattal then describes the cruel items in India's death-rate; the tremendous female mortality, due largely to too early childbirth, and the equally terrible infant mortality, nearly 50 per cent. of infant deaths being due to premature birth or debility at birth. These are the inevitable penalties of early and universal marriage. For, in India, "everybody marries, fit or unfit, and is a parent at the earliest possible age permitted by nature." This process is highly disgenic; it is plainly lowering the quality and sapping the vigour of the race. It is the lower elements of the population, the negroid aboriginal tribes and the Pariahs or Outcastes, who are gaining the fastest. Also the vitality of the whole population seems to be lowering. The census figures show that the number of elderly persons is decreasing, and that the average statistical expectation of life is falling. "The coming generation is severely handicapped at start in life. And the chances of living to a good old age are considerably smaller than they were, say thirty or forty years ago. Have we ever paused to consider what it means to us in the life of the nation as a whole? It means that the people who alone by weight of experience and wisdom are fitted for the posts of command in the various public activities of the country are snatched away by death; and that the guidance and leadership which belongs to age and mature judgment in the countries of the West fall in India to younger and consequently to less trustworthy persons."[269]

After warning his fellow-countrymen that neither improved methods of agriculture, the growth of industry, nor emigration can afford any real relief to the growing pressure of population on means of subsistence, he notes a few hopeful signs that, despite the hold of religion and custom, the people are beginning to realize the situation and that in certain parts of India there are foreshadowings of birth-control. For example, he quotes from the census report for 1901 this official explanation of a slight drop in the birth-rate of Bengal: "The postponement of the age of marriage cannot wholly account for the diminished rate of reproduction. The deliberate avoidance of child-bearing must also be partly responsible.... It is a matter of common belief that among the tea-garden coolies of Assam means are frequently taken to prevent conception, or to procure abortion." And the report of the

Sanitary Commissioner of Assam for 1913 states: "An important factor in producing the defective birth-rate appears to be due to voluntary limitation of birth."[270]

However, these beginnings of birth-control are too local and partial to afford any immediate relief to India's growing over-population. Wider appreciation of the situation and prompt action are needed. "The conclusion is irresistible. We can no longer afford to shut our eyes to the social canker in our midst. In the land of the bullock-cart, the motor has come to stay. The competition is now with the more advanced races of the West, and we cannot tell them what Diogenes said to Alexander: 'Stand out of my sunshine.' After the close of this gigantic World War theories of population will perhaps be revised and a reversion in favour of early marriage and larger families may be counted upon. But, (1) that will be no solution to our own population problem, and (2) this reaction will be only for a time.... The law of population may be arrested in its operation, but there is no way of escaping it."[271]

So concludes this striking little book. Furthermore, we must remember that, although India may be the acutest sufferer from over-population, conditions in the entire Orient are basically the same, prudential checks and rational birth-control being everywhere virtually absent.[272] Remembering also that, besides over-population, there are other economic and social evils previously discussed, we cannot be surprised to find in all Eastern lands much acute poverty and social degradation.

Both the rural and urban masses usually live on the bare margin of subsistence. The English economist Brailsford thus describes the condition of the Egyptian peasantry: "The villages exhibited a poverty such as I have never seen even in the mountains of anarchical Macedonia or among the bogs of Donegal.... The villages are crowded slums of mud hovels, without a tree, a flower, or a garden. The huts, often without a window or a levelled floor, are minute dungeons of baked mud, usually of two small rooms neither whitewashed nor carpeted. Those which I entered were bare of any visible property, save a few cooking utensils, a mat to serve as a bed, and a jar which held the staple food of maize."[273] As for the poorer Indian peasants, a British sanitary official thus depicts their mode of life: "One has actually to see the interior of the houses, in which each family is often compelled to live in a single small cell, made of mud walls and with a mud floor; containing small yards littered with rubbish, often crowded with cattle; possessing wells permeated by rain soaking through this filthy surface; and frequently jumbled together in inchoate masses called towns and cities."[274]

In the cities, indeed, conditions are even worse than in the country, the slums of the Orient surpassing the slums of the West. The French publicist Louis Bertrand paints positively nauseating pictures of the poorer quarters of the great Levantine towns like Cairo, Constantinople, and Jerusalem. Omitting his more poignant details, here is his description of a Cairo tenement: "In Cairo, as elsewhere in Egypt, the wretchedness and grossness of the poorer-class dwellings are perhaps even more shocking than in the other Eastern lands. Two or three dark, airless rooms usually open on a hall-way not less obscure. The plaster, peeling off from the ceilings and the worm-eaten laths of the walls, falls constantly to the filthy floors. The straw mats and bedding are infested by innumerable vermin."[275]

In India it is the same story. Says Fisher: "Even before the growth of her industries had begun, the cities of India presented a baffling housing problem. Into the welter of crooked streets and unsanitary habits of an Oriental city these great industrial plants are wedging their thousands of employees. Working from before dawn until after dark, men and women are too exhausted to go far from the plant to sleep, if they can help it. When near-by houses are jammed to suffocation, they live and sleep in the streets. In Calcutta, twenty years ago,[276] land had reached $200,000 an acre in the overcrowded tenement districts."[277] Of Calcutta, a Western writer remarks: "Calcutta is a shame even in the East. In its slums, mill hands and dock coolies do not live; they pig. Houses choke with unwholesome breath; drains and compounds fester in filth. Wheels compress decaying refuse in the roads; cows drink from wells soaked with sewage, and the floors of bakeries are washed in the same pollution."[278] In the other industrial centres of India, conditions are practically the same. A Bombay native sanitary official stated in a report on the state of the tenement district, drawn up in 1904: "In such houses—the breeders of germs and bacilli, the centres of disease and poverty, vice, and crime—have people of all kinds, the diseased, the dissolute, the drunken, the improvident, been indiscriminately herded and tightly packed in vast hordes to dwell in close association with each other."[279]

Furthermore, urban conditions seem to be getting worse rather than better. The problem of congestion, in particular, is assuming ever graver proportions. Already in the opening years of the present century the congestion in the great industrial centres of India like Calcutta, Bombay, and Lucknow averaged three or four times the congestion of London. And the late war has rendered the housing crisis even more acute. In the East, as in the West, the war caused a rapid drift of population to the cities and at the same time stopped building owing to the prohibitive cost of construction. Hence, a prodigious rise in rents and a plague of landlord profiteering. Says Fisher: "Rents were raised as much as 300 per cent., enforced by eviction. Mass-meetings of protest in Bombay resulted in government action, fixing maximum rents for some of the tenements occupied by artisans and labourers. Setting maximum rental does not, however, make more room."[280]

And, of course, it must not be forgotten that higher rents are only one phase in a general rise in the cost of living that has been going on in the East for a generation and which has been particularly pronounced since 1914. More than a decade ago Bertrand wrote of the Near East: "From one end of the Levant to the other, at Constantinople as at Smyrna, Damascus, Beyrout, and Cairo, I heard the same complaints about the increasing cost of living; and these complaints were uttered by Europeans as well as by the natives."[281] To-day the situation is even more difficult. Says Sir Valentine Chirol of conditions in Egypt since the war: "The rise in wages, considerable as it has been, has ceased to keep pace with the inordinate rise in prices for the very necessities of life. This is particularly the case in the urban centres, where the lower classes—workmen, carters, cab-drivers, shopkeepers, and a host off minor employees—are hard put to it nowadays to make both ends meet."[282] As a result of all these hard conditions various phenomena of social degradation such as alcoholism, vice, and crime, are becoming increasingly common.[283] Last—but not least—there are growing symptoms of social unrest and revolutionary agitation, which we will examine in the next chapter.

FOOTNOTES:

[239] I. e. the educated upper class.

[240] Vambéry, La Turquie d'aujourd'hui et d'avant Quarante Ans, p. 13.

[241] I. e. the priestly class.

[242] Vambéry, La Turquie d'aujourd'hui et d'avant Quarante Ans, p. 15.

[243] Vambéry, La Turquie d'aujourd'hui et d'avant Quarante Ans, p. 51.

[244] Bukhsh, Essays: Indian and Islamic, pp. 221-226.

[245] Bukhsh, Essays: Indian and Islamic, p. 240.

[246] The purdah is the curtain separating the women's apartments from the rest of the house.

[247] Bukhsh, Essays: Indian and Islamic, pp. 254-255.

[248] For progress in Western education in the Orient, under both European and native auspices, see L. Bertrand, Le Mirage oriental, pp. 291-392; C. S. Cooper, The Modernizing of the Orient, pp. 3-13, 24-64.

[249] In his Introduction to Sir Valentine Chirol's Indian Unrest, p. xii.

[250] Cromer, Modern Egypt, Vol. II., pp. 228-243.

[251] J. D. Rees, The Real India, p. 162 (London, 1908).

[252] Vambéry, Western Culture in Eastern Lands, pp. 203-204.

[253] H. E. Compton, Indian Life in Town and Country, p. 98 (London, 1904).

[254] Vambéry, La Turquie d'aujourd'hui et d'avant Quarante Ans, p. 32.

[255] Cooper, op. cit., pp. 48-49.

[256] On this point of comfort v. luxury, see especially Sir Bampfylde Fuller, "East and West: A Study of Differences," Nineteenth Century and After, November, 1911.

[257] L. Bertrand, op. cit., 145-147; J. Chailley, Administrative Problems of British India, pp. 138-139. For increased expenditure on Western products, see A. J. Brown, "Economic Changes in Asia," The Century, March, 1904; J. P. Jones, "The Present Situation in India," Journal of Race Development, July, 1910; R. Mukerjee, The Foundations of Indian Economics, p. 5.

[258] For higher cost of living in the East, see Chirol, Indian Unrest, pp. 2-3; Fisher, India's Silent Revolution, pp. 46-60; Jones, op. cit.; T. T. Williams, "Inquiry into the Rise of Prices in India," Economic Journal, December, 1915.

[259] Brown, op. cit.

[260] At the beginning of the nineteenth century the population of India is roughly estimated to have been about 100,000,000. According to the census of 1911 the population was 315,000,000.

[261] Sir W. W. Hunter, The India of the Queen and Other Essays, p. 42 (London, 1903).

[262] Cromer, "Some Problems of Government in Europe and Asia," Nineteenth Century and After, May, 1913.

[263] Archer, India and the Future, pp. 157, 162 (London), 1918.

[264] P. K. Wattal, of the Indian Finance Department, Assistant Accountant-General. The book was published at Bombay, 1916.

[265] Wattal, pp. i-iii.

[266] Wattal, p. 3.

[267] Ibid., p. 12.

[268] Wattal, p. 14.

[269] Ibid., pp. 19-21.

[270] Wattal, p. 28.

[271] Ibid., p. 82.

[272] For conditions in the Near East, see Bertrand, pp. 110, 124, 125-128.

[273] H. N. Brailsford, The War of Steel and Gold, pp. 112-113. See also T. Rothstein, Egypt's Ruin, pp. 298-300 (London, 1910), Sir W. W. Ramsay, "The Turkish Peasantry of Anatolia," Quarterly Review, January, 1918.

[274] Dr. D. Ross, "Wretchedness a Cause of Political Unrest," The Survey, February 18, 1911.

[275] Bertrand, op. cit., pp. 111-112.

[276] I. e., in 1900.

[277] Fisher, India's Silent Revolution, p. 51.

[278] G. W. Stevens, In India. Quoted by Fisher, p. 51.

[279] Dr. Bhalchandra Krishna. Quoted by A. Yusuf Ali, Life and Labour in India, p. 35 (London, 1907).

[280] Fisher, pp. 51-52.

[281] Bertrand, p. 141.

[282] Sir V. Chirol, "England's Peril in Egypt," from the London Times, 1919.

[283] See Bertrand and Fisher, supra.

CHAPTER IX

SOCIAL UNREST AND BOLSHEVISM

Unrest is the natural concomitant of change—particularly of sudden change. Every break with past, however normal and inevitable, implies a necessity for readjustment to altered conditions which causes a temporary sense of restless disharmony until the required adjustment has been made. Unrest is not an exceptional phenomenon; it is always latent in every human society which has not fallen into complete stagnation, and a slight amount of unrest should be considered a sign of healthy growth rather than a symptom of disease. In fact, the minimum degrees of unrest are usually not called by that name, but are considered mere incidents of normal development. Under normal circumstances, indeed, the social organism functions like the human organism: it is being incessantly destroyed and as incessantly renewed in conformity with the changing conditions of life. These changes are sometimes very considerable, but they are so gradual that they are effected almost without being perceived. A healthy organism well attuned to its environment is always plastic. It instinctively senses environmental changes and adapts itself so rapidly that it escapes the injurious consequences of disharmony.

Far different is the character of unrest's acuter manifestations. These are infallible symptoms of sweeping changes, sudden breaks with the past, and profound maladjustments which are not being rapidly rectified. In other words, acute unrest denotes social ill-health and portends the possibility of one of those violent crises known as "revolutions."

The history of the Moslem East well exemplifies the above generalizations. The formative period of Saracenic civilization was characterized by rapid change and an intense idealistic ferment. The great "Motazelite" movement embraced many shades of thought, its radical wing professing religious, political, and social doctrines of a violent revolutionary nature. But this changeful period was superficial and brief. Arab vigour and the Islamic spirit proved unable permanently to leaven the vast inertia of the ancient East. Soon the old traditions reasserted themselves—somewhat modified, to be sure, yet basically the same Saracenic civilization became stereotyped, ossified, and with this ossification changeful unrest died away. Here and there the radical tradition was preserved and secretly handed down by a few obscure sects like the Kharidjites of Inner Arabia and the Bettashi dervishes; but these were mere cryptic episodes, of no general significance.

With the Mohammedan Revival at the beginning of the nineteenth century, however, symptoms of social unrest appeared once more. Wahabism aimed not merely at a reform of religious abuses but was also a general protest against the contemporary decadence of Moslem society. In many cases it took the form of a popular revolt against established governments. The same was true of the correlative Babbist movement in Persia, which took place about the same time.[284]

And of course these nascent stirrings were greatly stimulated by the flood of Western ideas and methods which, as the nineteenth century wore on, increasingly permeated the East. What, indeed, could be more provocative of unrest of every description than the resulting transformation of the Orient—a transformation so sudden, so intense, and necessitating so concentrated a process of adaptation that it was basically revolutionary rather than evolutionary in its nature? The details of these profound changes—political, religious, economic, social—we have already studied, together with the equally profound disturbance, bewilderment, and suffering afflicting all classes in this eminently transition period.

The essentially revolutionary nature of this transition period, as exemplified by India, is well described by a British economist.[285] What, he asks, could be more anachronistic than the contrast between rural and urban India? "Rural India is primitive or mediæval; city India is modern." In city India you will find every symbol of Western life, from banks and factories

140

down to the very "sandwichmen that you left in the London gutters." Now all this co-exists beside rural India. "And it is surely a fact unique in economic history that they should thus exist side by side. The present condition of India does not correspond with any period of European economic history." Imagine the effect in Europe of setting down modern and mediæval men together, with utterly disparate ideas. That has not happened in Europe because "European progress in the economic world has been evolutionary"; a process spread over centuries. In India, on the other hand, this economic transformation has been "revolutionary" in character.

How unevolutionary is India's economic transformation is seen by the condition of rural India.

"Rural India, though chiefly characterized by primitive usage, has been invaded by ideas that are intensely hostile to the old state of things It is primitive, but not consistently primitive. Competitive wages are paid side by side with customary wages. Prices are sometimes fixed by custom, but sometimes, too, by free economic causes. From the midst of a population deeply rooted in the soil, men are being carried away by the desire of better wages. In short, economic motives have suddenly and partially intruded themselves in the realm of primitive morality. And, if we turn to city India, we see a similar, though inverted, state of things.... In neither case has the mixture been harmonious or the fusion complete. Indeed, the two orders are too unrelated, too far apart, to coalesce with ease....

"India, then, is in a state of economic revolution throughout all the classes of an enormous and complex society. The only period in which Europe offered even faint analogies to modern India was the Industrial Revolution, from which even now we have not settled down into comparative stability. We may reckon it as a fortunate circumstance for Europe that the intellectual movement which culminated in the French Revolution did not coincide with the Industrial Revolution. If it had, it is possible that European society might have been hopelessly wrecked. But, as it was, even when the French Revolution had spent its force in the conquests of Napoleon, the Industrial Revolution stirred up enough social and political discontent. When whole classes of people are obliged by economic revolution to change their mode of life, it is inevitable that many should suffer. Discontent is roused. Political and destructive movements are certain to ensue. Not only the Revolutions of '48, but also the birth of the Socialist Party sprang from the Industrial Revolution.

"But that revolution was not nearly so sweeping as that which is now in operation in India. The invention of machinery and steam-power was, in Europe, but the crowning event of a long series of years in which commerce and industry had been constantly expanding, in which capital had been largely accumulated, in which economic principles had been gradually spreading.... No, the Indian economic revolution is vastly greater and more fundamental than our Industrial Revolution, great as that was. Railways have been built through districts where travel was almost impossible, and even roads are unknown. Factories have been built, and filled by men unused to industrial labour. Capital has been poured into the country, which was unprepared for any such development. And what are the consequences? India's social organization is being dissolved. The Brahmins are no longer priests. The ryot is no longer bound to the soil. The banya is no longer the sole purveyor of capital. The hand-weaver is threatened with extinction, and the brass-worker can no longer ply his craft. Think of the dislocation which this sudden change has brought about, of the many who can no longer follow their ancestral vocations, of the commotion which a less profound change produced in Europe, and you will understand what is the chief motive-power of the political unrest. It is small wonder. The wonder is that the unrest has been no greater than it is. Had India not been an Asiatic country, she would have been in fierce revolution long ago."

The above lines were of course written in the opening years of the twentieth century, before the world had been shattered by Armageddon and aggressive social revolution had established itself in semi-Asiatic Russia. But even during those pre-war years, other students of the Orient were predicting social disturbances of increasing gravity. Said the Hindu nationalist leader, Bipin Chandra Pal: "This so-called unrest is not really political. It is essentially an intellectual and spiritual upheaval, the forerunner of a mighty social revolution, with a new organon and a new philosophy of life behind it."[286] And the French publicist Chailley wrote of India: "There will be a series of economic revolutions, which must necessarily produce suffering and struggle."[287]

During this pre-war period the increased difficulty of living conditions, together with the adoption of Western ideas of comfort and kindred higher standards, seem to have been engendering friction between the different strata of the Oriental population. In 1911 a British sanitary expert assigned "wretchedness" as the root-cause of India's political unrest. After describing the deplorable living conditions of the Indian masses, he wrote: "It will of course be said at once that these conditions have existed in India from time immemorial, and are no more likely to cause unrest now than previously; but in my opinion unrest has always existed there in a subterranean form. Moreover, in the old days, the populace could make scarcely any comparison between their own condition and that of more fortunate people; now they can compare their own slums and terrible 'native quarters' with the much better ordered cantonments, stations, and houses of the British officials and even of their own wealthier brethren. So far as I can see, such misery is always the fundamental cause of all popular unrest.... Seditious meetings, political chatter, and 'aspirations' of babus and demagogues are only the superficial manifestations of the deeper disturbance."[288]

This growing social friction was indubitably heightened by the lack of interest of Orientals in the sufferings of all persons not bound to them by family, caste, or customary ties. Throughout the East, "social service," in the Western sense, is practically unknown. This fact is noted by a few Orientals themselves. Says an Indian writer, speaking of Indian town life: "There is no common measure of social conduct.... Hitherto, social reform in India has taken account only of individual or family life. As applied to mankind in the mass, and especially to those soulless agglomerations of seething humanity which we call cities, it is a gospel yet to be preached."[289] As an American sociologist remarked of the growing slum evil throughout the industrialized Orient: "The greatest danger is due to the fact that Orientals do not have the high Western sense of the value of the life of the individual, and are, comparatively speaking, without any restraining influence similar to our own enlightened public opinion, which has been roused by the struggles of a century of industrial strife. Unless these elements can be supplied, there is danger of suffering and of abuses worse than any the West has known."[290]

All this diffused social unrest was centring about two recently emerged elements: the Western-educated intelligentsia and the industrial proletariat of the factory towns. The revolutionary tendencies of the intelligentsia, particularly of its half-educated failures, have been already noted, and these latter have undoubtedly played a leading part in all the revolutionary disturbances of the modern Orient, from North Africa to China.[291] Regarding the industrial proletariat, some writers think that there is little immediate likelihood of their becoming a major revolutionary factor, because of their traditionalism, ignorance, and apathy, and also because there is no real connection between them and the intelligentsia, the other centre of social discontent.

The French economist Métin states this view-point very well. Speaking primarily of India, he writes: "The Nationalist movement rises from the middle classes and manifests no systematic hostility toward the capitalists and great proprietors; in economic matters it is on their side."[292] As for the proletariat: "The coolies do not imagine that their lot can be bettered. Like the ryots and the agricultural labourers, they do not show the least sign of revolt. To whom should they turn? The ranks of traditional society are closed to them. People without caste, the coolies are despised even by the old-style artisan, proud of his caste-status, humble though that be. To fall to the job of a coolie is, for the Hindu, the worst declassment. The factory workers are not yet numerous enough to form a compact and powerful proletariat, able to exert pressure on the old society. Even if they do occasionally strike, they are as far from the modern Trade-Union as they are from the traditional working-caste. Neither can they look for leadership to the 'intellectual proletariat'; for the Nationalist movement has not emerged from the 'bourgeois' phase, and always leans on the capitalists....

"Thus Indian industry is still in its embryonic stages. In truth, the material evolution which translates itself by the construction of factories, and the social evolution which creates a proletariat, have only begun to emerge; while the intellectual evolution from which arise the programmes of social demands has not even begun."[293]

Other observers of Indian industrial conditions, however, do not share M. Métin's opinion. Says the British Labour leader, J. Ramsay Macdonald: "To imagine the backward Indian labourers becoming a conscious regiment in the class war, seems to be one of the vainest dreams in which a Western mind can indulge. But I sometimes wonder if it be so very vain after all. In the first place, the development of factory industry in India has created a landless and homeless proletariat unmatched by the same economic class in any other capitalist community; and to imagine that this class is to be kept out, or can be kept out, of Indian politics is far more vain than to dream of its developing a politics on Western lines. Further than that, the wage-earners have shown a willingness to respond to Trades-Union methods; they are forming industrial associations and have engaged in strikes; some of the social reform movements conducted by Indian intellectuals definitely try to establish Trades-Unions and preach ideas familiar to us in connection with Trades-Union propaganda. A capitalist fiscal policy will not only give this movement a great impetus as it did in Japan, but in India will not be able to suppress the movement, as was done in Japan, by legislation. As yet, the true proletarian wage-earner, uprooted from his native village and broken away from the organization of Indian society, is but insignificant. It is growing, however, and I believe that it will organize itself rapidly on the general lines of the proletarian classes of other capitalist countries. So soon as it becomes politically conscious, there are no other lines upon which it can organize itself."[294]

Turning to the Near East—more than a decade ago a French Socialist writer, observing the hard living conditions of the Egyptian masses, noted signs of social unrest and predicted grave disturbances. "A genuine proletariat," he wrote, "has been created by the multiplication of industries and the sudden, almost abrupt, progress which has followed. The cost of living has risen to a scale hitherto unknown in Egypt, while wages have risen but slightly. Poverty and want abound. Some day suffering will provoke the people to complaints, perhaps to angry outbursts, throughout this apparently prosperous Delta. It is true that the influx of foreigners and of money may put off the hour when the city or country labourer of Egyptian race comes clearly to perceive the wrongs that are being done to him. He may miss the educational influence of Socialism. Yet such an awakening may come sooner than people expect. It is not only among the successful and prosperous Egyptians that intelligence is to be found. Those whose wages are growing gradually smaller and smaller have intelligence of equal keenness, and it has become a real question as to the hour when for the first time in the land of Islam the flame of Mohammedan Socialism shall burst forth."[295] In Algeria, likewise, a Belgian traveller noted the dawning of a proletarian consciousness among the town working-men just before the Great War. Speaking of the rapid spread of Western ideas, he wrote: "Islam tears asunder like rotten cloth on the quays of Algiers: the dockers, coal-passers, and engine-tenders, to whatever race they belong, leave their Islam and acquire a genuine proletarian morality, that of the proletarians of Europe, and they make common cause with their European colleagues on the basis of a strictly economic struggle. If there were many big factories in Algeria, orthodox Islam would soon disappear there, as old-fashioned Catholicism has disappeared with us under the shock of great industry."[296]

Whatever may be the prospects as to the rapid emergence of organized labour movements in the Orient, one thing seems certain: the unrest which afflicted so many parts of the East in the years preceding the Great War, though mainly political, had also its social side. Toward the end of 1913, a leading Anglo-Indian journal remarked pessimistically: "We have already gone so far on the downward path that leads to destruction that there are districts in what were once regarded as the most settled parts of India which are being abandoned by the rich because their property is not safe. So great is the contempt for the law that it is employed by the unscrupulous as a means of offence against the innocent. Frontier Pathans commit outrages almost unbelievable in their daring. Mass-meetings are held and agitation spreads in regard to topics quite outside the business of orderly people. There is no matter of domestic or foreign politics in which crowds of irresponsible people do not want to have their passionate way. Great grievances are made of little, far-off things. What ought to be the ordered, spacious life of the District Officer is intruded upon and disturbed by a hundred distracting influences due to the want of discipline of the people. In the subordinate ranks of the great services themselves, trades-unions have been formed. Military and police officers have to regret that the new class of recruits is less subordinate than the old, harder to discipline, more full of complaints."[297]

The Great War of course enormously aggravated Oriental unrest. In many parts of the Near East, especially, acute suffering, balked ambitions, and furious hates combined to reduce society to the verge of chaos. Into this ominous turmoil there now came the sinister influence of Russian Bolshevism, marshalling all this diffused unrest by systematic methods for definite ends. Bolshevism was frankly out for a world-revolution and the destruction of Western civilization. To attain this objective the Bolshevist leaders not only launched direct assaults on the West, but also planned flank attacks in Asia and Africa. They believed that if the East could be set on fire, not only would Russian Bolshevism gain vast additional strength but also the economic repercussion on the West, already shaken by the war, would be so terrific that industrial collapse would ensue, thereby throwing Europe open to revolution.

Bolshevism's propagandist efforts were nothing short of universal, both in area and in scope. No part of the world was free from the plottings of its agents; no possible source of discontent was overlooked. Strictly "Red" doctrines like the dictatorship of the proletariat were very far from being the only weapons in Bolshevism's armoury. Since what was first wanted was the overthrow of the existing world-order, any kind of opposition to that order, no matter how remote doctrinally from Bolshevism, was grist to the Bolshevist mill. Accordingly, in every quarter of the globe, in Asia, Africa, Australia, and the Americas, as in Europe, Bolshevik agitators whispered in the ears of the discontented their gospel of hatred and revenge. Every nationalist aspiration, every political grievance, every social injustice, every racial discrimination, was fuel for Bolshevism's incitement to violence and war.[298]

Particularly promising fields for Bolshevist activity were the Near and Middle East. Besides being a prey to profound disturbances of every description, those regions as traditional objectives of the old Czarist imperialism, had long been carefully studied by Russian agents who had evolved a technique of "pacific penetration" that might be easily adjusted to Bolshevist ends. To stir up political, religious, and racial passions in Turkey, Persia, Afghanistan, and India, especially against England, required no original planning by Trotzky or Lenin. Czarism had already done these things for generations, and full information lay both in the Petrograd archives and in the brains of surviving Czarist agents ready to turn their hands as easily to the new work as the old.

In all the elaborate network of Bolshevist propaganda which to-day enmeshes the East we must discriminate between Bolshevism's two objectives: one immediate—the destruction of Western political and economic supremacy; the other ultimate—the bolshevizing of the Oriental masses and the consequent extirpation of the native upper and middle classes, precisely as has been done in Russia and as is planned for the countries of the West. In the first stage, Bolshevism is quite ready to respect Oriental faiths and customs and to back Oriental nationalist movements. In the second stage, religions like Islam and nationalists like Mustapha Kemal are to be branded as "bourgeois" and relentlessly destroyed. How Bolshevik diplomacy endeavours to work these two schemes in double harness, we shall presently see.

Russian Bolshevism's Oriental policy was formulated soon after its accession to power at the close of 1917. The year 1918 was a time of busy preparation. An elaborate propaganda organization was built up from various sources. A number of old Czarist agents and diplomats versed in Eastern affairs were cajoled or conscripted into the service. The Russian Mohammedan populations such as the Tartars of South Russia and the Turkomans of Central Asia furnished many recruits. Even more valuable were the exiles who flocked to Russia from Turkey, Persia, India, and elsewhere at the close of the Great War. Practically all the leaders of the Turkish war-government—Enver, Djemal, Talaat, and many more, fled to Russia for refuge from the vengeance of the victorious Entente Powers. The same was true of the Hindu terrorist leaders who had been in German pay during the war and who now sought service under Lenin. By the end of 1918 Bolshevism's Oriental propaganda department was well organized, divided into three bureaux, for the Islamic countries, India, and the Far East respectively. With Bolshevism's Far Eastern activities this book is not concerned, though the reader should bear them in mind and should remember the important part played by the Chinese in recent Russian history. As for the Islamic and Indian bureaux, they displayed great zeal, translating tons of Bolshevik literature into the various Oriental languages, training numerous secret agents and propagandists for "field-work," and getting in touch with all disaffected or revolutionary elements.

With the opening months of 1919 Bolshevist activity throughout the Near and Middle East became increasingly apparent. The wave of rage and despair caused by the Entente's denial of Near Eastern nationalist aspirations[299] played splendidly into the Bolshevists' hands, and we have already seen how Moscow supported Mustapha Kemal and other nationalist leaders in Turkey, Persia, Egypt, and elsewhere. In the Middle East, also, Bolshevism gained important successes. Not merely was Moscow's hand visible in the epidemic of rioting and seditious violence which swept northern India in the spring of 1919,[300] but an even shrewder blow was struck at Britain in Afghanistan. This land of turbulent mountaineers, which lay like a perpetual thundercloud on India's north-west frontier, had kept quiet during the Great War, mainly owing to the Anglophile attitude of its ruler, the Ameer Habibullah Khan. But early in 1919 Habibullah was murdered. Whether the Bolsheviki had a hand in the matter is not known, but they certainly reaped the benefit, for power passed to one of Habibullah's sons, Amanullah Khan, who was an avowed enemy of England and who had had dealings with Turco-German agents during the late war. Amanullah at once got in touch with Moscow, and a little later, just when the Punjab was seething with unrest, he declared war on England, and his wild tribesmen, pouring across the border, set the North-West Frontier on fire. After some hard fighting the British succeeded in repelling the Afghan invasion, and Amanullah was constrained to make peace. But Britain obviously dared not press Amanullah too hard, for in the peace treaty the Ameer was released from his previous obligation not to maintain diplomatic relations with other nations than British India. Amanullah promptly aired his independence by maintaining ostentatious relations with Moscow. As a matter of fact, the Bolsheviki had by this time established an important propagandist subcentre in Russian Turkestan, not far from the Afghan border, and this bureau's activities of course envisaged not merely Afghanistan but the wider field of India as well.[301]

During 1920 Bolshevik activities became still more pronounced throughout the Near and Middle East. We have already seen how powerfully Bolshevik Russia supported the Turkish and Persian nationalist movements. In fact, the reckless short-sightedness of Entente policy was driving into Lenin's arms multitudes of nationalists to whom the internationalist theories of Moscow were personally abhorrent. For example, the head of the Afghan mission to Moscow thus frankly expressed his reasons for friendship with Soviet Russia, in an interview printed by the official Soviet organ, Izvestia: "I am neither Communist nor Socialist, but my political programme so far is the expulsion of the English from Asia. I am an irreconcilable enemy of European capitalism in Asia, the chief representatives of which are the English. On this point I coincide with the Communists, and in this respect we are your natural allies.... Afghanistan, like India, does not represent a capitalist state, and it is very unlikely that even a parliamentary régime will take deep root in these countries. It is so far difficult to say how subsequent events will develop. I only know that the renowned address of the Soviet Government to all nations, with its appeal to them to combat capitalists (and for us a capitalist is synonymous with the word foreigner, or, to be more exact, an Englishman), had an enormous effect on us. A still greater effect was produced by Russia's annulment of all the secret treaties enforced by the imperialistic governments, and by the proclaiming of the right of all nations, no matter how small, to determine their own destiny. This act rallied around Soviet Russia all the exploited nationalities of Asia, and all parties, even those very remote from Socialism." Of course, knowing what we do of Bolshevik propagandist tactics, we cannot be sure that the Afghan diplomat ever said the things which the Izvestia relates. But, even if the interview be a fake, the words put into his mouth express the feelings of vast numbers of Orientals and explain a prime cause of Bolshevik propagandist successes in Eastern lands.

So successful, indeed, had been the progress of Bolshevik propaganda that the Soviet leaders now began to work openly for their ultimate ends. At first Moscow had posed as the champion of Oriental "peoples" against Western "imperialism"; its appeals had been to "peoples," irrespective of class; and it had promised "self-determination," with full respect for native ideas and institutions. For instance: a Bolshevist manifesto to the Turks signed by Lenin and issued toward the close of 1919 read: "Mussulmans of the world, victims of the capitalists, awake! Russia has abandoned the Czar's pernicious policy toward you and offers to help you overthrow English tyranny. She will allow you freedom of religion and self-government. The frontiers existing before the war will be respected, no Turkish territory will be given Armenia, the Dardanelles Straits will remain yours, and Constantinople will remain the capital of the Mussulman world. The Mussulmans in Russia will be given self-government. All we ask in exchange is that you fight the reckless capitalists, who would exploit your country and make it a colony." Even when addressing its own people, the Soviet Government maintained the same general tone. An "Order of the Day" to the Russian troops stationed on the borders of India stated: "Comrades of the Pamir division, you have been given a responsible task. The Soviet Republic sends you to garrison the posts on the Pamir, on the

146

frontiers of the friendly countries of Afghanistan and India. The Pamir tableland divides revolutionary Russia from India, which, with its 300,000,000 inhabitants, is enslaved by a handful of Englishmen. On this tableland the signallers of revolution must hoist the red flag of the army of liberation. May the peoples of India, who fight against their English oppressors, soon know that friendly help is not far off. Make yourselves at home with the liberty-loving tribes of northern India, promote by word and deed their revolutionary progress, refute the mass of calumnies spread about Soviet Russia by agents of the British princes, lords, and bankers. Long live the alliance of the revolutionary peoples of Europe and Asia!"

Such was the nature of first-stage Bolshevik propaganda. Presently, however, propaganda of quite a different character began to appear. This second-stage propaganda of course continued to assail Western "capitalist imperialism." But alongside, or rather intermingled with, these anti-Western, fulminations, there now appeared special appeals to the Oriental masses, inciting them against all "capitalists" and "bourgeois," native as well as foreign, and promising the "proletarians" remedies for all their ills. Here is a Bolshevist manifesto to the Turkish masses, published in the summer of 1920. It is very different from the manifestoes of a year before. "The men of toil," says this interesting document, "are now struggling everywhere against the rich people. These people, with the assistance of the aristocracy and their hirelings, are now trying to hold Turkish toilers in their chains. It is the rich people of Europe who have brought suffering to Turkey. Comrades, let us make common cause with the world's toilers. If we do not do so we shall never rise again. Let the heroes of Turkey's revolution join Bolshevism. Long live the Third International! Praise be to Allah!"

And in these new efforts Moscow was not content with words; it was passing to deeds as well. The first application of Bolshevism to an Eastern people was in Russian Turkestan. When the Bolsheviki first came to power at the end of 1917 they had granted Turkestan full "self-determination," and the inhabitants had acclaimed their native princes and re-established their old state-units, subject to a loose federative tie with Russia. Early in 1920, however, the Soviet Government considered Turkestan ripe for the "Social Revolution." Accordingly, the native princes were deposed, all political power was transferred to local Soviets (controlled by Russians), the native upper and middle classes were despoiled of their property, and sporadic resistance was crushed by mass-executions, torture, and other familiar forms of Bolshevist terrorism.[302] In the Caucasus, also, the social revolution had begun with the Sovietization of Azerbaidjan. The Tartar republic of Azerbaidjan was one of the fragments of the former Russian province of Transcaucasia which had declared its independence on the collapse of the Czarist Empire in 1917. Located in eastern Transcaucasia, about the Caspian Sea, Azerbaidjan's capital was the city of Baku, famous for its oil-fields. Oil had transformed Baku into an industrial centre on Western lines, with a large working population of mixed Asiatic and Russian origin. Playing upon the nascent class-consciousness of this urban proletariat, the Bolshevik agents made a coup d'état in the spring of 1920, overthrew the nationalist government, and, with prompt Russian backing, made Azerbaijan a Soviet republic. The usual accompaniments of the social revolution followed: despoiling and massacring of the upper and middle classes, confiscation of property in favour of the town proletarians and agricultural labourers, and ruthless terrorism. With the opening months of 1920, Bolshevism was thus in actual operation in both the Near and Middle East.[303]

Having acquired strong footholds in the Orient, Bolshevism now felt strong enough to throw off the mask. In the autumn of 1920, the Soviet Government of Russia held a "Congress of Eastern Peoples" at Baku, the aim of which was not merely the liberation of the Orient from Western control but its Bolshevizing as well. No attempt at concealment of this larger

147

objective was made, and so striking was the language employed that it may well merit our close attention.

In the first place, the call to the congress, issued by the Third (Moscow) International, was addressed to the "peasants and workers" of the East. The summons read:

"Peasants and workers of Persia! The Teheran Government of the Khadjars and its retinue of provincial Khans have plundered and exploited you through many centuries. The land, which, according to the laws of the Sheriat, was your common property, has been taken possession of more and more by the lackeys of the Teheran Government; they trade it away at their pleasure; they lay what taxes please them upon you; and when, through their mismanagement, they got the country into such a condition that they were unable to squeeze enough juice out of it themselves, they sold Persia last year to English capitalists for 2,000,000 pounds, so that the latter will organize an army in Persia that will oppress you still more than formerly, and so the latter can collect taxes for the Khans and the Teheran Government. They have sold the oil-wells in South Persia and thus helped plunder the country.

"Peasants of Mesopotamia! The English have declared your country to be independent; but 80,000 English soldiers are stationed in your country, are robbing and plundering, are killing you and are violating your women.

"Peasants of Anatolia! The English, French, and Italian Governments hold Constantinople under the mouths of their cannon. They have made the Sultan their prisoner, they are obliging him to consent to the dismemberment of what is purely Turkish territory, they are forcing him to turn the country's finances over to foreign capitalists in order to make it possible for them better to exploit the Turkish people, already reduced to a state of beggary by the six-year war. They have occupied the coal-mines of Heraclea, they are holding your ports, they are sending their troops into your country and are trampling down your fields.

"Peasants and workers of Armenia! Decades ago you became the victims of the intrigues of foreign capital, which launched heavy verbal attacks against the massacres of the Armenians by the Kurds and incited you to fight against the Sultan in order to obtain through your blood new concessions and fresh profits daily from the bloody Sultan. During the war they not only promised you independence, but they incited your merchants, your teachers, and your priests to demand the land of the Turkish peasants in order to keep up an eternal conflict between the Armenian and Turkish peoples, so that they could eternally derive profits out of this conflict, for as long as strife prevails between you and the Turks, just so long will the English, French, and American capitalists be able to hold Turkey in check through the menace of an Armenian uprising and to use the Armenians as cannon-fodder through the menace of a pogrom by Kurds.

"Peasants of Syria and Arabia! Independence was promised to you by the English and the French, and now they hold your country occupied by their armies, now the English and the French dictate your laws, and you, who have freed yourselves from the Turkish Sultan, from the Constantinople Government, are now slaves of the Paris and London Governments, which merely differ from the Sultan's Government in being stronger and better able to exploit you.

"You all understand this yourselves. The Persian peasants and workers have risen against their traitorous Teheran Government. The peasants in Mesopotamia are in revolt against the English troops. You peasants in Anatolia have rushed to the banner of Kemal Pasha in order to fight against the foreign invasion, but at the same time we hear that you are trying to organize your own party, a genuine peasants' party that will be willing to fight even if the Pashas are to make their peace with the Entente exploiters. Syria has no peace, and you, Armenian peasants, whom the Entente, despite its promises, allows to die from hunger in order to keep you under better control, you are understanding more and more that it is silly to hope for salvation by the Entente capitalists. Even your bourgeois Government of the Dashnakists, the lackeys of the Entente, is compelled to turn to the Workers' and Peasants' Government of Russia with an appeal for peace and help.

"Peasants and workers of the Near East! If you organize yourselves, if you form your own Workers' and Peasants' Government, if you arm yourselves, if you unite with the Red Russian Workers' and Peasants' Army, then you will be able to defy the English, French, and American capitalists, then you will settle accounts with your own native exploiters, then you will find it possible, in a free alliance with the workers' republics of the world, to look after your own interests; then you will know how to exploit the resources of your country in your own interest and in the interest of the working people of the whole world, that will honestly exchange the products of their labour and mutually help each other.

"We want to talk over all these questions with you at the Congress in Baku. Spare no effort to appear in Baku on September 1 in as large numbers as possible. You march, year in and year out, through the deserts to the holy places where you show your respect for your past and for your God—now march through deserts, over mountains, and across rivers in order to come together to discuss how you can escape from the bonds of slavery, how you can unite as brothers so as to live as men, free and equal."

From this summons the nature of the Baku congress can be imagined. It was, in fact, a social revolutionist far more than a nationalist assembly. Of its 1900 delegates, nearly 1300 were professed communists. Turkey, Persia, Armenia, and the Caucasus countries sent the largest delegations, though there were also delegations from Arabia, India, and even the Far East. The Russian Soviet Government was of course in control and kept a tight hand on the proceedings. The character of these proceedings were well summarized by the address of the noted Bolshevik leader Zinoviev, president of the Executive Committee of the Third (Moscow) International, who presided.

Zinoviev said:

"We believe this Congress to be one of the greatest events in history, for it proves not only that the progressive workers and working peasants of Europe and America are awakened, but that we have at last seen the day of the awakening, not of a few, but of tens of thousands, of hundreds of thousands, of millions of the labouring class of the peoples of the East. These peoples form the majority of the world's whole population, and they alone, therefore, are able to bring the war between capital and labour to a conclusive decision....

"The Communist International said from the very first day of its existence: 'There are four times as many people living in Asia as live in Europe. We will free all peoples, all who labour.'... We know that the labouring masses of the East are in part retrograde, though not by their own fault; they cannot read or write, are ignorant, are bound in superstition, believe in the evil spirit, are unable to read any newspapers, do not know what is happening in the world, have not the slightest idea of the most elementary laws of hygiene. Comrades, our Moscow International discussed the question whether a socialist revolution could take place in the countries of the East before those countries had passed through the capitalist stage. You know that the view which long prevailed was that every country must first go through the period of capitalism ... before socialism could become a live question. We now believe

149

that this is no longer true. Russia has done this, and from that moment we are able to say that China, India, Turkey, Persia, Armenia also can, and must, make a direct fight to get the Soviet System. These countries can, and must, prepare themselves to be Soviet republics.

"I say that we give patient aid to groups of persons who do not believe in our ideas, who are even opposed to us on some points. In this way, the Soviet Government supports Kemal in Turkey. Never for one moment do we forget that the movement headed by Kemal is not a communist movement. We know it. I have here extracts from the verbatim reports of the first session of the Turkish people's Government at Angora. Kemal himself says that 'the Caliph's person is sacred and inviolable.' The movement headed by Kemal wants to rescue the Caliph's 'sacred' person from the hands of the foe. That is the Turkish Nationalist's point of view. But is it a communist point of view? No. We respect the religious convictions of the masses; we know how to re-educate the masses. It will be the work of years.

"We use great caution in approaching the religious convictions of the labouring masses in the East and elsewhere. But at this Congress we are bound to tell you that you must not do what the Kemal Government is doing in Turkey; you must not support the power of the Sultan, not even if religious considerations urge you to do so. You must press on, and must not allow yourselves to be pulled back. We believe the Sultan's hour has struck. You must not allow any form of autocratic power to continue; you must destroy, you must annihilate, faith in the Sultan; you must struggle to obtain real Soviet organizations. The Russian peasants also were strong believers in the Czar; but when a true people's revolution broke out there was practically nothing left of this faith in the Czar. The same thing will happen in Turkey and all over the East as soon as a true peasants' revolution shall burst forth over the surface of the black earth. The people will very soon lose faith in their Sultan and in their masters. We say once more, the policy pursued by the present people's Government in Turkey is not the policy of the Communist International, it is not our policy; nevertheless, we declare that we are prepared to support any revolutionary fight against the English Government.

"Yes, we array ourselves against the English bourgeoisie; we seize the English imperialist by the throat and tread him underfoot. It is against English capitalism that the worst, the most fatal blow must be dealt. That is so. But at the same time we must educate the labouring masses of the East to hatred, to the will to fight the whole of the rich classes indifferently, whoever they be. The great significance of the revolution now starting in the East does not consist in begging the English imperialist to take his feet off the table, for the purpose of then permitting the wealthy Turk to place his feet on it all the more comfortably; no, we will very politely ask all the rich to remove their dirty feet from the table, so that there may be no luxuriousness among us, no boasting, no contempt of the people, no idleness, but that the world may be ruled by the worker's horny hand."

The Baku congress was the opening gun in Bolshevism's avowed campaign for the immediate Bolshevizing of the East. It was followed by increased Soviet activity and by substantial Soviet successes, especially in the Caucasus, where both Georgia and Armenia were Bolshevized in the spring of 1921.

These very successes, however, awakened growing uneasiness among Soviet Russia's nationalist protégés. The various Oriental nationalist parties, which had at first welcomed Moscow's aid so enthusiastically against the Entente Powers, now began to realize that Russian Bolshevism might prove as great a peril as Western imperialism to their patriotic aspirations. Of course the nationalist leaders had always realized Moscow's ultimate goal, but hitherto they had felt themselves strong enough to control the situation and to take Russian aid without paying Moscow's price. Now they no longer felt so sure. The numbers of class-conscious "proletarians" in the East might be very small. The communist philosophy might be virtually unintelligible to the Oriental masses. Nevertheless, the very existence of Soviet Russia was a warning not to be disregarded. In Russia an infinitesimal communist minority, numbering, by its own admission, not much over 600,000, was maintaining an unlimited despotism over 170,000,000 people. Western countries might rely on their popular education and their staunch traditions of ordered liberty; the East possessed no such bulwarks against Bolshevism. The East was, in fact, much like Russia. There was the same dense ignorance of the masses; the same absence of a large and powerful middle class; the same tradition of despotism; the same popular acquiescence in the rule of ruthless minorities. Finally, there were the ominous examples of Sovietized Turkestan and Azerbaidjan. In fine, Oriental nationalists bethought them of the old adage that he who sups with the devil needs a long spoon.

Everywhere it has been the same story. In Asia Minor, Mustapha Kemal has arrested Bolshevist propaganda agents, while Turkish and Russian troops have more than once clashed on the disputed Caucasus frontiers. In Egypt we have already seen how an amicable arrangement between Lord Milner and the Egyptian nationalist leaders was facilitated by the latter's fear of the social revolutionary agitators who were inflaming the fellaheen. In India, Sir Valentine Chirol noted as far back as the spring of 1918 how Russia's collapse into Bolshevism had had a "sobering effect" on Indian public opinion. "The more thoughtful Indians," he wrote, "now see how helpless even the Russian intelligentsia (relatively far more numerous and matured than the Indian intelligentsia) has proved to control the great ignorant masses as soon as the whole fabric of government has been hastily shattered."[304] In Afghanistan, likewise, the Ameer was losing his love for his Bolshevist allies. The streams of refugees from Sovietized Turkestan that flowed across his borders for protection, headed by his kinsman the Ameer of Bokhara, made Amanullah Khan do some hard thinking, intensified by a serious mutiny of Afghan troops on the Russian border, the mutineers demanding the right to form Soldiers' Councils quite on the Russian pattern. Bolshevist agents might tempt him by the loot of India, but the Ameer could also see that that would do him little good if he himself were to be looted and killed by his own rebellious subjects.[305] Thus, as time went on, Oriental nationalists and conservatives generally tended to close ranks in dislike and apprehension of Bolshevism. Had there been no other issue involved, there can be little doubt that Moscow's advances would have been repelled and Bolshevist agents given short shrift.

Unfortunately, the Eastern nationalists feel themselves between the Bolshevist devil and the Western imperialist deep sea. The upshot has been that they have been trying to play off the one against the other—driven toward Moscow by every Entente aggression; driven toward the West by every Soviet coup of Lenin. Western statesmen should realize this, and should remember that Bolshevism's best propagandist agent is, not Zinoviev orating at Baku, but General Gouraud, with his Senegalese battalions and "strong-arm" methods in Syria and the Arab hinterland.

Certainly, any extensive spread of Bolshevism in the East would be a terrible misfortune both for the Orient and for the world at large. If the triumph of Bolshevism would mean barbarism in the West, in the East it would spell downright savagery. The sudden release of the ignorant, brutal Oriental masses from their traditional restraints of religion and custom, and the submergence of the relatively small upper and middle classes by the flood of social revolution would mean the destruction of all Oriental civilization and culture, and a plunge into an abyss of anarchy from which the East could emerge only after generations, perhaps centuries.

FOOTNOTES:

[284] For these early forms of unrest, see A. Le Chatelier, L'Islam au dix-neuvième Siècle, pp. 22-44 (Paris, 1888).

[285] D. H. Dodwell, "Economic Transition in India," Economic Journal, December, 1910.

[286] Bipin Chandra Pal, "The Forces Behind the Unrest in India," Contemporary Review, February, 1910.

[287] J. Chailley, Administrative Problems of British India, p. 339 (London, 1910—English translation).

[288] Dr. Ronald Ross, "Wretchedness a Cause of Political Unrest," The Survey, 18 February, 1911.

[289] A. Yusuf Ali, Life and Labour in India, pp. 3, 32 (London, 1907).

[290] E. W. Capen, "A Sociological Appraisal of Western Influence on the Orient," American Journal of Sociology, May, 1911.

[291] P. Khorat, "Psychologie de la Révolution chinoise," Revue des Deux Mondes, 15 March, 1912; L. Bertrand, Le Mirage orientale, pp. 164-166; J. D. Rees, The Real India, pp. 162-163.

[292] Albert Métin, L'Inde d'aujourd'hui: Étude sociale, p. 276 (Paris, 1918).

[293] Albert Métin, L'Inde d'aujourd'hui: Étude sociale, pp. 339-345.

[294] J. Ramsay Macdonald, The Government of India, pp. 133-134 (London, 1920).

[295] Georges Foucart. Quoted in The Literary Digest, 17 August, 1907, pp. 225-226.

[296] A. Van Gennep, En Algérie, p. 182 (Paris, 1914).

[297] The Englishman (Calcutta). Quoted in The Literary Digest, 21 February, 1914, p. 369.

[298] For these larger world-aspects of Bolshevik propaganda, see Paul Miliukov, Bolshevism: An International Danger (London, 1920); also, my Rising Tide of Colour against White World-Supremacy, pp. 218-221, and my article, "Bolshevism: The Heresy of the Under-Man," The Century, June, 1919.

[299] See Chapter V.

[300] See Chapter VI.

[301] For events in Afghanistan and Central Asia, see Sir T. H. Holdich, "The Influence of Bolshevism in Afghanistan," New Europe, December 4, 1919; Ikbal Ali Shah, "The Fall of Bokhara," The Near East, October 28, 1920, and his "The Central Asian Tangle," Asiatic Review, October, 1920. For Bolshevist activity in the Near and Middle East generally, see Miliukov, op. cit., pp. 243-260; 295-297; Major-General Sir George Aston, "Bolshevik Propaganda in the East," Fortnightly Review, August, 1920; W. E. D. Allen, "Transcaucasia, Past and Present," Quarterly Review, October, 1920; Sir Valentine Chirol, "Conflicting

Policies in the Near East," New Europe, July 1, 1920; L. Dumont-Wilden, "Awakening Asia," The Living Age, August 7, 1920 (translated from the French); Major-General Lord Edward Gleichen, "Moslems and the Tangle in the Middle East," National Review, December, 1919; Paxton Hibben, "Russia at Peace," The Nation (New York), January 26, 1921; H. von Hoff, "Die nationale Erhebung in der Türkei," Deutsche Revue, December, 1919; R. G. Hunter, "Entente—Oil—Islam," New Europe, August 26, 1920; "Taira," "The Story of the Arab Revolt," Balkan Review, August, 1920; "Voyageur," "Lenin's Attempt to Capture Islam," New Europe, June 10, 1920; Hans Wendt, "Ex Oriente Lux," Nord und Süd, May, 1920; George Young, "Russian Foreign Policy," New Europe, July 1, 1920.

[302] Ikbal Ali Shah, op. cit.

[303] For events in the Caucasus, see W. E. D. Allen, "Transcaucasia, Past and Present," Quarterly Review, October, 1920; C. E. Bechhofer, "The Situation in the Transcaucasus," New Europe, September 2, 1920; "D. Z. T.," "L'Azerbaidjan: La Première République musulmane," Revue du Monde musulman, 1919; Paxton Hibben, "Exit Georgia," The Nation (New York), March 30, 1921.

[304] Sir V. Chirol, "India in Travail," Edinburgh Review, July, 1918. Also see H. H. The Aga Khan, India in Transition, p. 17 (London, 1918).

[305] Ikbal Ali Shah, op. cit.


CONCLUSION

Our survey of the Near and Middle East is at an end. What is the outstanding feature of that survey? It is: Change. The "Immovable East" has been moved at last—moved to its very depths. The Orient is to-day in full transition, flux, ferment, more sudden and profound than any it has hitherto known. The world of Islam, mentally and spiritually quiescent for almost a thousand years, is once more astir, once more on the march.

Whither? We do not know. Who would be bold enough to prophesy the outcome of this vast ferment—political, economical, social, religious, and much more besides? All that we may wisely venture is to observe, describe, and analyse the various elements in the great transition.

Yet surely this is much. To view, however empirically, the mighty transformation at work; to group its multitudinous aspects in some sort of relativity; to follow the red threads of tendency running through the tangled skein, is to gain at least provisional knowledge and acquire capacity to grasp the significance of future developments as they shall successively arise.

"To know is to understand"—and to hope: to hope that this present travail, vast and ill-understood, may be but the birth-pangs of a truly renascent East taking its place in a renascent world.

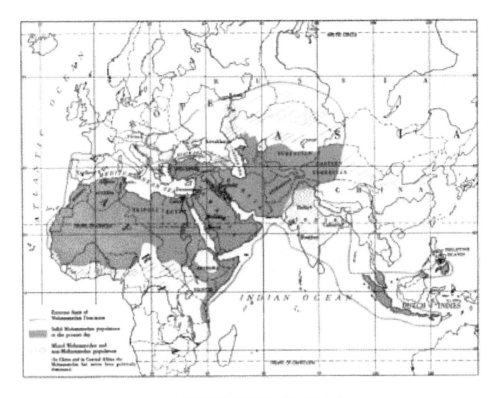

MAP OF THE WORLD OF ISLAM

7/24

Made in the USA
Las Vegas, NV
24 April 2021

21988364R00089